A HISTORY OF
FASHION

A HISTORY OF FASHION

J. Anderson Black
Madge Garland

Updated and revised by
Frances Kennett

ORBIS PUBLISHING
LONDON

Frontispiece: An exotic costume of about 1910 made for Madame Poiret by Paul Poiret, one of the most eminent designers of his time (Scala; Paris, Coll. Mme Poiret)

Right: This mid-seventeenth century gentleman wears his jacket open below a high waist to reveal his undershirt. The popular lace collar and diagonal sash and hat, together with the mid-calf boots and decorative garters, reflect the assertive taste and dress during this period. (The Mansell Collection, London)

First published in Great Britain by Orbis Publishing Limited, London 1975; reprinted 1978; second edition 1980

© Orbis Publishing Limited, London and Istituto Geografico de Agostini, SpA, Novara 1975, 1980

Printed in Italy by New Interlitho, Milan

ISBN 0 85613 205 5

Contents

FOREWORD

Below: Clothes express rank and status—
in this twelfth-century manuscript
illumination the clerical figure is clearly
distinguished from the Emperor Henry IV and
Matilda, Countess of Tuscany, whose richly
coloured and decorated garments could only
have been worn by the most important
personages in medieval Europe

A history of the way people dress is concerned with the story of man's first and most faithful addiction—his intense pre-occupation with the appearance of his own body. This obsession is hardly surprising as the body is all we have to begin life with and is the only thing we can be sure of keeping until death. Far less understandable is man's frequent dissatisfaction with what nature has given him, and this book illustrates some of his efforts to improve on his natural attributes. From time to time, people have desired larger heads, longer necks, smaller feet, a more pronounced bosom or a tinier waist. Had man been given the power, he might well have endowed himself with as many limbs as a Hindu deity but, frustrated, he has mutilated himself in countless different ways. Above all man has used clothing as a means of aspiring towards his fantasies of a better, or at least different, body.

It is a story in which myths, legends, fairy and folk tales and erotic taboos have all made their contributions, but so have such mundane considerations as political alliances, scientific discoveries, mechanical inventions and the conditions of international trade. Aesthetics are of course important, though always

REX ROGAT ABBATEM. MATHILDIM SuppLICAT ATQ;

7

On these pages: Each age uses different *means to achieve its ideal of elegance. The sumptuous materials and elaborate detail of the early seventeenth-century costumes on the right contrast vividly with the sensuous simplicity of the neo-classical gown (far right) painted by Ingres nearly two centuries later*

subservient to contemporary taste. Modesty comes and goes, but commonsense has always been absent and the most elementary anatomical facts have been consistently ignored.

Indeed, it is the unexpected traveller or the surprise mechanical or chemical innovation which have influenced fashion far more than any ostentatious queen or self-conscious designer. Merchant adventurers sailed into the unknown, founded the East India Company and the Indian Empire, and England found herself with a fabric novelty on her hands—muslin, forbidden by law to be imported into France because the silk textile workers threatened to strike. In this way a new fashion was set. Cotton seeds from the Orient germinated in America's virgin soil, leading both to a large increase in the slave trade and to voluminous cotton petticoats being worn by women the world over. A monk hid silkworms in his sleeve, and the resulting silk industry changed the dressing habits of the West. A trade treaty was made with the Indians in northern Canada and furs never seen before in Europe covered women's shoulders. The mainstream of change has constantly been diverted by such happenings or, less frequently, by a personality so

challenging that what he or she preferred was copied by lesser folk. Fashion is rarely 'set', however; more often it develops, with strong reactions between one generation and the next.

When man's pre-occupation with the appearance of his body becomes a true obsession, the fashion-conscious beauty or the over-dressed dandy materializes. Sometimes the desire to alter the human frame makes use of such optical tricks as the farthingale or the crinoline. Sometimes a fashionable figure is obtained by the sheer weight of machinery employed. The instruments of torture used by humans on themselves in the pursuit of fashion comprise an arsenal of horrors. The wooden planks of the Chinook Indians to elongate the skulls of their infants, the mutilated feet of pre-Revolution Chinese women when the smallness of the bride's foot was in direct ratio to the size of her bridal price, the high necks of the Burmese women who added ring after ring until, if they were removed, their weakened necks would break—these are only a few of the means which man has used against himself in an endless search to alter the body given to him.

Most vulnerable of all, the isthmus of flesh between the pelvis and the rib-

cage has attracted the greatest attention. The first pictures of civilized Europeans, the Minoan frescoes at Knossos, illustrate both men and women with tiny, corseted waists, and throughout the centuries innumerable variations of the corset have formed an essential part of changing fashions.

Most historians have attributed the origin of clothing to three causes: a need for protection against the elements, a desire for modesty and a love of display connected with sexual attraction. The first has only a limited role, for humans have always preferred decoration to comfort, which was hardly known before the last century when ideals of

courtly grandeur gave place to middle-class demands for bourgeois comfort. Earlier races were hardier—the Patagonians who inhabited a cold mountain climate, and the Marquesans a hot island climate both thought themselves suitably dressed in pigments alone, the British wore woad not wool, while North American Indians preferred feathers to furs. Very few styles of dress, therefore, have been designed to protect the wearers from any kind of climatic excess.

The desire for modesty can be expressed in clothing, but it is rarely a factor that determines fashion. Concepts of modesty vary enormously, and each period and each civilization has

developed totally different ideas of which parts of the human body should or should not be exposed. Women have gone bare-breasted when fashion decreed, as in ancient Crete or during the Directorate period of the French Revolution. On the other hand, they have sometimes covered even their faces in deference to custom, and Moslem women in some parts of the world wear the yashmak covering the entire body to this day. Victor Hugo wrote a violent letter of reproof to his fiancée in 1822 because she had lifted her skirts high enough to permit a glimpse of her ankles when crossing the road. As late as the 1950s, a nude photograph of Marilyn Monroe was suppressed at great expense because it was thought that it would be disastrous to her popularity. More recently, attitudes have changed and various degrees of nudity have been incorporated into fashion.

The love of display connected with the erotic urge is definitely the most important of the three factors contributing to the development of fashion, and the desire to attract is clearly the major reason for dressing-up. A drastic indication of this is to be found in the habit of certain African tribes whose women, when they are old, dispense with all covering, there no longer being any need for it.

Added to a love of sexual display, and intimately connected with the place people occupy in society, is the wish ostentatiously to display wealth and power. Until lately clothes were the easiest and most straightforward means of telling people just who you were and what you were worth, and this book is full of pictures of magnificent clothes intended to proclaim the wearer's status.

It is noticeable that clothes connected with sports, such as skiing and golfing, (where physical performance is all-important), have traditionally shown little difference between the sexes. This is also true of the overalls of factory workers, the tights of dancers and acrobats, and above all, it is true of the blue jeans of today. Before the Second World War male and female jackets could be discerned by whether the flap fastenings turned left or right, but this difference is now retained only for formal clothing. The prevalent play-clothes of today are the same for both He and She.

If, as many people believe, our coverings are the outward reflection of our philosophy of life, then today's fashions indicate that equality of sex, income and class are well on their way.

Most of the illustrations in this book show people of rank or wealth because in the past they were the only ones who could afford, or were permitted, to wear colourful clothes. They were also the people whose persons were recorded by the artists of their time. Now matters are very different, and the crowds that gather from all over the world to gaze at the creations of their ancestors in museums—while busily photographing each other—have the merit of adding notes of brilliant colour to the fashion scene.

Fashion is all pervading. Certain elements in dress remain constant throughout the detailed changes of shape, design and decoration. Corcos' young woman of the 1880s, for instance, displays in her posture and dress the essence of femininity projected in soft folds of fabric, the flattering line of her arms and shoulders, and the frame of ornament provided by her lace collar. Fashion has always reflected the individuality and personality of the social being and will continue to do so. Even the rebels against fashions of the time seem, to later eyes, to reflect them. Others, more successful, merely set a new fashion.

MADGE GARLAND

MESOPOTAMIA TO MYCENAE

The Ancient World

Left: The most important Sumerian garment was an ankle-length skirt which was either made of fur or a fur-like fabric called kaunakès. These warriors, depicted on a Sumerian mosaic from Mari, wear the long woolly pagne-skirt (which is a form of loincloth) and a leather stole reinforced with metal studs

Mesopotamia

In the third millennium there were two distinct peoples in the Valleys of the Tigris and Euphrates: the Akkadians to the north and the Sumerians to the south. It seems that the Sumerians were dominant for several centuries, at least during the first Ur Dynasty (about 2800–1600 B.C.). They were a highly sophisticated people with enormous technical resources, capable of producing advanced machinery and buildings and the most intricate goldwork. Their fashions and customs were adopted throughout Mesopotamia.

Unlike that of Egypt, Mesopotamia's soil is damp and fertile and no garments have survived the millennia of decay. We therefore have to rely entirely on other sources, such as statues and bas-reliefs which, although highly stylized, display a distinctive style of dress and show its development over the period.

The first and most striking feature of Sumerian dress is its simplicity.

The basic form for both men and women was a simple ankle-length, wrap-around skirt usually made in a fur called *kaunakès*, the torso being left bare.

In statues and bas-reliefs, the material is portrayed as having a thick flounced texture. This has given rise to a certain amount of controversy for most experts consider that the material used was sheepskin with the wool worn outwards, the symmetrical flouncing suggesting that the wool was trimmed and combed. But actual sheep, depicted at this period, have the same neat flounces which are possibly a stylized method of depicting wool. Fragments of woven material found in Sumerian tombs have led to the alternative theory, supported by some authorities who feel it is inconceivable that a nation as sophisticated as the Sumerians would have sweltered in sheepskins, that the material used was in fact a fabric with a woven back into which tufts of wool were knotted, much in the manner of rug-making, giving the effect of a fleece. This cloth was known as kaunakès. It is not known which of these two versions is the correct one, but the overall appearance of the Sumerian costume was of a long, shaggy skirt.

One of the finest three-dimensional statues ever discovered in Sumeria is the seated figure of Ebih-il, Superintendent of the Ishtar temple at Mari. He is wearing an ankle-length flounced skirt tied at the waist. At the back there hangs an eight-inch tail of the same fabric which

might be the surplus material from the waist-band, but is probably meant to suggest the animal skin from which garments were originally made. A slight variation on this basic style is depicted in a votive plaque of Ur-Nansche of Lagash. A longer piece of material has been used and the surplus thrown over the left shoulder to form a loose cloak, in the fashion of a Scottish kilt and plaid.

Both the statues mentioned above are of nobility, but the Royal Standard of Ur shows the dress of a wider cross-section of society. This mosaic, found by Sir Leonard Woolley in the Royal Tombs of Ur, depicts farmers, fishermen, musicians and soldiers. The form of dress is identical for all the figures but, with the exception of one seated figure, the skirts are portrayed without any discernible texture. The seated figure suggests that this could not have been an oversight on the part of the artist, and this suggestion is reinforced by the presence of sheep which are similarly depicted. It seems that either these skirts were made from sheepskin with the fleece removed or they were of linen without the tufting. Whichever of these alternatives is true, the flounced skirt appears to have been the preserve of the nobility and the army.

Above: The skirt and stole were the principal items of Sumerian costume. This limestone votive plaque of Ur-Nansche of Lagash, dating from the third millennium B.C. and now in the Louvre, shows figures of nobility dressed in the pagne-skirt with its stylized textured surface. The figure has its surplus material thrown over the left shoulder to form a loose cloak or stole

Right: A detail of mosaic from the Royal Standard of Ur, dating from early in the third millennium and now in the British Museum, shows how ordinary people such as farmers or soldiers dressed. The men wore calf or ankle-length skirts and cloaks

Left: The splendid sculpture of Ebih-il, the bearded superintendent of the Ishtar temple at Mari, now in the Louvre, shows the figure dressed in the characteristic Sumerian long skirt. The garment is tied at the waist and, at the back, the excess waistband forms an animal-like tail which is allowed to hang loosely

Right: The diorite statue of Gudea, now in the Louvre, shows the figure draped in a long, carefully-arranged shawl. Surplus material forms a half-cape over the left shoulder, but the right arm is left bare. Made from a single piece of material, this garment prefigures the Greek himation or Roman toga, two thousand years later.

Accessories and decoration

This simple, almost primitive, attitude towards clothes does not mean that the Sumerians were uninterested in their appearance. Their personal grooming, for instance, appears to have been meticulous. Some men shaved their heads and sported neatly trimmed beards without moustaches, while others had long hair and beards. Women's hairstyles were varied and complex and wigs may have been worn. Certainly wigs and wigstands were found in the tombs at Ur. One woman portrayed in a plaque from Khafajah exemplifies the sophistication of women's hairdressing. All the hair has been drawn up to the crown of the head, then plaited into six braids from the crown to the base of the skull. Here the small braids are plaited into one thick one which is passed round the head and across the top forming a coronet. The craftsmanship of contemporary goldwork discovered in the tombs is quite astonishing, showing an elegance of design and a fineness of execution which is in marked contrast to the simplicity of the Sumerians' basic costume. The most impressive single collection came from the grave of Queen Pu Abi of about 2500 B.C., which was full of lapis lazuli, cornelian and gold.

The Babylonians

The Babylonians did not assume dominance in Mesopotamia until the twenty-second century B.C., but their ideas and fashions had infiltrated the Sumerian way of life long before that date. The move away from fleeced skirts is apparent from the twenty-fourth century B.C. From this date, through the Babylonian and Assyrian empires, we see a development in both the form of clothes and their decoration: light woven materials replace the thick skins of the previous era. Clothes become much more practical and more suitable for the sub-tropical climate of Mesopotamia. Initially, wool was the material generally woven, rather than cotton or linen, but this was probably a result of availability. Statues show that these woven fabrics were richly decorated, very often with geometric designs.

Basic costume

During the last years of Sumerian and the first of Babylonian domination, the dressmaker's craft was more a question of artful draping of material than of producing complex garments. One of the earliest examples of these draped costumes, fashioned from a single rect-

angle of material, is shown in a statue of Gudea, ruler of Lagash (about 2350 B.C.) who, though a Sumerian, had adopted the typical Babylonian mode of dress. The figure is draped in a fashion not dissimilar to the Greek *himation* or Roman *toga* of two thousand years later. The material is draped round the body passing under the armpits, with the surplus material passed over the left shoulder encasing the left arm, leaving the right arm and shoulder uncovered.

Although pictorial representations of women in Mesopotamia are too rare for us to be able to make any generalizations about their costume, they seem to have followed the fashion of their menfolk. One rare exception is a statue of a woman from the time of Gudea, now in the Louvre, which, though damaged, gives us an idea of at least one fashion for women of this period. Again, the costume is made from a single rectangle of woven material, but, unlike the contemporary male costume, both shoulders are covered. The material is stretched tight across the bust, crossed over at the back with the loose ends passed over the shoulders and hanging loose to the waist.

A rather later statue of an Elamite woman (from about 2000 B.C.) shows a

variation on this theme. Here the fabric passes over the right shoulder and is draped round the body and on to the left shoulder, where the material is secured with a pin—one of the rare examples from this period where a pin is used to fasten material rather than the loose fabric being tucked away. The overall appearance of this form of drapery is strongly reminiscent of the Indian sari which is still worn today. Another interesting feature of this statue is an undergarment which protrudes from the fabric. This is generally thought to be a bust-bodice, a form which has also survived to the twentieth century in parts of India.

Wall paintings discovered at Mari in ancient Syria, dating from the eighteenth century B.C., give a further insight into the costume of the period. It would appear that these elaborate draped garments were only worn by the nobility—musicians and servants being dressed once more in simple skirts of linen. In one of the paintings, a figure, obviously a king or prince, is shown at an investiture wearing a skirt with a shawl folded in the same way as the Gudean woman's tunic. One of the most exciting qualities of these paintings is the colour. The costume is decorated with a dazzling

Right: The basic item of dress of the Assyrians was a short-sleeved ankle-length tunic, usually made of an elaborately decorated fabric. This Babylonian boundary stone shows the Babylonian king Marduk-Nadin-Akhe wearing the Assyrian style tunic and a tasselled shawl fastened by a broad sash. The tall cylindrical headdress and crimped hair are typical of the period

Far right: The early fourth-century B.C. frieze of glazed bricks from Susa depicts archers of the Royal Guard. They wear long loose tunics belted just below the ribs with voluminous full-length sleeves in rich, heavily patterned Persian fabrics. They wear purple stockings with yellow shoes and coronets on their heads. Beards and hair were crimped with hot tongs. It is interesting to note the use of laced shoes instead of bare feet or simple sandals

fringe of red, gold, grey and white, arranged to form a symmetrical pattern. Colour appears to have been one of the main areas for display in Babylonian costume.

Little is known about accessories. Shoes are never shown and jewellery appears to have been limited to bracelets and dog-collar necklaces.

The Assyrians

Babylonian rule in Mesopotamia lasted almost a thousand years and, once again, towards the end of this period, we see a dramatic change in costume, heralding the approach of a new civilization, that of the Assyrians. As Gudea, one of the last Sumerian rulers, had adopted the costume of the Babylonians, so Marduk-Nadin-Akhe in about 1050 B.C., at the end of Babylonian domination, is seen dressed in the costume of the Assyrians. He is depicted in a relief in the British Museum in a costume which bears no resemblance to that of his predecessors, a costume which can truly be described as Assyrian. The basic garment is a short-sleeved, ankle-length fitted tunic of richly decorated fabric. Over this is worn a tasselled shawl, also richly decorated,

which is wound round his hips and held in place by a broad embroidered sash which carries two daggers. On his head he wears a tall cylindrical hat similar to those worn by Greek Orthodox priests. Even his coiffure is Assyrian, with shoulder-length hair and a crimped beard. He wears shoes, rather than sandals, on his feet, which would previously have been bare. The stylized decorative motifs are typical of those which are to dominate the next few centuries.

The overall form of Assyrian costume, the short-sleeved fitted tunic covered with one or more shawls, remains virtually unaltered until the time of the Medes and Persians in the sixth century B.C. The fabric of both garments becomes increasingly elaborate, however, and there are significant developments in the field of accessories.

Between the ninth and sixth centuries B.C., costume can be divided into three main categories—ceremonial, military and hunting. The differences between the three probably owe more to functional considerations than to fashion.

One of the figures most commonly depicted from the ninth century is the great Assyrian king Ashurnasirpal II (884–859 B.C.). Apart from the arrange-

ment of the shawl, his basic costume is the same as that of Marduk-Nadin-Akhe, but the cylindrical hat is replaced by a soft felt cap, a forerunner of today's fez, and his feet are clad in simple, openwork sandals.

Military costume of the period has the same short-sleeved tunic, knee-length for greater mobility, with the shawl replaced by various items of protective wear and sandals rejected in favour of calf-length, laced boots.

The next important sources of pictorial evidence are the seventh-century bas-reliefs from Nineveh which were painted during the reign of King Ashurbanipal (669–630 or 626 B.C.). Again, changes in overall style are no more than marginal. The tunic, for example, is still ankle length but is now worn without the shawls. The most startling feature of the costumes depicted at Nineveh is the richness of the decoration of the fabrics themselves and the range of colours employed.

There are few portrayals of women's costume during this period. However, we know that a ruling was introduced by the Assyrians that all married women should be veiled in public, a forerunner of *purdah* which is still observed by some Moslem women.

The Medes and Persians

By the end of the seventh century B.C., the Assyrian Empire had fallen to the combined forces of the Medes and the Chaldeans. Their domination, however, was short-lived and they were overthrown by the Persians under Cyrus the Great in 539 B.C.

Little is known of the brief period of Median domination in Mesopotamia, but it appears that the Persians had great respect for the Medes and adopted many of their ideas. The Persians were originally mountain people from what is now Turkestan in the USSR. Their clothing, therefore, was basically unsuitable for their new domain and they evolved an eclectic style of costume which incorporated features of Median, Babylonian and Assyrian dress.

The Median contribution was the long flowing 'robe of honour' worn by the king and his retinue on ceremonial occasions. There are several excellent illustrations of this garment, a fine example being the fifth century frieze at Susa, which depicts archers from the Royal Guard. The form of the garment is extremely simple, consisting of two rectangles of cloth sewn across the top with an aperture for the head and sewn

down the sides from waist to hem. The generous width of the fabric provides voluminous full-length sleeves and the garment is belted just below the rib cage. It must have been an extremely comfortable garment in a hot climate and, skilfully adjusted, very elegant. The garments are decorated with geometric designs and rosettes and yellow, brown, ochre and blue are the predominant colours. On their heads the archers wear soft, felt hats held in position by a plaited band and, on their feet, ankle boots with three laces.

The Persians' contribution to this fluid situation was the most noticeable. As horsemen and mountain dwellers they had been used to making fitted clothes from skins and were skilled in the art of cutting and sewing material to follow the contour of the body—indeed, they were the first tailors. They rapidly adapted their ancient craft to new, lighter materials. This resulted in the first known trousers and jackets with set-in sleeves. The importance of this in the history of costume cannot be over-estimated. The basic style, adopted for everyday wear, consisted of tight-fitting trousers tucked into ankle boots and a tight tunic top with long sleeves. Sometimes this outfit was covered with an ankle-length overcoat which was frequently worn slung across the shoulders, the sleeves hanging free. They had a number of different styles of hats but one particular design is peculiar to them —a high, slightly rounded felt cap which sat perched on top of their bushy crimped hair.

In 331 B.C. Alexander the Great conquered Babylon and costume was influenced by the Greeks, whose style is described later. By the time the Persians regained their true independence, their costume had become divorced from developments in the West and was to follow quite different styles.

Egypt

Towards 4000 B.C., Egyptian civilization emerged on the banks of the Nile. Unlike Sumeria to the east, which was made up of a series of self-governing city states, Egypt was a nation in the true sense of the word. It enjoyed a certain unity and stability and did not experience the disruption of a continually shifting power base. For three thousand years, with a few temporary interruptions, the Pharaohs ruled a nation with a definite and highly ordered hierarchy, a nation of incredible sophistication and technical skill and, above all, a tradition so rigid that, in some areas, it precluded change for thousands of years. It is apparent that two of the most powerful forces in Egyptian society were religion (it should be remembered that Pharaoh was a living god) and tradition. Despite regular trade routes and the occasional invasions, the changes in their mode of dress over this period were minimal.

Unlike the Sumerians, the Egyptians abandoned the use of skins at a very early stage. Even the use of wool was frowned on as being unclean and, while it was used for heavy cloaks, it was forbidden in temples and was never buried with the dead. They generally preferred woven vegetable fibres such as linen, which produced lighter materials more suited to the climate. In the early days these were generally palm fibres but, as the Egyptians' irrigation system and agricultural methods improved, flax was used for the production of linen which was worn to the virtual exclusion of all other materials. The advantages of this material were manifold. It could be woven extremely finely to produce a light cool fabric, it was white, which was of religious significance, and it could be easily laundered. Egyptians, according

to Herodotus, took their cleanliness very seriously: he tells us that 'They wear garments of linen fresh washed, taking singular care to have them always clean . . .' for, he adds, '. . . they esteem cleanliness more than ornament.'

Basic costume

Egyptian costume for both sexes was extremely scanty and we are told that at the beginning of the dynastic period children and slaves went totally naked. They were seldom depicted in this state in tomb paintings since clothes were a status symbol and the presence of a naked figure might have jeopardized the status of the deceased in the after-life.

The oldest male garment was the simple loin-cloth or *schenti*, which consisted of a single strip of linen wrapped round the hips. It was adopted by all classes, although the material used by the Pharaohs, we are told, was much finer and often pleated. There were various methods of folding this garment, the most common being that employed today in India and parts of Africa with the material passing diagonally across the hips with one end tucked in at the waist and the other hanging free at the front. This garment was worn with a bare torso regardless of social status.

With the reign of Tuthmosis IV (1425–1405 B.C.), the schenti was generally abandoned in favour of a skirt. This again was made from a single rectangle of linen and could vary in length from mid-thigh to calf. The simplest form was drawn tight across the back and gathered in a single box pleat at the front, but the high-born had a much more elaborate version, in which the surplus material was gathered at the waist and a series of carefully arranged pleats fanned out. This arrangement was held in place at the waist by a decorated belt from which was suspended a wedge-shaped apron, embroidered and set with precious stones. A particularly fine example of this garment is shown on the panel from the back of the throne of Tutankhamun (c. 1361–c. 1352 B.C.) which can be seen in the Cairo Museum. The apron was also adopted by the lower classes, but the elaborate decoration was absent.

Another garment, introduced at the same time, was the sleeved tunic, which resembled a short-sleeved night-shirt. Again the length of garment varied, from knee to ankle length and, in the case of the Pharaohs, was made of such fine linen as to be totally transparent. It was worn over a schenti or decorated apron of the type mentioned above. An excel-

Far left: The elegant wooden figure of La Dame Tui wears a large wig and is dressed in a kalasiris of fine cotton

Left: Eventually the schenti was abandoned and replaced by a type of skirt made from a single piece of linen drawn tight across the back and gathered into a pleat at the front. This painting from a Noble's Tomb at Thebes, dating from about 1300 B.C., shows figures dressed in these garments

Right: This detail of a wall painting from the tomb of Mebamun at Thebes, c. 1400, demonstrates the simplicity of Egyptian dress which is typified by the very short loin-cloth known as the schenti. The detail shows a harvest scene in which the workers are wearing schentis

Below right: Royalty wore a more elaborate version of this skirt-like garment with the surplus material gathered at the waist and falling into pleats held in place by an ornate belt. This panel from the inside of the back of the throne of Tutankhamun shows him swathed in such a finely-pleated linen garment. The tomb of Tutankhamun, discovered in 1922, included remains of seven royal garments

lent example of this form is shown in a relief painting of Seti I and the Goddess Hathor, dating from the nineteenth dynasty. Another version of the tunic, generally worn by merchants and the middle classes, was made from thicker, opaque linen, tied at the waist with a girdle. From the sixteenth dynasty, princes used a large transparent veil of material which was draped around the body and knotted once at the neck. The elaborate folds on the shoulders and round the hips give the impression of a cloak, a tunic with sleeves and a short kilt. The robe is known as the royal *haik*.

The most elaborate and most unusual style of dress adopted by the Egyptians was a robe which is thought to be the only mode adopted by them from another civilization. The form is very similar to some of the costumes of Asia Minor—a single rectangle of linen about twice the height of the wearer, folded and with a slit cut for the head and the edges sewn from hem to waist. The fullness of the material formed voluminous sleeves and the skirt section was gathered at the waist in a knot.

Women's costume is represented in many of the tomb paintings but varies very little from men's, with an emphasis on scantiness and a tendency to veil the

23

body rather than to conceal it. Slaves and dancers are frequently represented naked or, if they are dressed, it is in a simple wrap-around linen skirt gathered at the waist with a cord. Women of higher birth often wore the same simple type of skirt, supplemented by a cape covering the shoulders and the upper part of the breasts. The simple nightshirt tunic (kalasiris) was also worn by women, either loose or belted, and sometimes decorated with an elaborate apron. The fabric was usually very finely pleated and, like the male version, virtually transparent.

One style which was peculiar to women was a long skirt starting just below the bust and reaching to the ankles. The skirt was supported by two broad shoulder straps, much in the style of the 'pinafore' dress which has been in and out of fashion at various times during the twentieth century. Again the robe, introduced from the East, was adopted by women. It was draped in the same way as the male version, but the material was generally gathered and tied in a slightly higher position, just below the bust.

It is not necessary to describe the clothes children wore, since they either went naked or were dressed as miniature

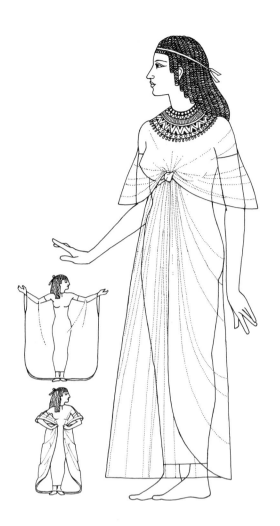

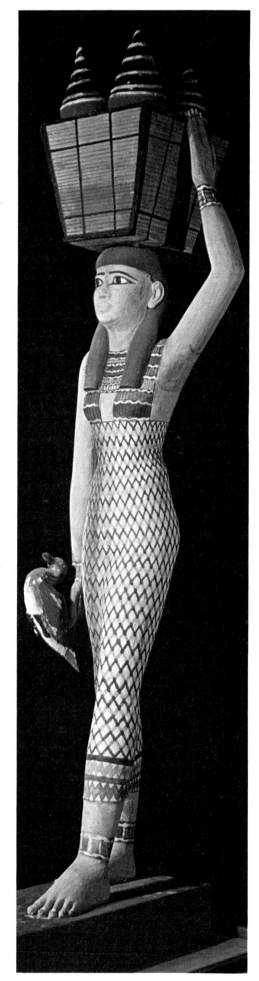

versions of their adult contemporaries. Even the military departed very little from civilian costume. They were, by comparison with warriors of other countries, very lightly clad with a linen loincloth or skirt covered with a leather apron, and breast-plate.

Men, women and children wore the same footwear, when they wore any footwear at all—a simple open sandal, either of leather or plaited papyrus, held in place by a thong between the big and second toe, with a strap passing over the top of the foot. Much more elaborate jewelled sandals were discovered in the tomb of Tutankhamun, but these can only have been for funerary or ceremonial purposes. It is thought that shoes were the most precious item of Egyptian dress; it was quite customary to carry them while making a journey and only to put them on after arrival at the wearer's destination.

Accessories and decoration
It is clear that Egyptian costume was simple to the point of being austere. Unlike their neighbours, the Egyptians were very restrained in their use of colour and decoration in their fabrics. They relied instead almost entirely on accessories and personal adornment to inject colour and interest into their costume.

There can be few people who have not seen, either first-hand or reproduced, the fabulous treasures discovered by Howard Carter from the tomb of the boy king, Tutankhamun, and who can therefore be unaware of the Egyptians' astonishing mastery of metalwork and lapidary techniques. Unlike that of many other nations, Egyptian jewellery can be genuinely considered as an integral part of costume. Because of the rigid adherence to tradition, jewellery forms were virtually standardized throughout the dynastic period and costume must have been designed with these forms in mind rather than treating them as optional extras. The most obvious example of this is the broad collar which was one of the most widely used forms of jewellery throughout the period. It was a series of strings of precious stones or *faience* (glazed earthenware) arranged in parallel rows and tied behind the neck forming a deep, semicircular chest ornament.

Another favourite neck ornament was the pectoral, which generally consisted of a rectangular plaque of gold openwork set with precious stones or faience and suspended at chest level from a decorated chain. The design of these

pectorals was again closely linked with tradition, superstition and religion and they invariably carried various amuletic devices to protect the wearer from all types of adversity.

The Aegean

Crete is thought to have been inhabited from the sixth millennium B.C., but it was probably not until the late fourth or early third millennium that immigrants from Asia Minor founded a genuine civilization. They brought with them the technology and organizational flair which transformed a nation of skin-clad cave dwellers into one of the most sophisticated civilizations of the ancient world.

The climate in Crete, as in Mesopotamia and mainland Greece, was not sufficiently dry to preserve actual examples of clothing, although tiny fragments of material were recovered from the shaft graves at Mycenae. Once again we are obliged to rely on the evidence of such other artefacts as statuettes, pots, reliefs and frescoes, all of which were predominantly figurative. Unlike so much sculpture from this period, the Minoan terracottas are polychromatic,

and this gives us an accurate guide not only to the forms of dress and their development but also to the colours and decorative forms favoured. However, the statuettes are very stylized and may give exaggerated versions of the clothing that was normally worn.

The Minoan civilization is considered to have started about 3000 B.C., but it is not until the start of the middle Minoan period, about a thousand years later, that we have any evidence of an individual style of costume emerging. Men, regardless of rank or status, appear to have favoured virtual nudity. They did wear belts with small cloth aprons, loincloths and even short skirts but these are very similar to those of pre-dynastic and Old Kingdom Egypt. The materials used for these limited garments certainly became more and more elaborate, as did those used for women's costume. The development of fabrics can be considered side by side with that of women's costume.

Minoan women's costume represents a complete departure from the styles observed in other contemporary civilizations. A statuette dating from 2000 B.C., found at Petsofa, depicts a woman in a bell-shaped skirt. It is highly stylized and it is quite difficult to make out the precise

outlines of the garment she is wearing, but most authorities consider it to be a dress cut from a semi-circle of stiff material with arm-holes which was worn as a cloak, tied at the waist with a cord. This would appear to be a forerunner of similar but more sophisticated dresses from the end of the middle period.

Like many early civilizations, the Minoans had started making garments from skins, but it is obvious from the decorative motifs on the Petsofa statue that they had already mastered the craft of weaving. This is confirmed by the discovery of weaving implements dating from the third millennium B.C. Minoan civilization was at its height at the end of the middle period—between 1750 and 1580 B.C. It was during this time that the palace at Knossos was built and that the most exciting developments in Cretan costume were seen. The Palace itself contained a complete spinning and weaving shop, along with some of the finest and most significant statuettes, which are still in a fine state of preservation.

The most striking feature of these costumes is the sheer technical virtuosity in the standard of the dress-making. Other civilizations of the time relied more on the fold and arrangement of the

Above: This late-Minoan sarcophagus painting from Hagia Triada shows Cretan religious costume. The leading priest wears a skirt with a 'tail' in a material reminiscent of the kaunakès of earlier civilizations; his two companions are dressed in the Cretan close-fitting embroidered robe

Above right: These Mycenean warriors wear close-fitting helmets pointed at the back and front with long plumes hanging behind

fabric than the cut of the garment itself. The Minoans, however, wore fitted clothes as we know them today.

While the overall line of the dresses is not dissimilar to those of the Petsofa figure, there are many refinements. The skirts fall straight from the hips and then fill out to a wide hem. It is not known for certain how this was achieved: some experts consider that the lower half of the skirt was stretched over hoops of rushes, wood or even metal. Others consider that these were the earliest boned crinolines. Many of the skirts were flounced with up to a dozen horizontal pleats. Above the skirt a tight-fitting short-sleeved bodice was worn. In most cases the breasts were entirely exposed, with the bodice laced up below the bust. Some frescoes, however, suggest that the breasts were in fact veiled with a transparent bolero top.

As has so often been true in the history of fashion, the Minoans obviously craved tiny waists and wore extremely tight belts. These were generally of some padded material which was wound round the waist twice with the ends hanging down the front of the dress. Other belts appear to be of metal, a fashion adopted by the men of the period. One common elaboration to this

mode of dress, particularly on the statues of goddesses, is a double apron falling in front and behind. It is possible that these aprons had some religious significance.

For the first time we encounter a race of hat-conscious women. Two entirely different styles are portrayed on the terracottas. One, the shape of an inverted plant pot, which is made from three tiers reflecting the flouncing on the dress and, the second, a simple beret.

Shoes for both sexes were exclusively for outdoor wear. This was deduced from various buildings in Knossos where the steps leading up to them were very worn, but this damage stopped abruptly at the door. Courtiers and royalty are invariably portrayed barefoot, whereas soldiers and hunters are more usually shown wearing leather sandals or calf-length boots.

Not only was the Minoan costume extremely sophisticated in construction, but the decoration of the fabrics themselves was unsurpassed in the ancient world. Once again we are limited by the sources of information available to us and it is impossible to say whether the designs were woven into the material, embroidered or dyed, but it is obvious that the Minoan women had an unprecedented love of colour and display

Above: Another fresco from the Royal Palace at Knossos depicts the ladies of the Minoan court. Cretan women of this period left much of the upper part of their bodies exposed. Their hair was held in place by a ribbon and a single long curl fell from above the ear to the neck in the characteristic fashion of Crete. Some sort of hair ornament was usually also worn

in their fabrics. Most designs were geometric with a preference for repeated patterns. In other cases, however, the decorative themes were drawn from nature using flowers, fish and birds. It is also impossible to say what dyes they used, but it is obvious from the statuettes and frescoes that a considerable range was available. The colours most commonly depicted are purple, red, blue and yellow.

During the fifteenth century B.C., Knossos was overrun by invaders from mainland Greece and eventually the Minoan government collapsed and Crete was controlled from Mycenae. Culturally, however, the normal procedure was reversed. Instead of the conquerors imposing their culture on the conquered Minoans the Myceneans adopted the Minoan culture with the result that Mycenean costume is virtually indistinguishable from late Minoan. Women's costume retained the same basic form but with rather more complex flouncing and pleats of varying depths starting from the hips. The double apron appears to have disappeared but the desire for lavishly decorated material continued unabated.

In men's costume there was one development worth noting. The double apron and loin-cloth, at least in the case of warriors, appear to have been replaced by very tight shorts decorated with tassels.

These overall forms survived without any major change until the Dorian invasions of about 1200 B.C. which brought about the downfall of the Minoan/Mycenean civilization and plunged the Aegean into centuries of cultural stagnation.

CLASSICAL PERFECTION
Greece and Rome

Greece

Greek costume is noted for its unchanging styles, which are to be found with only minor modifications from the twelfth century B.C. until the third century B.C. In the early centuries after the Illyrian conquest of Greece, presumably Cretan outlines continued in fashion, that is, the bell-shaped skirts and tight bodices, but these existed alongside the shape which became the basic form of classical Greek dress: the Doric chiton. This draped double rectangle, loosely held on the shoulders and gathered in various ways round the wearer's body, was worn by men and women for well over five centuries. Fortunately, Greek costume is well documented for us through surviving pieces of sculpture and in written descriptions by contemporary historians.

During the periods under discussion, generally referred to as Archaic and Classical, there were two basic styles of costume for both men and women: Dorian, in existence at the beginning of the Archaic period, and Ionian which was adopted later. Within these two categories, however, there were numerous variations and, as time passed, a conglomerate style emerged.

The most basic outer garment for women was the Doric peplos which was worn universally up to the beginning of the sixth century B.C. It was made from a rectangle of woven wool measuring about six feet in width and a variable amount longer than the height of the wearer. The fabric was wrapped round the wearer with the excess material folded over at the top. The excess flap could fall as far as the waist or as low as the hips. The garment was pinned at both shoulders and the excess material allowed to fall free, giving the impression of a short cape. At its simplest, the Doric peplos was worn without a belt and the side was left open, but there were other more sophisticated variations. The open side, for example, might be sewn from waist to hem and the excess material, instead of being folded over at the top, could be tucked through a girdle worn just below the bust and allowed to fall free. This loose fold of material concealed the belt, giving a skirt and blouse effect. A second belt was sometimes worn over the fold at about waist level, which strengthened the impression of it being two garments. The pins which were used to fasten the shoulders of the peplos were originally open pins with decorated heads, but these were later replaced by *fibulae* or brooches.

Right: This dish illustrates the Doric costume of both men and women. The man's chiton or long tunic is topped by a himation which covers the shoulders like a stole. The woman's chiton could be draped in several different ways. In this archaic representation the features of the man are still very stylized

Below: The Doric chiton was the basic garment worn by Greek women up to the beginning of the sixth century B.C. It was folded so that there was an overlap of material on the bodice, which was held in place by pins

The Ionic chiton which followed and which, to some extent, overlapped with the Doric style was similar in overall construction. The woollen fabric introduced to Greece by the Dorians was replaced by thin linen or occasionally silk, reflecting the increased influence of Asia Minor on the country. Again this costume was made from a single rectangle of material but substantially wider than that used for the peplos, measuring anything up to ten feet wide. Unlike the peplos, it had no surplus material in its length but was measured from shoulder to ankle. Its enormous width required some eight or ten fibulae to fasten the top edge, leaving an openwork seam either side of the neck which ran across the shoulders and down the arms to form elbow-length sleeves. Being shorter than the peplos, it had no blousing effect but was generally girded just below the bust. The top of the garment was sometimes sewn rather than pinned, and a few examples are shown with fitted sleeves.

The other garment worn throughout this period was an outer garment usually worn by men, the *himation*. This was formed from a rectangle of woven wool and started life as outdoor wear, but, with the arrival of the lighter material of the Ionic chiton, it could be worn at any

time. At the beginning of the Archaic period the himation was comparatively small and was generally worn round the shoulders as a cloak but, as time passed and Greek taste became more sophisticated, methods of draping it became more elaborate and its dimensions increased to ten or twelve feet by five feet.

With the himation we see for the first time the complex and highly stylized fabric arrangements which typify Greek dress. By the middle of the Archaic period the commonest method of folding was to wrap the material round the torso so that it passed under the left arm and to pin it at the right shoulder, the excess material falling down the right arm being fastened by several small pins in the same way as the sleeves of the Ionic chiton. A simpler method of folding, widely adopted during the fifth century B.C., and similar to that used for a present-day evening stole, was to pass the material behind the back and drape the loose ends over the forearms.

Opinions differ as to how the most elegant method of draping the chiton was achieved, but most experts agree that one corner of the material was taken over and fastened at the right shoulder; the full width of material was then pulled tight across the chest, half passing over the left

Left: This figure shows how the short cloak was worn. The pointed hat is of a type that became popular later

arm and half enveloping the head; it was then passed round the back, over the right arm, around the body once again and the loose end held in the left hand. The effect of this arrangement was not only extremely elegant, it was also feminine and flattering, lending an air of mystery.

Forms of male dress throughout the Archaic and Classical periods were very similar to women's. The two basic garments, the chiton and himation, were adopted by both sexes, but there were some differences which may be noted. During both the sixth and seventh centuries B.C., the male chiton was a full-length garment made from a rectangle of woven wool measuring approximately seven feet wide and falling from shoulder to ankle with no surplus material. Unlike the female version, the male chiton was always sewn up the side and was girded differently. Men found it necessary to secure the garment at the shoulders in the form of a harness. A narrow cord passes round the back of the neck, over the shoulders and under the arms; the loose ends are then attached to the loop of cord behind the neck.

The full-length chiton was standard wear for all Greek men until the fifth century B.C. when, except for the elderly, it was abandoned in favour of the short chiton, which was knee-length. It was sometimes pinned on the left shoulder only, leaving the right arm and shoulder free. On other occasions both shoulders were pinned, and, in the case of soldiers, the shoulders and arms were sewn, leaving a wide slit for the head. The short chiton was generally girded at the waist and a certain amount of material could be gathered above the belt to draw the hem-line to mid-thigh level.

Greek men also wore the himation; as with the women's chiton, it was made from a single rectangle of woven wool, comparatively small at the beginning of the Archaic period and becoming increasingly large. At first the himation was worn loosely over the shoulders. Later it was pinned at the throat or on the right shoulder with a fibula but, by the middle of the fifth century B.C., methods of draping became increasingly elaborate. It could be worn either over the long and short chiton or on its own.

When worn alone, a fashion much favoured by philosophers and orators, the draping of the himation was at its most complex. One popular way of wearing it, enveloping the entire body, was to pass the material right round the body, holding one end under the left

Left: The himation reached its most complex state at the end of the fifth century. It is worn here by a lady and her maid as the outer garment. Indoors the chiton was the most usual garment to be worn. The himation was draped over the head, partly masking the face

Below: During the Hellenistic period sculptures became even more lifelike and broke away from the rigidity of earlier periods. This sculpture of Persephone holding a pomegranate shows her swathed in the himation, which has become voluminous

Below right: One way of draping the Doric peplos involved covering the pouching formed by the belt with another section of the long woollen rectangle. This maiden from the Acropolis dates from the sixth century B.C. The Marble was originally brightly painted

arm and throwing the remainder of the material from behind over the left shoulder, across the chest enveloping the right arm, over the right shoulder, across the back again and finally draping the end of the loose material over the left arm. A simpler version of this is shown in a statue of Demosthenes where the material is folded round the body under the armpits with one end tucked in at the top and the other thrown over the left shoulder from behind, leaving most of the upper torso and the right arm uncovered.

The chlamys, a short outer garment, was one Greek form which was worn by men only. Generally worn over the short chiton, it was particularly fashionable with horsemen, travellers and soldiers, being less cumbersome than the himation. This again was a rectangle of woven wool, generally draped round the shoulders and fastened at the throat or right shoulder with a fibula.

It is a popular misconception that all Greek costumes were white. This idea probably arose because most Greek statues are of marble, bronze or some other monochromatic material, and even those which were originally polychromatic had generally lost their colour by the time they were discovered. It may be that clothes during the Archaic period were generally white or off-white, certainly the commoners were forbidden to wear red chitons and himations in theatres or public places, but by the fifth century costumes were decorated with a wide range of colours.

Greek decoration was either woven into the material or embroidered on afterwards. Homer tells us of extravagant costumes woven with threads of silver and gold. Pottery, statues and the written word have given us some knowledge of the decorative themes employed. These could be geometric or figurative, the commonest being the fret, or Greek key pattern—a clean, geometric design, which was used for bordering fabrics, and has been used as a decorative motif ever since. Other designs used for borders include the wave and egg and dart patterns, together with numerous stylized floral designs. More complex borders depicted representational themes ranging from animals, birds and fish to complex battle scenes. The coloured threads available for these embroideries appear to have been virtually limitless. Certainly, the historian Herodotus mentions an instance of yellow, indigo, violet, red and purple being used together in a single garment.

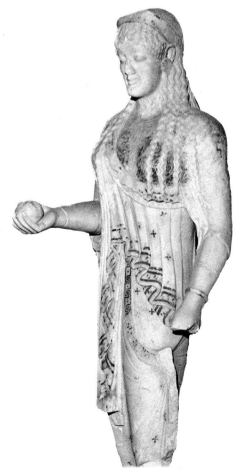

Accessories and decoration

Indoors the Greeks went barefoot, regardless of social status, but only the lower orders went barefoot in the street. Sandals were the main form of footwear among the upper ranks. The simplest version comprised a stiff leather sole with a thong between the big and second toe attached to a strap passing behind the ankle. There were numerous types of more complex sandals, some equipped with tooled leather tongues not unlike Scottish brogues. Others had criss-cross thonging up to the ankle. One interesting example found in Egypt and presumed to have belonged to a prostitute had nails on the sole which left the imprint 'follow me' in the sand. Soldiers, hunters and others engaged in active occupations usually wore boots. Again there were a number of different styles. They were generally calf-length, some lacing up and others held in place with cross-cross thonging in the fashion of sandals.

Hats were not commonplace at any time during this period, except for travelling when both men and women wore a petasos, a broad brimmed felt hat with a rounded dome, similar to those worn by French priests today.

Until the fifth century both sexes wore their hair long but, after that date, it was considered effeminate for adult men, although the fashion continued among women and boys. Young men cut off their hair at puberty and dedicated it to the gods. Beards were also abandoned, except by philosophers and intellectuals who, according to Herodotus, retained them in order to give them an air of seriousness. Women's hairstyles changed radically around this period. Previously hair had been styled in carefully curled ringlets, now it was tied back neatly and held in place with a fillet, or band.

Pictorial and written evidence show that the Greeks inherited their predecessors' love of jewels, and the few surviving examples display the same mastery of the goldsmith's and lapidary's craft. The only goldwork so far discovered has come from tombs and may not be representative of what was used in everyday life. Diadems, for instance, found in the tombs at Eritrea are wafer-thin and can be bent between the finger and thumb. It is possible that the tomb jewels are lighter versions of the real pieces, as the Greeks, pitifully short of gold, might well have resented burying too much of the precious metal with the dead.

Left: The Girl from Verona, here shown in a Roman copy of the lost Greek original, wears a later and more sophisticated style of female dress, although it is still composed of the same basic elements: chiton and himation

Below: This garment, the Ionic chiton, was an alternative to the Doric peplos. The main difference lay in its greater width. The top edges of the material were fastened on the shoulder with clasps, so giving the wearer greater opportunity for the display of jewellery

The Etruscans

The Etruscan civilization flourished from the seventh century B.C. in an area to the north of Rome between the rivers Tiber and Arno. These peoples were probably migrants from Western Asia who became minority rulers over the Villanovans, who were already established in the area. Certainly they had the only Indo-European language ever found in Western Europe which, with the exception of a few words, has never been satisfactorily translated.

The main source of information for this period is once again painting, sculpture and pottery. It is obvious from these that the Etruscans, while intensely independent, were influenced by older cultures. The whole civilization appears to be split neatly into two phases: the Oriental Phase from 700 to 675 B.C., where the influence of Middle Eastern civilizations is apparent; and the Greco-Etruscan phase, during which the Etruscans came into contact with the western colonies of Greece and assumed some of their artistic disciplines. Our knowledge of Etruscan costume is sadly limited, unsupported as it is by written commentary, but it is obvious, from the frescoes which have been discovered

recently, that there was a definite connection between the late Etruscan and early Roman periods.

The earliest statues show both men and women dressed in tunic-robes of various lengths ranging from the knee to ankle with half sleeves. These were either sewn across the top or fastened with fibulae on the right shoulder. Over this tunic men wore a long cloak, while women preferred a semi-circular cape which reached the base of the spine and had two panels thrown forwards over the shoulders, reaching the waist. Tunics were fastened with wide belts, and the boots with turned-up toes were the same as these worn in the Middle East. By the beginning of the fifth century B.C., the long cloak was abandoned in favour of a semi-circular cape worn over the shoulders which, many experts consider, was the inspiration for the Roman toga. The Etruscans themselves probably adapted the garment from the Greek short cloak, the chlamys.

Changes in women's costume during this period were even more noticeable. The tunic became a delicately tailored garment of much finer material. The sleeves were still elbow-length, but the garment was waisted without the help of a belt. Some of the statues from the

Above: These two figures from the Triclinium Tomb at Tarquinia are among the few surviving representations in colour of Etruscan dress, with tunic-robes and semi-circular capes, which may have provided the inspiration for the Roman toga

Above: The early Etruscans' draped cloak derived from those of the Greeks and earlier Mediterranean peoples. By the fifth century the long cloak had become a short toga called a trabea. This page shows the dancers and musicians from the Tomb of the Leopards at Tarquinia which dates from the early fifth century B.C. Great importance was attached to personal ornament by the Etruscans. The flute player (right) wears a fillet to keep his hair in place. His cloak, which is decorated with stripes, is reminiscent of the Greek chlamys, and his strapped sandals are also similar to those worn by the Greeks

fifth century B.C. show a slit up the back of the tunic which is then laced with ribbons.

The new Greek influence is also apparent in footwear, with pointed boots ousted in favour of sandals. One area of self-adornment adopted by the Etruscans about which we know a great deal is jewellery. The Etruscans were perhaps the most brilliant goldsmiths the world has ever seen. They were able to achieve results, particularly with the use of their favourite technique of granulation, that have kept the experts baffled to this day.

The Romans

The story of Rome's expansion from a small city-state to the greatest empire of the ancient world is well known. Roman citizenship was highly prized and, within its well-ordered hierarchy, every aspect of daily life, including costume, was closely regulated by the government. Never since dynastic Egypt had such restrictions been placed on the behaviour of the individual.

The period under discussion stretches from the beginning of the Republican

era (500 B.C.) to the end of the Imperial period (A.D. 330) when the capital of the Empire was moved to Byzantium. The legendary founding of Rome was in about 750 B.C., but our knowledge of the civilization before the Republican period is so scanty that it is from this period that the first written evidence about costume is drawn.

Like that of the Greeks, Roman costume consisted of two basic garments, the tunic and cloak. The Romans classified these under two headings: *indumenta*, those garments which were slipped over the head, and *amictus*, any garment which was wrapped round the body.

In the very early days of the Republic, men wore a simple linen loin-cloth, but this was soon replaced by the *tunica* which was adapted from the Greek chiton. At its simplest it was made from two pieces of cloth, generally wool, sewn together with a slit for the head and two slits for the arms, gathered in at the waist with a belt. This, in fact, remained the sole garment for workers who frequently wore it off the shoulder to allow greater freedom of movement. The well-ordered hierarchy of Roman society demanded that there should be different types of tunica to denote social status.

During the Republic, the tunica was worn to the knee without sleeves but, during the first century A.D., the *dalmatic*, with wide elbow-length sleeves, was introduced. These were later extended to reach the wrist and were decorated with fringes. For the common people, the tunica was white or the colour of natural wool, but knights and magistrates decorated the garment with two narrow purple stripes down the front and back. This garment was called *tunica angusticlavia*. A garment with a wider purple stripe, *tunica laticlavia*, was worn by senators but, by the beginning of the third century A.D., these stripes had ceased to have any real significance and were used for purely decorative purposes.

The *tunica palmata* was worn by victorious generals with the *toga picta*. These were truly magnificent garments of purple silk embroidered with gold thread and decorated with pictorial motifs appropriate to the military campaign. They are forerunners of the magnificent imperial costumes of Byzantium.

The *tunica recta* or *regilla*, an ungirdled garment, was worn by young men before reaching the age of majority and by women on their marriage, although no full accounts of it exist.

Sometimes more than one tunica was worn at the same time. The one next to the skin was known as a *subucula* and the outer garment was called a *tunica exteriodum*.

The tunica continued to be worn short until the third century A.D., except by dandies who wore it just below the knee, but after this date it was frequently worn at ankle-length and became known as a *caracalla*. Girdles were not worn at home, but it was considered effeminate to appear in the street in a loose tunica. The girdle was often equipped with a purse in which money and valuables were carried.

The basic garment, the *stola*, worn by women throughout this period was even more closely derived from the Ionic chiton. The stola was fuller than the tunica with the sleeves being drawn from the fullness of the material. It was invariably ankle-length and was sometimes unsewn at the top and secured by fibulae. It was generally made of wool in the early period, but this was later abandoned in favour of linen and cotton or, for the very rich, silk. Colour was widely used with reds, blues and yellows embroidered with gold thread predominating. Under the stola a simple sleeveless shift was worn which, like the male

version, was called a subucula. In addition to this, women wore an unstiffened bust bodice, the *strophium*. The stola was generally girded in two places, at the hips with a wide belt known as a *succincta*, and under the bust with a girdle called a *cingulum*.

The origin of the toga is a matter for speculation. Some experts believe that it derived directly from the Etruscan cloak, while others consider that it owes its origins to the Greek himation. The truth probably lies somewhere between the two. What is certain is that the toga was the one garment which distinguished a Roman citizen from his contemporaries and was a mark of social status.

The true toga probably emerged during the sixth century B.C. At this time it was comparatively small, little bigger than the chlamys, but its size gradually increased with the complexity of its arrangement. The great Imperial toga of the first and second centuries A.D. could measure more than twenty feet across. The sheer quantity of material needed for such a garment, together with the complexity of arranging it, and the limitations it imposed on the wearer, meant that it was suitable only for the rich or leisured classes. The toga was the right of every Roman citizen.

The toga was basically a semi-circle of wool, and the dignity and beauty of the garment depended entirely upon the way in which it was draped round the body. In the early days of the Republic it was the sole garment, being worn over a simple loin-cloth until the introduction of the tunica. We are told that Cato the Censor aped his ancestors by appearing at the Tribune dressed in a toga without a tunica. The complicated social attitude towards the toga extended to various methods of decoration, and it is interesting to look at the different categories of toga which denoted status or profession.

The commonest form was the *toga virilis* or *pura*. This was made from plain untreated wool and was generally about six inches shorter than all other togas. It was worn by citizens of no particular account on ceremonial occasions. The *toga praetexta* was the garment of public office and was worn by magistrates, consuls, censors and other high government officials. It was also worn by young men of high birth before they reached puberty and took the toga virilis which, as a sign of humility, they wore for one year with both arms enveloped in the folds of the material. The praetexta had a single broad purple stripe woven

41

into its upper straight edge. Julius Caesar, however, who was known for his eccentricity of dress, wore his toga praetexta with the stripe running down the arm.

The *toga candida*, as the name suggests, was worn by candidates for public office. It was identical to the toga virilis except that the wool was bleached to remove the yellowness of the natural colour. It was fashionable for candidates to wear their toga without a tunica— ostensibly as a sign of humility but, as Plutarch tells us, it offered an ideal opportunity for them to show off scars acquired as a result of having served in the army.

The *toga picta* was the triumphal garment worn with the tunica palmata by generals after victorious campaigns. These were the property of the state and were lent to the generals for special ceremonies. Like the tunica palmata, the toga picta was decorated with a purple background embroidered with gold thread. Later, it became the official robe of the emperor and was retained for his exclusive use.

Another form, the *toga pulla*, was black, dark brown or grey, and this was generally worn by those in mourning. The last type, *toga trabea*, came in three

styles: all purple for those consecrated to the gods; purple and white for pre-Republican rulers; and purple and crimson striped for augurs (interpreters of omens).

It would be impossible and confusing to attempt to explain all the folding methods for these various togas. They changed continually throughout the thousand years of Roman civilization, reflecting the changing dimensions of the garment and fluctuations in public taste. The purple stripe of the toga praetexta originally ran along the curved edge of the segment, but it was later transferred to the straight edge.

Different methods of folding the toga could also signify particular occasions, and a fold of material drawn over the head, for example, was recognized as the accepted practice for religious ceremonies and times of mourning.

Once again, the women's overgarment, the *palla*, is more closely related to Greek dress than is the toga. It was formed from a single rectangle of woven wool, normally undyed. Like the toga, it started life with modest proportions, but it too became larger and more complex towards the end of the Republican period. It was originally folded much like the toga with the fabric being

allowed to fall forward over the left shoulder to the feet and passing across the back towards the right. Later it enveloped the whole body and both arms but, unlike the toga, it was secured with a fibula at the left breast.

The Romans did not enjoy the stable weather conditions of the civilizations so far discussed and, with their Empire expanding to the north, they were constantly faced with extremely cold conditions. For the first time we see the introduction of sturdy overgarments in civilized society. There were, of course, several types, each with its own social significance. None of them, however, were of any great social status since they were adapted from rustic costume. The commonest cloak was the *lacerna*, a rectangular woollen garment with rounded corners, which was worn draped over the shoulders and fastened at the neck or shoulder with a fibula. It had a detachable hood and, as time passed, it was produced in finer materials, dyed various colours and worn by Roman citizens. Even when the lacerna had been generally adopted, however, it was frowned on by authority. Augustus forbade it in both the Forum and the Circus and, while it was popular at both the theatre and the games, it was always laid to one

side as a sign of respect when the Emperor entered. A heavier version of the lacerna in fur or leather was also produced for winter in the northern colonies.

Another cloak which seems to have been socially more acceptable was the *paenula*. This was also wool, but it was cut from a semi-circle of cloth and worn round the shoulders. It could vary in length from hip to ankle and was adopted by both men and women, although the Emperor Alexander Severus forbade women to wear it within the city boundaries. The front of the garment was secured with hooks, ties or pins, or sewn up leaving a gap for the head.

The two other outer garments mentioned by Roman writers appear to have been for workers only: the *birrus*, a rectangle of thick wool with a hood, and the *laena* which was of course wool dyed red and used as a blanket at night.

Accessories and decoration

The overall simplicity of their costume is in contrast to the Romans' attitude towards make-up, hairdressing, and other forms of self-adornment. Roman men had their hair cut comparatively short, but it was carefully crimped with hot irons and perfumed—a self-conscious practice observed even by warriors and athletes. Ovid tells us that baldness was considered a deformity and suggests that Julius Caesar wore his celebrated laurels to cover up this very defect. It is also reported that, during the Imperial period, baldness was often concealed by false hair-pieces, glued to the scalp.

The men of Ancient Rome allowed their beards to grow until barbers were introduced in the second century B.C., after which mature men went clean-shaven. This practice continued until the reign of Hadrian who, we are told, reintroduced beards to disguise his own wart-covered chin. After his death, beards were once again abandoned, with the exception of certain philosophers who wished to emulate their Greek mentors. Slaves shaved their heads when they were freed and, in order to be distinguished, wore a woollen cap called a *pileus*. Youths allowed their hair and beard to grow until they assumed the toga virilis when, like the Greeks, they had a celebration of manhood. Beards were not always shaved but were plucked or clipped and experiments were made with depilatories although these were frowned upon as being effeminate. The upper classes retained slaves solely as hairdressers, and barbers' shops were available for commoners.

BYZANTIUM AND THE DARK AGES

From the Fall of Rome to the Norman Conquest

Left: Byzantine costume influenced styles throughout the medieval world. It was particularly remarkable for its lavish use of colour and rich fabrics, usually of silk. Records of Byzantine costume have survived in quantity, often in the form of mosaics, such as this one depicting Salome from St Mark's, Venice

The most striking feature of Byzantine costume is its colour. After the comparative simplicity of Greek and Roman fabrics, we enter an age of dazzling ornament. Most of the evidence is derived from mosaics or illuminated manuscripts, but actual examples of Byzantine fabrics have survived. These are for the most part ecclesiastical garments and reliquary cloths, but written reports suggest that these textiles are very similar to those worn by the nobility.

Wool and linen were used, but it is for their work with silk that the Byzantine textile-workers will be remembered. There was a well-established trade route between the Middle East and China by the time Byzantium was founded and great quantities of silk were imported in the early days. In 552, however, travelling monks returned from the East with silkworms and started a flourishing silk industry in the city itself. One fabric which they produced was *samite*, a thick, strong silk which was ideally suited to the majestic Byzantine costume. Into their silks they sewed gold threads and, on some occasions, the reverse process was used with silk being sewn into sheets of gold. Precious stones and pearls were also used in fabrics to make them even more splendid.

Colours used for garments appear to have run right through the spectrum, but the Imperial court favoured purple with gold embroidery, influenced by the toga picta which had been adopted by emperors towards the end of the Roman Imperial period. Where they gained the expertise to produce these elaborate fabrics is uncertain, but many experts believe that either Egyptian Copts were employed in Byzantium or the fabrics were produced in Egypt to Byzantine design.

The motifs employed reflect the mixed heritage of the society—simple geometric patterns from the Classical lands, mythological beasts from the East and religious scenes from the new Christian faith. The designs were applied in a number of ways. Geometric patterns were often used all over the fabric, while other motifs were used only as a border. There were also stripes similar to those used by the Romans. The most unusual form, however, was the *tablion*, a rectangular decorative panel sewn onto the front of cloaks.

The most striking aspect of the costumes pictured in mosaics is their ecclesiastical appearance, and it should be remembered that the Emperor had considerable religious power. He was

considered to be Christ's representative on earth, and, while he did not officiate at religious ceremonies, he had many other duties attached to the Church and his whole life was controlled by Christian legislation.

The basic garments of early Byzantium were, not surprisingly, similar to those of the late Roman Empire. The undergarment was a simple tight-fitting tunic with long sleeves which could vary in length from knee to ankle. Over this was worn a tunic-robe similar to the dalmatica with loose sleeves. The undergarment was usually white, but the tunic-robe offered more opportunity for decoration. The most significant break away from the Roman mode of dress was the abandoning of the toga, although even this was retained as the official dress of consuls in Byzantium until the middle of the sixth century A.D.

The toga was replaced by a cloak: there were three basic styles, all derived from Roman cloaks and these again were highly decorated.

The simplest form was a rectangle of fabric which was worn round the shoulders and reached the ground, fastened at the right shoulder with an elaborate brooch. An excellent example is that worn by the Emperor Justinian in the famous mosaic from the Church at San Vitale, Ravenna. The tablion is clearly portrayed on the Emperor's gown.

A semi-circular cape of similar dimensions, fastened at the right shoulder, was also adopted. The third type of cloak was similar to the Roman paenula, a circular cape sewn up at the front with an aperture for the head. This last type was sometimes provided with a detachable hood.

The only garment included in Byzantine costume which is derived from the toga is the *pallium* which should not be confused with the Roman cloak of the same name. This was a simple band of stiff cloth, about eight inches wide, which was wound round the neck and body in a number of different ways. Again, this was richly decorated and worn by Byzantine emperors and later by kings of Western Europe as a part of their ceremonial dress.

Some authorities maintain that *bracchae*, or tight breeches, were worn under the tunic-robe but, since legs are invariably shown covered in pictorial sources, it is impossible to ascertain this. Some form of hosiery, either of knitted wool or soft fabric and tailored to follow the contours of the foot and ankle, was

Above: Byzantine men wore trousers which were similar to the pantaloons of the Persians. They were made of a rich material often patterned or embroidered. The three kings bearing gifts to Christ in the mosaic in the Church of Sant' Apollinare Nuovo at Ravenna wear trousers topped by a tunic which appears to be fastened between the legs. The mosaic dates from the sixth century A.D.

Right: The basic Byzantine garments were derived from those of the late Roman Empire. A simple tight-fitting tunic was worn under a tunic robe with loose sleeves. The toga was replaced by a cloak which was often richly decorated. Leather sandals were retained for footwear, as shown in this illustration which is part of the Byzantine mosaic at Ravenna

certainly worn. Shoes show a distinct Eastern influence, with calf-length boots and shoes richly decorated with gems.

Women's costume followed that of their male contemporaries. Women wore a light, tight-sleeved chemise reaching the ankle. Over this they wore a tunic-gown with a slightly shorter hem and sleeves so that a band of the under-garment was visible. The outer garment could be girded or not according to the width of the material used. Women are also depicted wearing a veil with a long piece of material from it falling behind or folded forward and draped over the forearm.

The few illustrations of farmers and workers date from the ninth century A.D. by which time the Oriental in-fluence had increased. They are por-trayed wearing light breeches tucked into knee-length boots. Over this they wear a thigh-length tunic with loose sleeves and an ankle-length cloak. The fabrics shown are by no means as elaborate as those of the court but the social barriers governing clothes, so strict in Rome, had broken down by this time and in Byzantium the only re-straints were economic.

Most representations of Byzantine men and women show them bare-headed, except for the Emperor who wears a crown and farmers who wear a petasos, a wide-brimmed type of hat. Men's hair is generally cropped or bobbed, while women retain the elaborate hairstyles of the late Imperial Period, sometimes held in place with a turban, another Oriental influence.

The Byzantine love of colour was also apparent in their jewellery. The Ravenna mosaics depict jewels of great magnifi-cence, and many examples have sur-vived to this day. Gold and unfaceted precious stones were used, but it is cloisonné enamelling that most distin-guished Byzantine jewellery. Although the forms used were inherited from Rome, the decorative themes once again reflect the combined influence of East and West.

From the Barbarians to the Norman Conquest

By the beginning of the fifth century A.D., Britain and Gaul, after centuries of Roman domination, were vulnerable to attacks by the nomadic tribes which had so long existed on the borders of the Roman Empire, and eventually the

Above: The simplest form of cloak was a rectangle of fabric worn round the shoulders and fastened at the right shoulder by a brooch called a tablion. This mosaic from the Church of San Vitale at Ravenna portrays the Empress Theodora, who wears an elaborate crown with rows of pearls suspended from her diadem. The richness and variety of Byzantine fabrics is evident

Roman Empire collapsed, all traces of the classical life-style vanishing, after raids by Saxons, Franks and other Barbarians.

Little is known of the life and costume of the Barbarians; they were largely illiterate and few representations of their costume have ever been discovered. Occasional examples of their garments, however, have been recovered from peat bogs in Germany, Holland and Scandinavia. These, together with isolated written descriptions, give us enough information to build a sketchy picture of Barbarian dress. Men, it would appear, wore a short fitted tunic of coarsely woven material, fastened at the waist with a belt. Below this they wore either short breeches with leg bandages or cross-gartered trousers. On their feet they wore crude leather shoes and, over the tunic, striped cloaks of heavy woollen material. In winter they wore animal skins with the fur outwards, as did other nomadic peoples.

Our knowledge of Barbarian women's costume is even more inadequate, but archeological discoveries suggest that they wore a simple skirt with a drawstring at the waist and a short bloused top with elbow-length sleeves. Both sexes wore their hair long and plaited and men sported heavy moustaches.

THE MEROVINGIAN PERIOD

In the Merovingian period in France, between 481 and 752, there were significant developments in Western costume. The Merovingians, unlike the Romanized Gauls, buried their dead fully-clothed, and excavations at Lorraine and Le Mans have yielded fragments of clothing. It would appear that the Merovingians adopted the general styles of their predecessors but produced their garments in finer fabrics. The most important garment for men was the *gonelle*, a knee-length full tunic top made in linen and decorated at the hem with embroidery. This garment was again belted at the waist and worn with breeches of differing lengths secured by leg bandages.

Few examples of female clothing have yet been discovered, but we know from written reports that Merovingian women wore an ankle-length tunic robe called a *stole* which, like the male version, was secured at the waist with a wide belt and decorated with embroidered designs. An example of Merovingian royal costume was discovered recently at the Church of St Denis near Paris in the tomb of the Merovingian Queen Arnegonde (A.D. 550–570). She was buried

Above: This illustration from a sixth-century book of Genesis portrays Joseph and Potiphar's wife and shows Coptic influence on civilian dress. Narrow breeches are tucked into high boots and tablions decorate the cloaks

49

Above: Relatively few representations survive showing the costume worn by Barbarian tribes who reigned in western and northern Europe after the centuries of Roman domination. These two ninth-century reliefs show Pictish figures dressed in woollen cloaks. There is little resemblance between the Classical costume of the Romans and the rather simple style shown here

Left: This relief from a sixth-century bronze plate found at Björnhofda, Torslunda, in Sweden, shows men fighting wild animals. One wears a sleeved smock of animal skin with the hairy side outward. The other man wears trousers with the fur inward

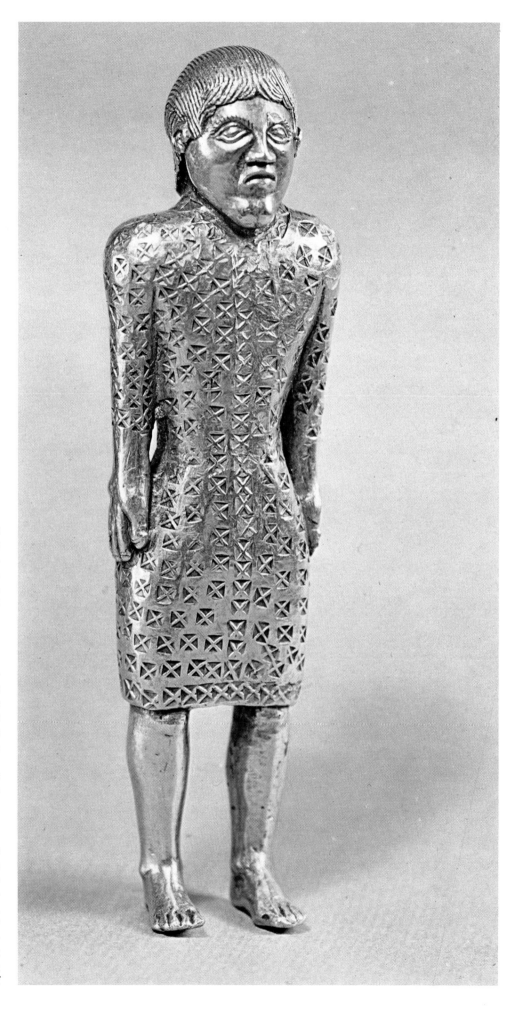

Right: This unique gold statuette found near Le Mans in France and now in the Dumbarton Oaks Collection, Washington D.C., shows exactly what Merovingian costume looked like. The statuette wears a knee-length tunic, a gonelle, closely-fitted at the waist, decorated all over with geometric ornaments. The legs and feet are bare and the hair is medium-length and combed

in a tunic of fine wool over which she wore a violet satin tunic-robe and an open silk gown with wide sleeves. Attached to the gown by a gold fibula, or brooch, was a waist-length veil and on her feet were short boots of black leather.

THE CAROLINGIAN PERIOD

When the Merovingian rulers were succeeded by the Carolingians in 752, the situation throughout Western Europe was generally more settled and leaders had more time to turn their thoughts to luxury and self-adornment. Christian burial customs were widely adopted, however, and the idea of interring the dead with all their finery was discouraged.

Men's costume

The shirt appears to have been a quite simple undergarment which was worn next to the skin and was the only garment worn while sleeping. It is frequently mentioned in manuscripts but, since it was invariably covered by other clothing, it is never shown in illustrations and its exact form is unknown. It is fair to presume, however, that it was a simple chemise of linen since mention of

ubi angelus dm ostendit
sem iohannem mea et
con magnam cum qua for
nicati sunt reges terra
& reges septem sunt:

& bestiam quam uidi habet capita vii & cornua x· supquos multis· sedet·

Above: Costume remained relatively static for several centuries. This illustration from a mid-twelfth century English manuscript depicts a wedding scene at St Albans. All the basic elements of Carolingian dress from the eighth century can be seen: short tunics sewn up at the sides and decorated with embroidered borders; longer tunics, as worn by the nobility, and the all-encompassing cloak, derived from the Roman toga style, worn principally by young men of the period

Left: Women in Carolingian times wore either one tunic on top of the other, or a long tunic with a mantle fastened at the shoulder. The Whore of Babylon depicted in this ninth-century Apocalypse wears a costume derived from Eastern models that would not normally have been seen

wool shirts is only made in connection with penance. The tunic, as in the Merovingian period, was the most important garment to the Anglo-Saxons, but they wore it at different lengths. The short tunic fell to about ankle length and had a simple aperture for the head and tight wrist-length sleeves. This garment was worn by all ranks, but workers and peasants are generally shown with their tunic slit from hem to waist and girded with a cord or strip of material. The short tunic of an Anglo-Saxon nobleman was sewn up both sides and decorated with an embroidered border. The long tunic is frequently portrayed on kings and other members of the Anglo-Saxon nobility. This garment was of the same basic construction as the short tunic but reached the ground and, it is thought, was worn only on ceremonial occasions—kings shown walking or taking part in any active pursuit are always portrayed wearing the short tunic.

Another garment which appears to have been the preserve of the nobility was the surcote. This was a second tunic robe with loose elbow-length sleeves made in a fine linen or silk and richly decorated with embroidery. When worn over the short tunic, the surcote would

reach the waist and when worn over the long tunic it would reach the knees.

The other garment allowed to common men was the cloak or mantle. Like the short tunic, this was accepted wear for all classes, but there were different styles denoting social status. The most common was a simple rectangle of material fastened on the left shoulder with a fibula. It covered the back and gathered into sloping folds enveloping the left arm and leaving the right arm free. The cloak generally fell just below the short tunic, but there was a longer version to be worn with the long tunic. This was ankle-length and only worn by the nobility on ceremonial occasions.

Young men of the period wear a completely different type of cloak, much like a herald's tabard, fastened on both shoulders with fibulae and open down both sides to allow the arms complete liberty. A more complex cloak, reminiscent of a Roman toga, was worn by noblemen in the eighth century: this covered one shoulder and was wrapped round the body.

Hats appear to have played no important part in Anglo-Saxon costume of the period. Kings are always shown wearing a simple coronet, and workers wore small caps of animal skins. The Barbarian habit

of plaiting the hair appears to have been abandoned, and hair was parted in the middle and allowed to flow over the shoulders. The upper lip and top of the chin were generally shaved, but the beard was allowed to grow long and was often combed and trimmed into two points.

Anglo-Saxons of the eighth century were seldom shown bare-footed, and it may be assumed that shoes were within the reach of even the lowest classes. They appear to have been simple leather slip-on shoes, laced either at the side or on top. The leg-colouring in some Anglo-Saxon illustrations shows that stockings of some sort were worn, using linen for the wealthy and wool for rustics or poorer people.

Women's costume

A number of Saxon women are represented in illuminated manuscripts of the eighth century. They probably wore an undergarment similar to a man's shirt— a simple linen chemise with wrist-length sleeves, although, of course, this is never visible. The word gown originates from this time and is derived from the Saxon word *gunna* which was used to describe the female equivalent of the tunic. The gown was a simple ankle-length tunic-

robe which changed very little during this period, except for the length of the sleeves which varied from wrist to elbow. The gown was invariably girded at the waist with a strip of material of the same colour as the gown. It was made in a variety of materials which depended on the wearer's financial position and the climatic conditions in which it was worn. Once again the women portrayed from this period belong for the most part to the nobility, and the fabric of their gowns is generally shown in portraits of the wealthy as being richly decorated with floral and geometric motifs.

Women also wore a mantle, but this was a totally different garment from that of their male contemporaries. The upper part of the mantle was always covered by a *coverchief* and it is difficult to say how the mantle was secured at the shoulders. Most authorities consider that it was a simple circle of material with a hole cut for the head. If this was the case, the hole was obviously cut off-centre as the back of the mantle always appears to hang lower than the front and sides.

The coverchief, worn by Saxon women above the cloak, appears to have been obligatory in public. The coverchief

covered both the head and shoulders, with the surplus material either hanging loosely down the side or drawn across the bosom and passed round the neck. Both mantle and coverchief were produced in a number of colours, but they seldom matched. There are few examples of hairstyles, but women usually used pins and ribbons to plait and curl their hair underneath their veils.

THE NINTH AND TENTH CENTURIES

Basic categories of dress changed little over the next three hundred years, but the design and decoration of each individual item underwent many developments.

Men's costume

Anglo-Saxon writers of the ninth century give little description of costume, and it is necessary at this point to move to France, where the ninth-century writer Eginhart gives us a detailed description of the costume worn by Charlemagne at the beginning of the century. It appears from his account that there was no substantial difference between the costume of the two nations at this period.

Charlemagne, Eginhart tells us, adhered rigidly to the fashions of his ancestors and scorned any innovations from outside. He mentions nine items of dress worn by the Emperor and describes each of them individually—the shirt, drawers, tunic, stockings, leg bandages, shoes, sword and sword belt and, in winter, the thorax and Venetian cloak.

Eginhart tells us that the shirt was made from linen, but he gives no hint of its form. It can be assumed, however, that it was a simple long-sleeved chemise of the older type. The word shirt, derived from the Saxon word *sherte*, was used to describe the garment which came next to the skin. Later, Chaucer used the word to describe the garment worn both day and night by a new-born baby.

Eginhart describes Charlemagne's tunic as being made from linen bordered with silk. It may be assumed that this was a short tunic since the writer assures us elsewhere that his Emperor wore the long tunic not more than twice in his life. Anglo-Saxon illustrations of the ninth century show little change in the short tunic. A rather wider and more elaborate variety of decorative borders is shown and buttons are occasionally used to secure the blouse section.

Developments in dress below the waist during the ninth century were much more complicated. Eginhart tells us that Charlemagne wore drawers, stockings and leg bandages. This was one distinct style of dress but there was another known as *coxalia*, which consisted of trousers with socks.

Drawers were about knee length and extremely tight fitting—those worn by Charlemagne were made from linen. The drawers were worn with stockings, much in the fashion of twentieth-century breeches. The nobility wore stockings of some fine material, probably linen, which actually met the bottom of the drawers at the knee and were fastened with a garter. Peasants on the other hand wore stockings of some coarser material which only reached the calf and were often ungartered. Eginhart describes the leg bandages worn by Charlemagne as 'long fillets which were bound crossways to the stocking in such a way as to keep them properly extended on the leg'.

Drawers and stockings were also adopted in England, and Anglo-Saxon illustrations show various different ways in which leg bandages were used. The nobility appear to have used a narrow band of material in a criss-cross fashion up the full length of the stocking. A second method was to use a wider bandage, wound in a spiral from foot to knee, which covered the entire stocking. A third and simpler version, much used by the lower orders, was a simple garter at the top of the stocking. We are told that most leg bandages were made from wool, but that canons insisted that monks should wear linen bandages to distinguish them from the laity. They came in numerous different colours and were often embroidered.

The three main forms of leg covering were, firstly, 'braies' or drawers, reaching from the waist to the knee; secondly, '*long* braies' or trousers, reaching to the ankles and sometimes crossed with leg bandages. The third style of long hose or stockings was sometimes worn with socks over the top.

It is quite difficult to discern from Anglo-Saxon illustrations the exact forms of footwear adopted during this period, but it is obvious that both boots and shoes were worn by all classes. An unusual method of lacing is shown in one such illustration, where the shoes are fastened with a thong around the ankle which passes through a loop at the back of the shoe and then fastens at the instep.

The *thorax*, which Charlemagne apparently wore during the winter, was made from otter's skin and covered the shoulders and chest. No evidence exists of such a garment, but Strutt surmised that it was worn under the tunic.

The mantle was once again an important item of dress. That belonging to Charlemagne, we are told, '. . . was of a blue or grey colour, square in shape and so doubled that, when it was placed upon his shoulders, it hung down as low as his feet before and behind; but on the sides it scarcely reached to the knees.' This was his mantle for normal wear but on ceremonial occasions his garments were extremely magnificent. The tunic he wore was '. . . interwoven with gold, his shoes were adorned with gems; his mantle fastened with a fibula of gold; a diadem ornamented with gold was placed upon his head.'

Shortly after A.D. 800, a short cloak was adopted in France which was referred to by contemporary writers as *saga fresonica*. Charlemagne, who established himself as an arbiter of fashion, is reported to have scorned this garment: 'Of what use,' he asked, 'are such trifling little cloaks? When we are in bed they cannot cover us; when we are on horseback they are insufficient to defend us

from the wind and rain; and when we retire to ease nature they will not protect our legs from the cold and frost.'

The French mantle or *sagum gallicum* which replaced this inadequate garment was much more suitable for the northern climate. It was large and square and sometimes folded four times. All the evidence shows that Anglo-Saxon mantles and cloaks varied little from the previous century.

The Anglo-Saxon fashion for wearing hair long continued from the previous century and was reinforced by the arrival of the Danes. These immigrants from the North were, it appears, dandies of a high order and were in the habit of combing and decorating their hair daily to win the favours of Anglo-Saxon ladies.

By the time Edward the Confessor came to the throne, hair was being worn extremely long by all classes and this caused the Church much displeasure. We are told that the fashion was preached against by Wulfstan, Bishop of Worcester, who considered it so effeminate as to constitute an offence against God.

In France, long hair was a mark of high rank and various laws were passed restricting shoulder-length hair to the nobility of the first order and princes of royal blood. People of lower ranks were obliged to cut their hair in a line drawn from the middle of their forehead. Beards were also important status symbols—to touch the beard was a mark of great reverence.

Women's costume

Changes in women's dress during the ninth and tenth centuries were even less marked than those of their male contemporaries. The under-tunic appears to have been identical to that worn in the eighth century, except for a rather more elaborate decorated border at the wrist and hem. The gown also remained virtually unaltered until the latter part of the tenth century when the sleeves became fuller at the cuff. Once again the fabrics were more decorative. The mantle was also retained, but a second style made a short-lived appearance during the early years of the tenth century. This was a rectangle of material which was wrapped round the waist, from where it passed over the shoulder with the remainder of the material hanging loosely at the side.

Coverchiefs were also generally worn throughout the period, with the result that once again hairstyles were still seldom seen.

THE FEUDAL AGE
The Eleventh and Twelfth Centuries

The most dramatic and far reaching event in Western Europe during the eleventh century was, without doubt, the Norman conquest of Britain. One might expect an equally dramatic change in costume during the period which followed, either with the Normans imposing their costume on the Saxons, the Normans adopting Saxon costume, or possibly a merging of the two styles. The effect on costume on both sides of the Channel, however, was marginal. It should be remembered that Harold's predecessor, Edward the Confessor, was of Norman stock and that Harold himself spent several years in Normandy before acceding to the throne. Naturally they both introduced ideas from across the Channel. The Normans themselves had abandoned the customs and dress of their Norse forefathers and were by this time completely integrated into the French way of life and, as we have seen, French and English costume had been virtually indistinguishable for several centuries.

The materials used in costume underwent some changes. Furs, for instance, which were seldom used by the Saxons before the Conquest, became much sought after. Silk also became more generally used by the nobility as the supplies increased from the Norman territories in the South, notably Sicily. A silk industry as such is not thought to have existed in Northern Europe at this time.

Both the Saxons and the French were excellent weavers with a high degree of technical skill, and the situation improved still further with the arrival of Flemish weavers who had sailed with William's army. Flanders was generally accepted as the finest producer of woollen fabrics even at this early date and, after the Conquest, many Flemish weavers settled in Britain. Their fabrics were much sought after by the nobility and, as news of their success and prosperity spread, others were tempted to try their hand so that, during the reigns of Henry and Stephen, their numbers increased considerably.

It was during this period that weavers and tailors organized themselves for the first time, and state controls over the two trades were introduced. Laws were also passed to control the manufacture and retail of fabrics. In the reign of Richard I a ruling was passed in England that all cloths should be sold in a standard width, namely two ells—about 90 inches—and should be of the same quality in the middle as at the edges; and that no merchant should stretch in

ꞇodꝭxın fu ꞇꞇaꞇꞇꝛe aꞇeınꞇ ☉ ꝺꞇꞓ la bele ꞓa ꞓœmꞇꞇꞓe ꞓ n ſemble meınꞇoꞇ aıꞇ o ꞇꞇꞇꝛ3

Above: Both Harold and his predecessor, Edward the Confessor, had close ties with Normandy and naturally they introduced elements of French costume into Britain. This illustration depicts the marriage of Edward to Eadygth. Both men and women wear long draped tunics with lavishly-trimmed cloaks

front of his shop '. . . red or black cloth, or any other thing by which the sight of the buyers might be deceived in the choice of good commodities . . .' A metal rule was introduced to ensure that the ell measure was consistent throughout the country.

Eleventh-century writers were unanimous in their admiration for the elegance and refinement of the Normans and of the way they dressed and conducted themselves. They also spoke with some envy of their rich finery and decoration. What differences existed between the costume of the two nations were allowed to continue without interference while William I ruled, but his son, William Rufus, became notorious for his love of change and gimmickry. In addition, he insisted that any changes should also be adopted by members of his court and so by the nobility generally. These changes were not of form but more of decoration. For instance William Rufus, unlike his father, adopted the Saxon custom of wearing shoulder-length hair which was much criticized by writers of the day. William of Malmesbury, an English chronicler of the first half of the century, was one of the most outspoken critics of this fashion. 'They resembled women rather than men', he wrote in disgust,

'they also adopted a mincing gait . . . and seem to pride themselves on the effeminacy of their appearance.'

With the support of the King and the Court, the nobility ignored such criticism. When Henry came to the throne, however, he managed to stem the flow towards excess in fashion by personal example and brought some order into the dress of the court and nobility.

Men's costume

There was no change to the shirt and drawers during this period. Trousers also appear to have remained unaltered but were evidently abandoned by the nobility and were worn solely by peasants and the lower classes, for whose working conditions they were most suitable.

The Norman short tunic was always somewhat longer than its Saxon counterpart, reaching two or three inches below the knee. In the case of noblemen, it was also much more richly decorated with patterned borders, and the main fabric was embroidered with threads of silver and gold. Reports are made of precious stones being incorporated into the most magnificent garments.

The long tunic had been reserved for Saxon nobility on ceremonial occasions.

Right: Two illustrations from the medieval Encyclopedia by Rabanus Maurus, Abbot of Fulda, depict Normans in a characteristically simple style, dressed in short tunics, breeches, hose and shoes

The Normans, however, appear to have been rather more relaxed about the long tunic and, while it was never worn by the common man, it was used quite freely by the nobility as everyday wear. This was another feature of eleventh-century dress which brought cries of derision from contemporary writers, who felt that the garment was grotesquely effeminate. The Normans generally wore two tunics regardless of their length. The undertunic was generally of linen with long tight sleeves and decorated cuffs, and the outer tunic was a dalmatic, flared from the waist with wider, rather shorter sleeves. This over-tunic underwent several changes during the period. Towards the end of the eleventh century, there was a vogue for voluminous sleeves which, if they were allowed to hang loose, would cover the hands. By the middle of the twelfth century, attempts were made to accentuate the profile of the figure, and the blouse section of the outer tunic was laced behind. There was also a fashion for wearing the short outer tunic with a long inner tunic, both lavishly decorated.

The mantle or cloak was, of course, a well-established item of both Saxon and Norman wardrobes long before the Conquest. The merging of the two nations

and subsequent changes in public taste, however, brought about several important changes both in the form and decoration of this garment. By 1066 the Norman mantle came in a variety of lengths, ranging from knee-level to the longest version which trailed along the ground. This garment was generally constructed from a simple semicircle of fabric which could be worn in two different ways. It could cover both shoulders and be fastened at the throat with a fibula or it might cover the left side only and be fastened on the right shoulder, leaving the right arm completely free. Both the length and manner of wearing the mantle appear to have depended more on practicality than on any desire to indicate the wearer's rank.

The Normans also introduced the hooded mantle. This was generally worn with the hood falling behind and only drawn over the head when the weather justified it. These mantles were widely worn by the Anglo-Norman nobility but were more useful to farmers and working people, for whom they were made in thick wool. Shepherds are often portrayed in hooded mantles of sheep or goatskin with the wool worn outwards. Hooded mantles belonging to monarchs of the eleventh and twelfth

Above: The numerous representations of figures that decorate medieval cathedrals give us clear indications of medieval costume. These shepherds from Chartres Cathedral, c. 1150, wear the short tunic or cottelle of common people and leg coverings made of narrow bands of material. One shepherd wears a hood or sayon

Left: These two figures in the Museum of Catalan Art, Barcelona, are dressed in the Romanesque style. They are shown wearing trousers, which had not been worn since Barbarian times. Their green and red tunics are edged with geometric designs and the loose elbow-length sleeves are typical

centuries were described as being made from silk and fine linen. Many of these garments were either lined or faced with fur, but there was one mantle, the *reno*, which was made from precious furs and only worn by the very wealthy.

Stockings and socks were also worn by the Normans, and there appears to have been little difference in the style of hose in the two countries. It is obvious from contemporary writers, however, that the Norman nobility prized stockings more highly as items of dress than did their Saxon counterparts. Leg bandages were almost abandoned by the nobility by the end of the eleventh century when the long tunic came into more general use, but they continued to be worn for some time by commoners with their short tunics.

Another novelty introduced by the Anglo-Normans under William Rufus was a fashion for pointed shoes. We are told by Orderic Vitalis that they were first worn by a man with deformed feet who, so that no one should mock them, encouraged his friends to adopt the same fashion and from this they spread throughout the English court. Even commoners adopted pointed shoes but, for practical reasons, they wore other footwear when working. The most usual

was a simple calf-length leather boot.

The Normans also brought with them a variety of head coverings quite apart from the mantle hood. Contemporary writers group them together under the heading of *pileus* but it is obvious from illustrations that they came in many different shapes. The most common were the Phrygian cap, the simple skull cap and a tight-fitting bonnet which covered the ears and was tied under the chin. This last form hardly constitutes a hat, it was more a made-to-measure headscarf designed to keep the hair in place in windy weather. The main difference between the headgear of the nobility and commoners was the materials from which it was made. Peasants would have hats of leather, sheepskin, felt or wool, while their masters would wear finest linen lined with fur and decorated with embroidery.

The Church's fight against long hair was still in full swing when Henry I succeeded his brother William Rufus in 1100. Henry had followed the trend and is reported to have had shoulder-length hair during the early years of his reign but, during a church service conducted by the Norman Bishop Serlo, he was so strongly reprimanded that he agreed to cut it as an example to his subjects.

Above: The Normans had a choice of tunic styles. There was a short version which reached just below the knee and a longer, grander version. The third style was to wear two tunics together: an outer tunic called a dalmatic was worn over an undertunic. The dalmatic had much wider sleeves, a laced-up back, and it emphasized the cuff

Left: A detail from a twelfth-century illuminated manuscript in Stuttgart showing the Martyrdom of St Alban: this shows the new use of fur in a pelisse with the fabric of the garment serving as the lining, and the fur mounted decoratively upon it. St Alban's collar shows the new vertical opening which replaces the slit. The garment was quite long and wide on the hips, a style made possible by inverted V-shaped insertions

Below: These rustic figures wear simple hoods typical of those worn by ordinary people. The headgear of the nobility was of richer and more expensive material often elaborately embroidered

Far right: An illustration from Matthew Paris which shows a rustic working in the fields. Particularly interesting is the conical helmet

Right: Eleventh-century innovations in dress introduced by the Normans are typified by the secular use of shapes which in the main would be considered clerical in style. The hooded mantle, shown in this illustrated manuscript, became the standard outer garment for rustics and clerics alike for the following two centuries

Only twenty-five years later, however, the public predilection for flowing locks was again indulged. Towards the end of the twelfth century, long loose locks did fall out of fashion, and men curled their hair with irons and tied it up with ribbons.

It has been established that, before the Conquest, it was customary for Saxon nobles to grow their beards and shave their top lips. The Normans, on the other hand, were generally clean shaven and William passed a law which compelled all Saxons to remove their beards. This edict caused great public indignation amongst those who had otherwise proved quite happy to adopt Norman customs. A luxuriant beard had long been considered a mark of great distinction and the order to remove them was considered a deprivation of personal liberty.

By the time Henry I came to the throne, however, the law had either been repealed or fallen into disuse and the fashion for long beards was once again re-established. But when Henry was persuaded to shave his hair, his beard was also removed and this too was copied by his followers. Unlike the fashion for long hair, it was a long time before beards became fashionable again.

Women's costume

The basic forms of women's garments were much the same after the Conquest, but one new item, the *surcote*, was added to their wardrobe and the cut and decoration of the other garments underwent several significant changes between 1066 and the end of the twelfth century. Like men's clothes, women's costumes were to show a growth in sophistication during this period.

The undertunic was still never shown in illustrations, but there is no reason to believe that it was any more than a simple linen chemise, and, since it was invariably covered, it is unlikely that any form of decoration was applied to the fabric.

The most important garment for women was once again the gown. At the time of the Conquest it is doubtful whether there was any substantial difference between Norman and Saxon gowns, but by the beginning of the twelfth century it had become a more complex and sophisticated garment altogether. The bodice was slit down either side from arm to hip and fitted with ribbons which could be adjusted to stretch the material tight across the upper part of the body. The flared skirt was long and fell around the wearer's

Above: A more sophisticated style of dress emerged in the twelfth century. The sleeve became an exaggerated feature, which progressed from a flared cuff to a trailing streamer—the tippet—and became, finally, a pleated trumpet-shaped style. The bodice became tighter as the skirt became fuller and more flared. The structure of the garment also changed; the simple layer effect of two tunics worn over each other becomes, by the end of the period, a complicated seamed gown with a finely pleated skirt

Left: In earlier medieval times women's costumes were similar to men's, with tunics covered by cloaks predominating. Cloaks could be very richly decorated like the one shown

feet. The most remarkable development of the gown, however, was in the sleeves which were tight from shoulder to elbow, then flaring out into enormous cuffs. Sometimes these were so wide that they trailed along the ground. To prevent this, there was a fashion for tying knots in the sleeves. By the middle of the twelfth century, there were further developments to the gown—the skirt was even fuller with dozens of knife-edged pleats, and the tightness of the bodice was accentuated with a body belt worn over the gown. This resembled a deep cummerbund which reached from just below the bust to the hips and was fastened behind with ribbons. The sleeves of this gown were as wide if not wider than the previous version and, like the skirt section, had knife-edge pleats. The materials for women's gowns were fine linen and silk decorated with embroidery, again reflecting the contact with the East made by the Norman colonies in southern Europe and by the Crusaders, who brought back rich fabrics from the East.

The mantle was common to both Norman and Saxon women in the eleventh century, but its form underwent a considerable change during this period. At the time of the Conquest it was usually a circle of material with a single hole cut for the head. Later this changed to a simple semi-circle or three-quarter circle which, like the male cloak, was worn over both shoulders and fastened at the throat with a fibula. By the middle of the twelfth century it became longer, forming a train behind, and fibulae were often replaced by thongs.

The coverchief, which had been fashionable for almost three centuries, continued to be worn. At first it covered the entire head and neck leaving only the face exposed, but this style was gradually modified until it only covered the top and sides of the head and was held in place with a decorative metal fillet.

These modifications to women's head-dresses give us our first opportunity for several centuries to examine their coiffure. The most distinctive style emerged about halfway through the twelfth century when women wore their hair in enormously long plaits which were thrown forward over the wearer's shoulders, occasionally even reaching the knees. Reports of the time assure us that few women had enough hair to achieve this effect naturally and there was a great demand for false hairpieces.

sine coniugibus de fou beniamin latent uit uineas i die festo. et uirginibz
ro solēmnitate uenientibz isylo et choros ducentibs erumpēt e la
trēs z singli singlas ereis accipēt z ad domo suas ducerēt uxores.

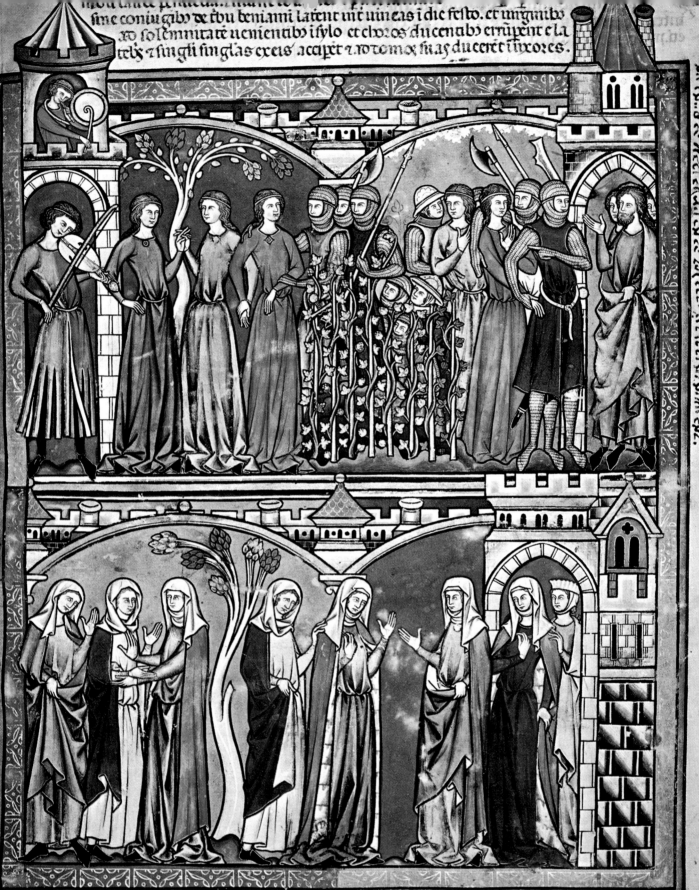

valiter Noemi mulier hebrea. uidua et duobs filijs orbata. in patriam Ex libro Ruth.
suam Bethleem rediens nurus suas hortat ut in patria inwe erant maneant: cuius cō
silio una acquieuit et māsit. Alia cui nomen erat Ruth nullo modo ab ea uoluit separi. sz secuta
est eam. et ita āwe Bethleem ueniut. et ibi mulieres Noemi reducem recognoscint.

CHURCH AND STATE
The Thirteenth Century

Left: These scenes from the Old Testament in a thirteenth-century manuscript depict contemporary dress of both men and women of various age groups. The musician on the left in the upper half is at the height of fashion with a shorter decorated hemline. The young women have long gowns with simple decoration at the neck. Their hair is long as a sign of their unmarried status. The knights, although armoured, also wear surcotes of fashionable shape. Below, the women's heads are covered, sometimes even the chin as well. This signifies that they are older married women, wearing mantles over their long dresses. Later this was to become a style of dress exclusive to nuns

The thirteenth century was a period of great aesthetic, cultural and political importance. Gothic architecture superseded the severity of the Romanesque style; universities were established in various parts of Europe; pageantry and chivalry became the order of the day. The Christian church was at last united, with the Pope as its head, and the Crusades, although perhaps losing their religious character, provided a link with the East. All these factors combined to have a significant effect on costume and the attitude towards self-adornment in Western Europe.

Costume was generally more elegant and more practical than that of the preceding era. This change was due, in part, to the introduction of new materials and the increase in supply of traditional ones, a result of improved trade relations within Europe and beyond. Soft, heavy materials were the fabrics of thirteenth-century costume.

Wool had long been the most important material in European costume. Camelot, a very fine and expensive woven cloth, had previously been imported but was now produced in France. Jersey was manufactured in Italy and camelhair could be obtained from Cyprus. Elsewhere in Europe, flannel and serge were produced. Linen of every variety, from heavy canvas to sheer lawn, was available, and cotton fabrics covered the same enormous range. Silk weaving was also introduced to Europe and, with a reduction in price, it came within the reach of a wider market. Again the range of fabrics produced was vast. Some of the names were doubtless similar, but the dozens of different silk fabrics mentioned in contemporary reports appear to cover all those known to us today as well as a few which have long since disappeared. Heavy matt silk brocade was used for mantles, as was velvet, satin was used for lining garments, and chiffon was fashionable for those who could afford it as an alternative to lawn.

Of particular importance in making this wide variety of fabrics available throughout Europe were the great fairs that became an established part of the pattern of annual events during the thirteenth century.

The first and most famous of these were the fairs of Champagne. Lying at a focal point of Europe, where roads from Calais, Flanders, Vienna, and Italy met and crossed, the province of Champagne was a convenient rendezvous for Spanish and African leather dealers,

Above: This shows some forms of ecclesiastical dress which were at an early stage of development in the thirteenth century. In the variety of sleeve shapes and necklines, an increasing desire to shape garments to the body can be seen, providing alternatives to the traditional forms, which were very often determined by the uncut rectangle of material as it came off the loom

Flemish weavers, English wool merchants, and the importers of dyes and alum from the ports of the Mediterranean. Under the protection of the Counts of Troyes (from which comes Troy weight), the fairs each lasted seven weeks, and were held in rotation in the towns of Lagny, Bar-sur-Aube, Provins and Troyes. The traders came from as far afield as Scotland, Egypt, Constantinople and even Novgorod in Russia. Not only fabrics but made-up goods, all in the latest fashion, were on sale, and within weeks of the fair's end all Europe was dressed in the same new styles.

One of the great luxuries in costume was the use of fur. Furs played an important part in the costume of the previous two centuries, but in the thirteenth century they were even more widely used throughout Europe and a wider variety of skins was adopted. The furs of sable, fox, beaver, cat and lamb were all common in the twelfth century, but to these were now added the skins of marten, squirrel, ermine and rabbit. The demand for skins increased rapidly and they were used not only for warmth but also for decoration. The necks, cuffs and hems of many garments were now trimmed with precious furs.

A definite hierarchy emerged in the use of furs: sheepskin, badger, muskrat, cat and other coarse furs were used by the lower classes while, as today, the pelts of finer, rare and smaller creatures were only within reach of the very wealthy.

The most prized fur of the thirteenth century is described in writings of the time as *vair*. This is thought to have been a grey-coloured squirrel. The glossary of the *Romance of the Rose* tells us that: 'The fur most esteemed was the skin of an animal of the squirrel-kind, called *vair*, whose back was bluish grey resembling the colour of a dove, and its belly white.' Other authorities consider that the word vair was a collective noun used to describe all prime fur including such things as ermine and sable.

Developments in costume were not, however, confined to the production of fabrics. The decorative arts also showed a considerable improvement during this period. Embroidery was known as *acupictus* (Latin still being the working language of most writers in Europe) which means painting with a needle, and the complexity and fineness of the compositions undertaken at this time fully justified the description.

The attitude towards clothing reflects the atmosphere of the time, which was

one of pomp and pretension. A contemporary report tells us of the costume worn by Richard the Lion Heart at his coronation in 1189. The whole ceremony, we are told, was conducted with much more pomp and magnificence than had been seen in preceding eras.

This love of parade and pomp was not peculiar to England. A report of the coronation of Queen Mary in Paris in 1275 says, 'It was extremely grand, in so much that it would be almost impossible to describe the different displays of pomp and ceremony. The barons and the knights were habited in vestments of divers colours: sometimes they appeared in green, sometimes in blue, then again in gray, and afterwards in scarlet, varying the colours according to their fancies. Their breasts were adorned with fibulae or brooches of gold; and their shoulders with precious stones, of great magnitude, such as emeralds, sapphires, jacinths, pearls, rubies and other rich ornaments. The ladies who attended had rings of gold, set with topaz stones and diamonds, upon their fingers; their heads were ornamented with elegant crests, or garlands, and their wimples were composed of the richest stuffs, embroidered with pure gold, and embellished with pearls and other jewels.'

Men's costume

Just before the turn of the thirteenth century there were some very definite changes in the dress of both men and women. Men continued to wear the shirt and drawers which, apart from being much shorter, followed the pattern of the preceding centuries. The tunic, or *cote* as it was by then known, underwent several changes. Gone were the huge exaggerated cuffs. The fullness of the sleeves was now at the other end, emanating from enormous arm holes and tapering to a fitted cuff. Gone, too, was the laced bodice. The garment was now altogether fuller and waisted with a belt. The skirt section was generally split from the crotch to a hem which fell several inches below the knee. Twenty years later the enormous arm holes disappeared and the cote was fitted with more conventional tight sleeves. The hem remained at calf level, but the skirt was often *dagged* in several places to allow greater mobility. Again, the garment was generally girded with a broad decorated belt.

By the middle of the thirteenth century a totally new tunic had emerged, the *surcote*, which was worn over a cote similar to that described above. The *surcote* was a form of tabard, sleeveless with a scooped neck and open at the sides. This was a style which doubtless owed its origins to the Crusades and was frequently emblazoned with the heraldic devices which had originally enabled the wearer to be identified in the field of battle. This garment was also slit up the front and girded with a loose belt sitting just above the hips. It was often made from the richest fabrics—samite, a type of heavy silk, and cloth of gold lined with fur.

The other garment usually worn over the tunic was once again the mantle, which appears to have been made in the same way as the twelfth-century mantle. Again it was generally of a rich material, lined with fur and fastened on the right shoulder with an ornamental brooch. Towards the end of the century a more elaborate outer garment appeared, the *garde-corps*, or *herygoud*; a calf-length coat which fell freely from the shoulders and was generally ungirded. The full, flared sleeves could either be fitted in the normal manner, or the arms could be put through two slits at the armpit with the material allowed to hang loose. The garde-corps was worn in place of the mantle and was generally made from heavy woollen material, lined with fur and fitted with a hood.

The tunic became shorter and shorter, while hose became a more important item of dress. It is thought that stockings were usually made from an elastic woollen fabric which was tailored to the leg and fitted with a seam. They were, in fact, still separate stockings, not tights, and were either held up by their own elasticity or secured on the thigh by a garter. Many stockings were made without feet and resembled gaiters held by a strap under the sole of the foot. Reports also suggest that stockings were padded to improve the shape of the wearer's leg, making it appear more muscular than nature had intended. The colour of stockings varied considerably —at the beginning of the century there was a preference for plain practical colours such as bluish-grey, but later there was a vogue for patterned stockings decorated with floral or geometric motifs.

There were several different types of footwear worn during the thirteenth century. Most fashion-conscious men favoured simple black leather shoes with a pointed toe, but a refined version of the peasants' soft leather boot was also fashionable for town wear. In some cases, towards the middle of the fourteenth century, shoes were discarded altogether in favour of a sole attached to the stockings. During the most ostentatious periods, however, shoes of heavy silk and embroidered leather were worn which, at their most extreme, were studded with precious stones.

Long hair at last went out of fashion— a result of public taste rather than religious edict. The new style was both more practical and more elegant. Hair was now bobbed at about jaw level and worn with a straight fringe. It was, however, anything but casual. The nobility curled the end of their hair so that it flowed straight from the crown and ended in a neat roll. Beards were not common, and when they were worn they were neatly clipped to a point and worn with a pencil moustache.

Hats were very much in evidence: the Phrygian cap and white bonnets were joined by fur caps, wide brimmed felt hats and linen night-caps.

Women's costume

The changes in women's dress between the twelfth and thirteenth centuries were virtually parallel to those of men. Their tunics, unlike the male version, remained at ankle length, but otherwise underwent similar modifications. At the beginning of the century wide cuffs were

Above: This picture from Alfonso's Book of Chess shows the variety of upper-class Spanish dress in the thirteenth century. Spain was somewhat isolated from Europe and more open to exotic influences from the South. A greater range of shapes could now be achieved by more skilful tailoring. The sleeves are fitted at the wrists, hats are elaborately arranged and dresses often tailored closely to the waist

Right: The lower half of this manuscript page shows poorer people in contemporary dress, although of course depicting Old Testament scenes. The men in the left scene have hitched up their loose tunics for convenience of movement. The straw hat typical of countrymen is seen at the right. At the top left the open-sided gown is displayed —a very popular style usually associated, as in this scene, with higher social ranks. At the right the long cloak shows a striped edging made with small untrimmed furs. (A more costly cloak would be lined with trimmed fur and appear plain)

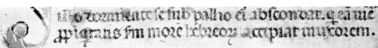

yaluter uentilantibus aream meſſoribꝰ. Booz in aceruo manipulorum cormiente.
Ruth iuxta conſilium ſocruſ ſue abſcondit ſe ſub pallio eiꝰ.

abandoned and replaced by tight cuffs and voluminous sleeves. The material at the back of the skirt was frequently longer than at the front, forming a short train. Tunics were sometimes fastened at the neck with a ring brooch and girded with a decorated belt. Later in the century the sleeves were tight from shoulder to wrist and the belt was replaced by a sash.

By the middle of the century, the tunic was considerably tighter, and a *surcote* was worn. This was the female version of the cyclas. It was a full length sleeveless gown worn directly over the tunic, slit from armpit to hip and laced tight across the torso.

Women continued to wear the mantle as their basic outer garment throughout the early part of the thirteenth century. Once again, this was considerably longer than the male version with the material forming a train at the back. It was usually worn over both shoulders and fastened across the chest with a cord, revealing the front of the tunic underneath. Mantles were made from a variety of rich materials and were generally lined and faced with fur.

At the end of the century a new outer garment appeared, the *pelicon*, which was the female equivalent of the garde-corps. It was made from an enormous, elliptical piece of material, approximately twelve feet across at its widest point, with holes cut for the head and arms. When worn, the material fell freely from the shoulders, reaching the feet in front and forming a train behind. Like the garde-corps, the pelicon was made of heavy material lined with fur and fitted with a hood.

Since both the tunic and outer garments reached the floor, it is difficult to study women's hose, but there is no reason to suppose that it was different from men's. Certainly, there was little difference between the footwear of the two sexes except that women did not wear boots.

Coiffure and headwear changed at the beginning of the thirteenth century, but then remained constant for almost a hundred years. Unmarried girls wore their hair loose, flowing over their shoulders and sometimes decorated with a simple circlet. This style was considered unsuitable for married women who tied their hair up, securing it with a net. A piece of white linen was then taken under the chin and fastened on the top of the head, and a small pill-box hat, with or without a veil, was worn over this arrangement.

Above: This outer garment is called a pelicon, the female equivalent of the garde-corps. On the right it can be seen that it was made from a large elliptical piece of material, measuring some 12 feet at its widest point. The black, unbroken line denotes the pattern for a hood which was attached to the pelicon. A hole was cut for the head about three-quarters of the way down the material, and two slits were made for the arms. When placed over the head, the bulk of the material fell from the shoulders forming a train behind the wearer. The hood buttoned up to the neck

Right: These figures from an allegorical fresco in northern Italy show that upper-class dress had reached a new degree of sophistication. Principally, the women liked long willowy silhouettes, with elaborate sleeves to add a grandeur to their style. The man wears a typically decorated tabardor surcote

DEFENCE OF RANK
The Fourteenth Century

Left: This band of Italian street musicians, from a fresco in Assisi, demonstrates the more imaginative styles of dress to be found in Italy in this period. The checked garment on the left shows details of seams and construction and the upward movement of the collar on men's dress. A new freedom for personal expression is seen in the fashions of both sexes at this time

At the beginning of the fourteenth century, the first major change in costume throughout Europe for several centuries became apparent. Although changes were initially no more than adaptations of existing styles, in about 1340 a revolution occurred both in form and in social attitudes towards dress. Long flowing costume for both sexes was gradually abandoned.

By the middle of the fourteenth century, the wool trade and weaving were important and lucrative industries in England. Wool fabric was imported from Flanders and Holland, imposing strains on the English Exchequer. In 1332 a famous Flemish woollen manufacturer, John Kempe, moved to England, and he was soon followed by many others. After initial hostility from native weavers, King Edward gave the Europeans legal protection, and thereafter the domestic industry flourished.

The King also passed legislation governing the type and quality of fabrics which could be worn by various classes. Never since Republican Rome had there been such a carefully preserved hierarchy of dress. The law delineates the mores of fourteenth-century civilian dress. There was no attempt to restrict the forms of dress worn by different classes; the law concentrated entirely on the materials and methods of decoration in order to establish a rigid hierarchy of status in dress. The punishments for disobeying these laws ranged from confiscation of the cloth to a substantial fine. Contemporary writers, however, make it clear that the laws were frequently ignored, and they found it necessary to criticize excesses in dress as they had during the previous century.

Coinciding with this radical reappraisal of the value of dress and the morality of display was a dramatic change in the form of dress. Communications in Western Europe were slowly improving and fashions spread from country to country. In about 1340 the long, full-flowing garments of the thirteenth century were gradually abandoned throughout Europe in favour of tailored, form-fitting garments. This change is recorded coincidentally by historians in Germany, Italy, England and France.

Men's costume

The most obvious change in men's costume after 1340 was its decreasing length. Ankle-length robes for men had been generally abandoned in the thirteenth century, but they were now

tans : qui fingis laborem in precepto.

Captabunt in animam iusti : ϟ san

guinem innocentem condempnabūt.

even shorter and generally worn above the knee. This particular mode is thought to have originated in Italy and found its way to Britain via France.

The cote and surcote were now replaced by the doublet and *cote-hardie*. The cote-hardie was a tight-fitting, long-waisted garment with a skirt falling from just below the hips. It was generally buttoned from neck to hem and fitted with long, tight sleeves and a low boat-shaped neckline. The cut of the cote-hardie was designed to emphasize a small waist and broad shoulders and marked a considerable development in the tailor's craft. It could be worn directly over a simple linen chemise, but an even shorter garment, called a *gipon*, was worn between them in winter. This garment could be either sleeved or sleeveless and was frequently quilted or lined with fur. It was the forerunner of the doublet which became the basic dress of the fifteenth and sixteenth centuries, but at this time it was seldom, if ever, worn without a cote-hardie.

The new length of leg made visible required much better-fitting hose, and the replacement of long drawers by linen stockings became inevitable. The legs were, however, still covered with stockings as opposed to tights, and these were often made to measure and represented an expensive item of dress. Another unusual feature of both the cote-hardie and stocking was the colouring which portrayed the heraldic device of the wearer. It was quite common to have parti-coloured or rayed (diagonally striped) garments. For instance, the left-hand side of the cote-hardie might be yellow and the right-hand side vermilion. With this would be coupled a vermilion stocking on the left leg and a yellow one on the right, giving a checkerboard effect. This decorative technique was particularly fashionable at the English court in the middle of the century.

The sleeves of the cote-hardie were frequently buttoned from elbow to wrist and decorated with *tippets*, long flowing streamers measuring anything up to three feet.

The long semi-circular mantle survived to the end of the century, but it was then generally replaced by the houppelande, which once again showed a considerable development in tailoring. This was an ankle-length overcoat of rich material flared from shoulder to hem and fitted with a high standing collar. The coat was slit down the front and buttoned from neck to crotch, from

Right: This detail from a fresco in the Spanish Chapel in Florence was painted in 1365 and shows the new long-waisted style of dress for women alongside the older looser style. These women are dancing and their parti-coloured garments may have been specially made for the occasion. Hair was by now elaborately styled—bound or plaited and sometimes dyed. The pendant sleeve on the right and the flowing skirts suggest the softness and quality of the fabric available at this time

Below right: This famous scene from the Luttrell Psalter shows Sir Geoffrey Luttrell bidding his family farewell. The women have adopted a fashionably willowy stance which is accentuated by the extreme length of their skirts and tight bodices. The heavily padded cloth on the horse displays splendidly the heraldic devices which were probably painted directly onto it. The lady's open-sided gown was a stylish feature very popular at this time, and later it became a sign of high rank. Under her crown this lady wears the traditional coif

Right: In the fourteenth century the dress of the nobility evolved continuously. This woman's costume, characteristic of northern Europe, is higher waisted than before, and has the widest possible neckline. The headdress had by now stiffened and become an independent feature of the greatest importance for a fashionable lady

Above: In northern Europe fashionable styles were often more extreme than elsewhere and here is an example of the taste which critics there sometimes complained of. The man in the background has his short cape so padded at the shoulders that it makes a box shape under which no other garment is visible. In the foreground we see the alternative, more formal-looking long styles

where it generally fell open. The most remarkable feature of the garment, was the sleeves which were enormously wide at the wrist, on some occasions falling to the ground, and narrowing to tight points. The houppelande was generally made of a rich embroidered fabric, lined and faced with fur. It was sometimes worn ungirded, but more frequently it was belted just below the chest.

There was also a change in the form of the cote-hardie at this period. When worn without a houppelande it was fuller, pleated, fitted with a high neck and lined with fur. It is thought that this heavier cote-hardie was worn directly over a linen undergarment, without a second doublet. The sleeve design also changed, fitting the upper arm and billowing out into full bagpipe sleeves. These were sometimes allowed to hang loose but were more often gathered into a tight wristband.

In about 1350 pointed shoes became extremely fashionable, and by the end of the century this fashion had reached an unprecedented height of extravagance. Some reports tell us of points which were so long they had to be held to the knees by chains. Certainly, six-inch points beyond the toes reinforced

with whalebone were common among the leisured classes.

The chaperon and linen bonnet were the most popular modes of headdress. Hats with brims, pot-shaped hats, and soft caps were produced in a wide range of materials and were trimmed with fur and decorated with brooches, feathers or medals.

Women's costume

Changes and developments in women's costume during the fourteenth century appear to have been consistent throughout Western Europe. With the introduction of the short costume for men, there was for the first time in several centuries a clear differentiation between the costume of the two sexes. The overall changes in style, however, were similar. Gone were the full garments, and in their place tight-fitting, figure-revealing dresses now appeared. By the middle of the century, women wore three layers of clothing—the sleeveless chemise as an undergarment, the under-robe and a cote-hardie. The under-robe had a tight-fitting bodice, flared skirt and tight wrist-length sleeves buttoned from the elbow. The cote-hardie worn over this was of similar construction to the male version, but it was long, trailed on the

Left: This scene, from the Spanish Chapel in Florence, allegorically depicts the activities of the Church and the Dominican Order. In the background are Church dignitaries shown wearing clothes of the older, looser cut, but the man to the left in short white hood and tunic is the most obviously fashionable. The old woman kneeling with her staff on the right wears what was by then an old-fashioned head and chin cover, but the young women next to her have contemporary hair styles, which were lifted up to the back of the head to increase the appearance of height and slenderness

ground, and had elbow-length sleeves decorated with tippets. The neckline was lower than that of any previous European costume, a feature which attracted a great deal of disapproval from the Church.

In about 1380 the open *surcote*—perhaps the most elegant garment to emerge from the Middle Ages—was introduced. It was not unlike the sideless gown of the mid-thirteenth century but was much better tailored and more decorative. The material at the side of the gown was scooped away from the armhole to the hips, revealing much of the under-robe. The remaining panel was quite narrow and formed a bib, usually trimmed with ermine or some other expensive fur. The skirt was full and flared and often several inches longer than the wearer. It was generally ungirded, but the under-robe was kept in place with a highly ornamented belt worn round the hips which was partially visible.

At the end of the fourteenth century, the houppelande was also adopted by women. This was virtually identical to the male version, with a high neck, enormously voluminous sleeves and girded just below the bust.

Since the costume of fourteenth-century women frequently covered the feet, it is difficult to get an accurate idea of the stockings or shoes worn, but it is reasonable to presume that they were very similar to men's. Contemporary writings certainly refer to women adopting the ridiculous, pointed shoes towards the end of the century.

Women's hairstyles and headdresses underwent a considerable change during this period. At the turn of the century women continued to wear their hair loose until they were married, from which time they wore it up, covered with a wimple and veil. Towards the middle of the fourteenth century, women adopted the fashion of wearing plaits of hair down either side of the face.

The most remarkable change in women's hairdressing, however, was the development of the *crespine*. Cylinders of wire mesh encased the hair on either side of the head and were supported by a metal circlet. The mesh itself was frequently decorated with jewels, and the back of the head covered by a short veil. These face-framing arrangements were the forerunners of the many fantastic headdresses which were to become one of the most significant developments in women's costume of the fifteenth century.

Above left: Inventive designs on woven fabric now became common and these women display some very fine examples. The styling of their hair is also intricate and anticipates later, more formal, devices for containing the hair. These dresses were cleverly tailored, probably with insets in order to make a wide skirt flow from a tight bodice with no break for the waist

Above: The crespine which appeared at the end of the fourteenth century was a device whereby two wire cylinders—joined by a metal band—encased the hair on either side of the face. The wire mesh was often decorated with pearls and jewels. The headdress could be worn with a fillet across the brow and a veil bound tightly round the back of the head, or a veil which was draped over the crespine and fell to the shoulders

Right: Guidoriccio da Fogliana was painted by Simone Martini. Under his splendid surcote can be seen plate armour. His very high collar is rather unusual. The bright fabric of his surcote and matching cover for the horse are well chosen, for the pattern accentuates the shapes and movement underneath and suggests again the new individualism which was then developing in fashion

Below: These three drawings of upper-class female dress show what large quantities of fabric were required. Often the headdresses alone used up several yards. The central figure has closed cuffs on very full sleeves, known as the 'bird's-crop' sleeve, and this was as acceptable as the completely open type worn by the women to the left and right of her. The 'V' opening to the neck of the bodice was by now becoming a separate, stiffened turned-up collar

85

CHIVALRY IN FLOWER
The Early Fifteenth Century

Left: Pisanello drew these courtly dress designs in the first half of the fifteenth century, and captured the stalking movement of the figures. Inventive variations of layering using extravagant quantities of fabric seemed unending, as if European fashion was first spreading its wings and preparing the way for the prolific repertoire of styles to follow

The early fifteenth century was a confusing time for costume throughout the West. Not that there were any major changes in form, but there were changes in attitude and in emphasis. New and more eccentric versions of the garments worn at the end of the previous century were adopted, each change bringing with it a howl of protest from the clergy, historians and even the courts.

Materials used during the fifteenth century were much the same as those of the previous century. The rich silks, previously imported from the East, were now imitated with great skill by European textile manufacturers. Linen, cotton and wool continued to be the basic materials for dress manufacture, but the nobility greatly favoured velvet and taffeta, and fur once again played an important part in lining and facing garments.

There were, of course, plain coloured fabrics, but fifteenth-century textile designers excelled in the use of all-over patterns using stylized flowers, vines and geometric motifs. Larger, all-over patterns were brocaded, damasked and stamped or cut on velvet, a mode of decoration very much associated with the Renaissance. Stripes, both vertical and horizontal, continued to be fashion-able, although parti-coloured hose declined in popularity.

By the beginning of the fifteenth century, the sumptuary laws, introduced by Edward III in England and by other monarchs throughout Europe, had fallen into disuse, and new laws were introduced to replace them. In England these were every bit as severe as the ones they replaced, but they placed more emphasis on style than on the material employed. No one lower than the rank of baronet could wear crimson, gold or velvet, for example, and only senior court officials or High Church officers could wear hoods lined with fur. The use of silver and gold was subjected to even stricter controls: this had an obvious financial implication, whereas the other conditions were clearly concerned with maintaining privilege.

The stringent conditions were nevertheless infringed frequently, and Thomas Occliff, writing at the beginning of the fifteenth century, was typical of many historians of his day. 'And this', he says, 'in my thinking, is an evil, to see one walking in gowns of scarlet twelve yards wide, with sleeves reaching to the ground, and lined with fur, worth twenty pounds, or more; at the same time, if he had only been master of what he paid for, he would not have had

Above: In this Italian wedding group the International Gothic fashions are slightly softened in accordance with Italian taste and mixed with that country's liking for parti-coloured garments. The men's stockings are a reminder of previous fashions

Left: The Burgundian court exerted great political and cultural influence in Europe in the early fifteenth century and here they are assembled in a hunting party. These northern garments seem particularly angular when compared with contemporary Italian versions. By now, considerable variety in dress was possible and yet each suit of garments is chosen as a balanced combination in itself

enough to have lined a hood.' Of the extravagance of the lower classes he writes, '. . . and certainly the great lords are to blame, if I dare say so much, to permit their dependents to imitate them in their dress. In former time, persons of rank were known by their apparel; but, at present, it is very difficult to distinguish the nobleman from one of low degree.'

Men's costume

The overall forms which emerged towards the end of the fourteenth century continued well into the fifteenth. The doublet was if anything slightly shorter and more definitely padded; colour was less exaggerated; the collar rose to chin level and did not fit quite so tightly; sleeves were once again tight. Buttons, however, were abandoned. The doublet was also known as a *pourpoint, jupe* or *cote-hardie*.

Towards the middle of the century, the long houppelande was partly replaced by the short houppelande. This was basically the same garment but terminated at knee level with slits in the sleeves for the arms, leaving the remainder of the material to fall free by the wearer's sides, much in the fashion of the late thirteenth-century garde-corps. The short houppelande was usually of heavy, richly embroidered fabric trimmed at the neck, hem and cuffs with ermine or some other rich fur. It was considerably looser and fuller than the earlier version, giving more emphasis to the breadth of the shoulders than to the smallness of the waist.

Parti-coloured hose appear to have gone out of fashion for a time, and they were replaced by black or dark coloured stockings of the same style; shoes continued to be pointed.

Nowhere is change more apparent for both sexes than in headdresses. A short shoulder-cape with hood, the chaperon, continued to be fashionable and the liripipe or taper grew and grew until, by about 1420, it sometimes reached the ground and, to avoid tripping over it, the wearer frequently tucked it into his belt or wrapped it round his neck. One eccentric way of wearing the chaperon was briefly popular: the opening, which was originally intended to surround the face, was put on the crown of the head. The cape part with its jagged edge was then draped at the side of the head and the liripipe wrapped round the head turban-style.

The chaperon itself now came in a great number of styles. Some had a tail at the front and back, some two points, and others a bag instead of a tail. Each of these styles could be arranged on top of the head according to the wearer's taste. Not unnaturally, people soon grew tired of arranging these elaborate constructions daily and began to sew them into position so that they could be removed complete. The other hat styles which had been fashionable in the late fourteenth century survived well into the fifteenth.

The sumptuary laws once again placed severe restrictions on jewellery, and most jewels produced during this period were either for the court or the Church and so cannot be considered part of civilian costume. Some items of jewellery were functional: buttons, pins and buckles were frequently made as jewellery, and belts were made from linked gold plaques decorated with precious stones. Here again, however, it is important to remember that such luxuries would be available only to a tiny minority of the population.

Belts were invariably fitted with an envelope-shaped leather purse. These varied considerably in size and for the nobility were often produced in rich fabrics decorated with gems. Pomanders, small balls of filigree containing a

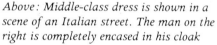

Above: Middle-class dress is shown in a scene of an Italian street. The man on the right is completely encased in his cloak

Above right: This famous scene from the Duc de Berry's manuscript shows a riding party dressed in elegant International Gothic fashions. The court officials playing trumpets on the left are in the old parti-colour styles which by now constituted a uniform instead of a fashion, although serrated edges have been added to the sleeves in deference to contemporary taste. The diagonally draped braids and chains which are worn by the riders are a particularly decorative feature, suggesting a leisurely ride rather than a vigorous hunt

Right: Giovanni Arnolfini celebrated his marriage with this double portrait of himself and his wife by Jan van Eyck in 1434. Although these two people are of Italian origin, their dress epitomizes Northern fashion. The careful decoration of the woman's blue under-dress suggests it was intended to be seen. The covering of the 'horn' headdress is beautifully intricate. Arnolfini himself wears the sombre, open-sided mantle lined with fox fur which was characteristic of the upper middle-class

sponge soaked in perfume, were also popular, and these were worn suspended from the belt. Gloves worn by the nobility were of tight-fitting chamois leather with wide wrists, virtually indistinguishable from a gentleman's glove of the twentieth century. The leather on the back of the hand was frequently decorated with coloured embroidery, and sometimes part of the glove's fingers was cut away to allow the wearer to display his finger rings.

Women's costume

Women's costume showed less change in the first half of the fifteenth century than did that of their male contemporaries. The silhouette became rather longer, with a high waist and small bosom, and it was fashionable to walk with the stomach protruding and the hips thrust forward. This effect was sometimes achieved with padding.

The sideless gown continued to be worn right through this period until the end of the century. The later versions of the gown had a V-shaped panel cut from the shoulders to the abdomen revealing the under-robe.

The sideless gown existed alongside the houppelande which had been introduced just before the turn of the century,

but the high collar was generally abandoned in favour of a wide, sailor collar or a small, round, turned-over collar. The gown, which was also introduced as an over-garment during this period, had a high-waisted and close-fitting bodice, long tight sleeves and a very full skirt. One feature common to all women's overgarments was their ample length. They were always several inches longer than the wearer and had to be lifted when walking. This no doubt provided a good opportunity for a fashionable lady to show off the contrasting fabrics and decoration of the outer garment, its fur lining and the inner garment. Many outer garments were even fuller at the back, falling into a train.

The most obvious change in women's fashion during this period, however, was not in clothes but in headgear. Never had there been such elaborate hairstyles and headdresses—and nothing provided a better opportunity for moral indignation and satirical lampooning. Women's headdresses fell into three main categories: reticulated, turban and horned. The reticulated was a development of the crespine of the previous century, but the *cauls* were now much larger, and the hair was completely covered by a metal mesh. The turban style was constructed

with a thick padded roll of velvet which ran across the forehead and behind the ears, hiding the hair completely. The roll was frequently decorated with jewels and held in position by a veil which fastened under the chin.

Both these styles of headdress were quite elegant if somewhat impractical. It was the horned headdress which caused the greatest outrage when it appeared soon after 1410. It was perhaps the most ludicrous garment to invade the world of fashion in Western Europe in the Middle Ages. Again, this was a development from the crespine. The cauls by this time had reached astounding proportions, extending anything up to a foot on either side of the head. As if this were not enough, they were frequently surmounted by enormous branches of wire, like cows' horns, which supported the veil. The wingspan of this arrangement could be anything up to four feet. It is hardly surprising that, at a time when sumptuary laws were supposed to be in force, there were fierce protests as this form of headdress became fashionable throughout Western Europe. One of the earliest writers on the subject, a Norman knight, tells us of a bishop who exclaimed against the fashionable foibles of the fair sex and accused them of being '. . . marvellously arrayed in divers and quaint manners, and particularly with high horns.'

Such remonstrations once again were to prove more useful as a source of information to twentieth-century writers than as an effective means of changing contemporary public taste. Lidgate, a monk of Bury, writing in the second half of the century, was still entreating women to discard their horns for, he insisted, they were no aid to beauty. He also used the somewhat naïve argument that the Virgin Mary never resorted to such a disguise.

The same problem was being faced in France where, we are told, Isabel of Bavaria, the vain consort of Charles VI, insisted that the doors of her palace at Vincennes were made higher and wider so that they might admit her headdress and those of her ladies-in-waiting.

Another French author describes a horned headdress: 'It consisted of a mixture of woollen cloth and silk, with two horns resembling turrets; and was cut and pinked after the fashion of a German hood, or crisped like the belly of a calf.'

Needless to say, not many women had enough hair to achieve these monumental arrangements and they resorted to a variety of wigs and hair pieces.

Above left: These two figures wear quite elaborate costume; the decorative detail, on the hem of the cape on the left, for example, is representative of this period. The cape has an opening at the shoulder so that it could also be worn as a coat

Above: Figures to the centre and right of this English court interior scene illustrate the popular elongated fashions and love of ostentatious display and movement of fabric. (Note the short tunics of the men)

Above right: To achieve the fantastic shapes of International Gothic costume, copious padding and quilting was employed as in the dress of this upper-class couple

Right: These peasant costumes are much less decorative than those of the wealthier classes and the women have folded their overskirts, and the men their tunics, while at work. This illustration is taken from the Duc de Berry's illuminated manuscript, Les Très Riches Heures

CLASSICISM REVIVED

The Early Renaissance

Left: A painting of Henry VIII from the school of Holbein. Male dress reached this impressive and bulky splendour during Henry's reign. The doublet was stuffed and padded and then slashed to display the fine white chemise or shirt worn beneath. In the case of Henry's own expensive suit of clothes, the slashing was interspersed with jewels and heavy embroidery. At this time the codpiece protruded through the skirt of the doublet and was decorated too. The tight stockings or hose were tied up to the doublet with laces. The wide, round sleeves of Henry's over-jacket are accentuated by embroidery

Fifteenth-century fashions demonstrate a complete break from the traditions of the Middle Ages, reflecting the new artistic energy awakening throughout Europe. The influence of secular life overshadowed religious preoccupations, and clothing became a more overt expression of status and material well-being. With the new affluence and increased availability of fabrics came a broadening of the silhouette and a shift of emphasis from vertical to horizontal lines. As trade with the New World developed, a new middle class emerged, eager to spend its wealth imitating the style of the aristocracy.

In keeping with the new prosperity, fabrics had become more and more elaborate and gorgeous. They were intended purely for the use of the nobility but, despite attempts throughout Europe by monarchs and moralists of the period, the new and affluent merchants were not to be deterred from their share of the glory. In England, Henry VIII once again introduced sumptuary laws which, considering his own love of display, must be among the most hypocritical pieces of legislation ever recorded. The laws introduced on this occasion place less emphasis on the financial status of the individual and more on his birth, and they appear solely to protect the King,

his family and the court from being copied. Moralists of the period, however, continued to criticize ostentatious dress and felt that the less wealthy should not waste their funds on self-adornment.

The deliberate cutting of velvet and brocade exemplified the development of extreme and daring fashions which were accentuated by the use of extravagant fabrics. The practice of slashing involved cutting slits in the material of the garment and pulling the lining through. This strange innovation is thought to have started after the victory of the Swiss over Charles the Bold, Duke of Burgundy, in 1477. The Swiss plundered great quantities of silk, velvet and other expensive materials which they cut up and used to patch their ragged clothes. This style was first copied by German mercenaries and then spread to the rest of Germany. It was introduced to the French court by the Guise family, who were half German, and then to England on the marriage of Louis XII to Mary, sister of Henry VIII.

Slashing was then adopted throughout Western Europe, but it was in Germany that it was taken to the greatest extremes with hundreds of cuts inflicted on the doublet and breeches. Women's clothes were also slashed but not to the same extent since skirts were unpadded.

Right: The bodice of women's dresses was squared at the top and very close-fitting. The dresses had elaborately built-up shoulders to the sleeves, with tight-fitting arms, and divided skirts revealing the rich fabric of underskirts beneath. Close-fitting caps or veils restrained the hair, ornamented with rich jewellery. Note that children of this period wore exact replicas of adult clothing. This wedding portrait from Italy also illustrates the southern European tendency for men to avoid the heavy padding and distortion of the silhouette seen in northern Europe, notably England, at this time (early sixteenth century)

Before describing the individual items of dress, a few general points which typified different countries in Europe and their taste in costume should be made. The Italians were the most restrained and avoided grotesque distortion of the outline of the figure, and they never adopted the heavy padding popular in the North. Spain generally followed the fashions of Italy at the beginning of the sixteenth century but, with their new wealth from the Americas, they soon broke away and initiated their own styles. After Charles VIII's 1494 invasion of Italy, France was much affected by Italian taste and this in turn was passed on to England. After about 1510, however, both France and England became less and less influenced by their Southern neighbours. Instead they looked to Germany for their inspiration, and it was here and in the Low Countries that costume had become most extreme. From head to foot, costumes bulged with enormous quantities of padding, making the slightest man appear enormous. Headdresses sprouted huge feathers and elbows were decorated with ribbons. Parti-coloured hose were halved, quartered and decorated with variegated patterns. Neither in England nor in France did people ever take costume to

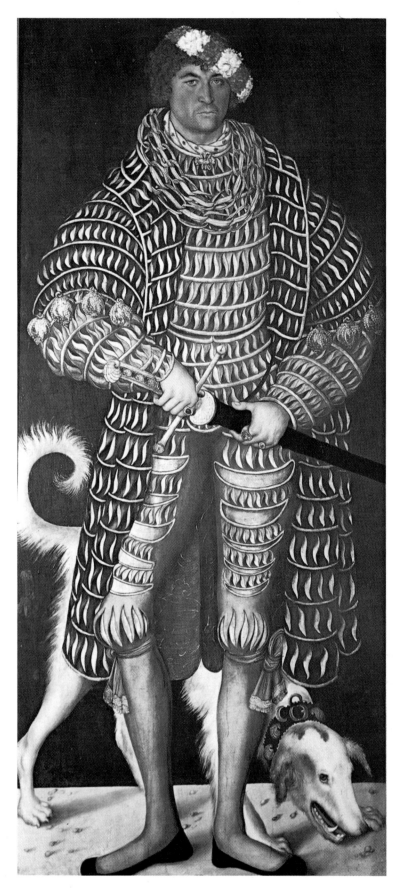

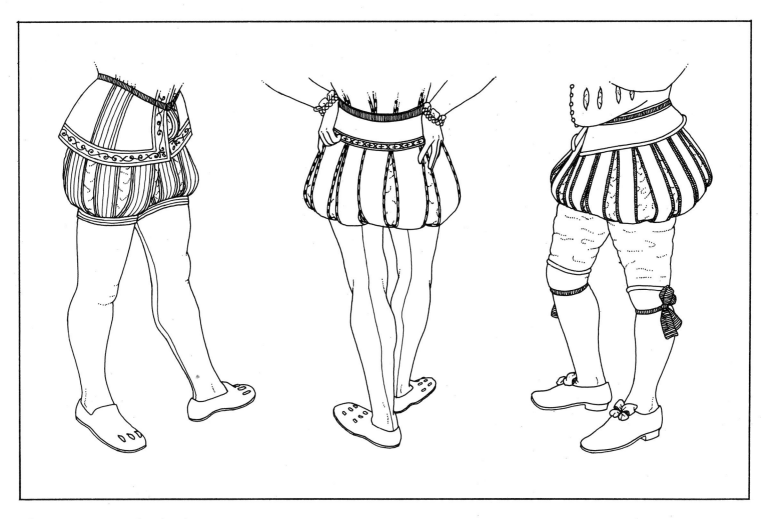

these extremes, but one would have to classify their costume between 1510 and 1550 with that of Germany rather than that of Italy.

Male costume throughout Europe from 1500 to 1550 is characterized by broad shoulders, large padded sleeves, tight jackets and padded thighs. In every country, the simple linen chemise vanished for the last time and was replaced by the shirt as we know it today. This garment was sometimes, but by no means always, of white linen. Inventories mention silk and taffeta shirts in a number of different colours. This garment had full sleeves gathered into a band or ruffle at the wrist. The neck, which reached to the base of the throat, was a simple aperture through which the head would just pass, and it was then shirred—drawn into pleats with a cord. As the necklines of outer garments became lower this frill was frequently visible, but after about 1530 it was generally replaced by a simple turn-over collar. There are many paintings which date from this period that clearly show the shirt embroidered at both the wrist and the collar.

The doublet, worn directly over the shirt, was a very different garment from the one worn in the previous century. It terminated at the waist without a skirt. Its padded sleeves generally reached the wrist with the shirt ruffle protruding and were attached at the shoulder by cords. The neckline was generally square with the shirt once again showing. Sometimes there was a narrow V-shaped slit down the front to the waist, but more often the doublet fastened behind with a flat area of fabric stretched tight across the chest. The materials used were sometimes plain, but it was the one garment which frequently carried decorative motifs. In England, Germany and France, the material would be slashed in several places across the chest. This practice allowed the shirt beneath to be glimpsed, and also effectively displayed the padding of the sleeves.

When the doublet was worn without an outer garment, as was sometimes the case, the sleeves would be very heavily padded, particularly at the shoulders, and would usually be sewn in. It is thought that, when worn with an outer garment, the doublet was not actually a complete garment, but more like a false front, such as the dicky.

The garment worn over the doublet had several names, the most common of which was the vest or jerkin—this was

Far left: The young men of the Swiss Guard (painted here by Raphael in the Vatican) show that Italian dress was equally bulky as that of the rest of Europe, but it also displayed its own national characteristics in the loose long hair, and very wide-necked bodice. Not only is the choice of colour most subtle and effective, with contrasting shades, but so is the use of different fabrics: here shiny, there soft. There is no slashing here, but an equally varied pattern is created by checks and stripes

Left: Women retained the close-fitting cap which helped to emphasize the spreading skirt below, with the underskirt revealed at the front. The wide padded shoulders add to the accentuated silhouette

the equivalent of a present-day suit-jacket, while the doublet was the equivalent of the waistcoat. The jerkin could vary considerably in length from hip to knee, and the longer version had a pleated skirt. The front was almost always open or cut away, to reveal the magnificence of the doublet, and tied at the waist with a belt or cord. Like the doublet, the sleeves were frequently tied to the shoulders with metal-ended laces and were sometimes of a totally different material. It is even possible that sleeves were interchangeable, thus giving the wearer a greater variety of outfits from a limited wardrobe. The sleeves were usually shorter than the doublet, terminating just above the elbow after puffing enormously at the shoulder. It is this feature which makes both Henry VIII painted by Holbein and Francis I by Clouet appear vast. Some-

times, however, the jerkin sleeves are seen to reach the wrist padded all the way from the shoulder and this served to exaggerate the silhouette even more noticeably.

From the waist down, Renaissance costume shows even more development. The amount of hose visible depended, of course, on the length of the upper garment. When worn with the short doublet alone, the fashion of the previous century, two individual stockings were of course useless, and they were replaced by tights. After about 1510, however, a second lower garment was added, at which time the two became known as the *upper-* and *netherhosen*. When the two were worn together, the style for two individual stockings returned as netherhosen. The upper-hosen were virtually breeches which could vary in length from thigh to knee;

some were tight, while others were much fuller and looser. In Germany, particularly, padding was much admired and became an integral part of dress, with the upper-hosen padded out at the thighs.

Codpieces were also introduced at the end of the fifteenth century. At first this was for purely practical reasons when a short doublet was worn alone, but later the codpiece became a definite feature of fashion and often protruded through the jerkin and became so voluminous it could serve as a pocket. It was generally made from the same fabric as the garment it juxtaposed or was superimposed as a separate piece of material.

Garters were worn either above or below the knee, initially for purely functional reasons to prevent the nether-hosen from wrinkling and later as a decorative feature.

101

THE AGE OF OSTENTATION
The Sixteenth Century

Left: Sir Philip Sidney was an Elizabethan of many talents, a famous poet who died for his country in the war against Spain, and we are reminded of his role of soldier by the shining plate armour which covers his shoulders and collar. His doublet, shaped in the fashionable 'peascod', is decoratively slashed and may have been made of leather

The cloak or mantle, which had been one of the few constants in European dress over the preceding centuries, at last fell out of favour. While it remained popular with the working classes for some time to come, the nobility replaced it with the gown. This was not only worn as an outdoor garment but was also used as a decorative overgarment for all occasions. The gown was sometimes worn over the doublet and jerkin or sometimes over the jerkin alone. It was generally about knee-length, open at the front with revers which developed into a huge square sailor collar at the back. It was invariably lined and faced with fur. Some gowns were sleeveless with wide arm-holes trimmed with fur, some had large padded sleeves, and still others had open sleeves with a slit along the top for the arm, allowing the fabric to hang loose at the wearer's side. The gown was sometimes belted, but more often it was allowed to fall open and display the magnificence of the garments beneath.

In Italy, young men wore their hair extremely long, and they were severely criticized for the effeminacy of this style. By the middle of the sixteenth century very short hair, similar to that worn in the early twentieth century, was generally popular. Beards were very much out of fashion during the later decades of the fifteenth century and were not generally adopted even during the early sixteenth. But when two of the most powerful monarchs in Europe—Henry VIII and Francis I—sported neatly clipped beards and moustaches, courtiers followed the fashion as, in turn, did their own retainers.

At the end of the fifteenth century the exaggerated pointed shoes of the early Renaissance disappeared, but they were replaced by a style almost as absurd: enormous broad-toed, low-cut shoes fitted with ankle straps. These shoes were sometimes even slashed to display the stockings underneath. In about 1540, however, the style was generally modified and a more sensible round-toed shoe was adopted. Shoes were generally made of leather, but mention is made of highly ornamental shoes of velvet and silk decorated with embroidery and precious stones.

Needless to say, a fantastic display of portable wealth was not within the reach of the masses in any country in Europe. Peasants wore a simple tunic or jerkin, a linen chemise and thigh-length stockings, leather shoes and hooded capes. The newly prosperous middle

classes, however, strove to emulate the profile of their more exalted contemporaries, wearing the same basic forms of garments manufactured in materials more suited to their pockets.

Women's costume

Changes in women's costume during this period were neither as dramatic nor as sudden as those of their male contemporaries. Until the beginning of the sixteenth century, the transitional period, women's basic appearance remained virtually unaltered. They continued to wear the short-waisted gown with the deep V-neck as described in the previous chapter. A variation on this style was most commonly found in the Netherlands and Germany, where the bodice was laced up the front over an underdress. The chemise underwent the same changes as the man's shirt. Since the cuffs and collar were almost always visible, it was also fitted with ruffs at the wrists and the neck was shirred in the same fashion as men's shirts. In Italy during the transitional period there was a vogue for the surcote, which is more typical of the early fifteenth century.

After 1510 the true Renaissance gown emerged. Like their male counterparts, noblewomen appear to have been striving for a horizontal effect with wide square shoulders. The deep V-neckline vanished in favour of a low-cut shaped square neckline. A strange feature of women's gowns was the sleeves. The Italians were the most extreme, favouring heavily padded upper arms, whereas the Germans, French and British adopted a fairly tight conventional sleeve. This, however, was only true of the sleeves of the undertunic. The overtunic would usually have wide sleeves which were turned back to the elbow, revealing the rich fur lining.

Skirts throughout the period were full and formed a train at the back. By 1510 they were cut separately from the bodice but were otherwise similar in appearance to those of the fifteenth century. In about 1530, however, there was an important innovation. The skirt of the gown was often split down the front from waist to hem and fell apart to reveal a large triangle of undergarment, the mirror image of the V-neckline mentioned above. At about the same time skirts became more voluminous and bell-shaped.

The gown was invariably decorated, rather than girded, with a long belt or sash of embroidered material which was tied loosely above the hips and hung

Above: In this painting entitled The Ambassadors by Holbein, the men shown are Jean de Dinteville and Georges de Selve, two members of the French embassy at the English court. Their dress is slightly different from that worn in England, though it is, of course, similarly sumptuous and refined as befitting the nobility

Above right: A successful moneylender weighs a piece whilst his wife holds the account book. The Flemish painter, Marinus van Reymerswael, has carefully recorded minute details of dress and domestic life. The delicate lace pattern of the woman's horn-shaped headdress is visible, and so too is the fine fabric of her chemise which shows at her open neck

down the front of the skirt to about knee-level. Other items of women's dress, such as shoes and stockings, were virtually identical to those worn by men at this time.

Hats showed perhaps the most noticeable and dramatic development during the fifteenth century, and styles were often quite extreme. Italy was the one country which did not favour covering the hair. Italian women preferred to display elaborate hairstyles involving braids and coils decorated with bands, ribbons and jewels, rather than to use hats which were fashionable elsewhere in Europe.

By the 1570s the fashionable headdress had become taller than wider in Northern Europe. It covered the hair completely, with a cone-like shape over which a veil was draped or pinned. The most extreme version was the *hennin* or butterfly headdress, sometimes nearly two feet in height. A mid-century variation included a broad band attached to the base of the hennin, framing the face and falling to the shoulders; the veil was not worn with this style.

As the horizontal influence of Renaissance architecture spread, the effect on women's headdresses was very obvious, and high-domed hats were replaced by hoods which were to remain the basic

form for almost sixty years. The hood is thought to have originated in the Low Countries.

At its simplest the hood was a round crown with a band of material across the forehead falling to the shoulders. This was a logical development from the hennin. Later, however, more elaborate versions evolved, particularly in England. Of these, the most notable looked like a classical Greek temple with the crown shaped like an angular roof and the side pieces like two walls covering the ears. These were constructed in rich fabric stretched over a metal frame. Later this style was further modified so that the walls turned inwards towards the neck, surrounding the face with an angular diamond frame. Like men's headdresses, these were frequently embellished with lavish embroidery and precious stones.

The French hood, which became fashionable after about 1530, was a rather more sympathetic garment. It exposed some of the hair which was almost always parted in the middle and tied back over the ears. The main feature of this headdress was a crescent of stiff material covered with velvet which fitted around the back of the head. The velvet in turn was richly decorated with

Overleaf: This tapestry is one of a series made for Catherine de Médicis in about 1575. The ladies have long, flowing sleeves and, at this stage of transition in fashion, both types of ruff, the closed and the open, can be seen. Note the small, low caps of the men, often decorated with rich jewels or ostrich plumes

goldwork and precious stones. The crescent was generally worn over an under-cap of pleated linen and was fitted with a broad strip of black velvet falling down the back.

Women also wore a version of the man's brimmed cap. It was worn over a pleated linen under-cap and, like the male version, was of velvet richly decorated with jewels, badges and feathers. It was generally worn straight, towards the back of the head, and it often revealed a narrow band of centre-parted hair at the front.

In Italy, women did not cover their heads entirely, for they preferred to decorate their hair in a number of ways. The most elegant of these had strings of pearls woven into the hair. Finger rings were worn by both sexes, as were jewelled belts. Perhaps the most extravagant use of gold and precious stones, however, was in the decoration of the fabric of various garments—a fashion which was taken to its greatest extremes during the latter part of the century. Other accessories adopted by men during the period include long canes with silver or gold knobs and purses which were still worn on the girdle. Gloves worn by both sexes were generally slashed at the knuckles to reveal the finger rings

Above left: Anne of Cleves, bride of Henry VIII, came from Flanders and her costume in this portrait demonstrates certain differences between the Flemish and English dress of the time. Her square headdress, although still kept in place by a stiff under-structure, is delicately covered in the fine fabric for which her country was so famous. The high, tight bodice is closed by a typical Flemish belt, and the unusual width of the sleeves also distinguishes her from her companions at the English court

Above centre: Here Françoise de Foix shows the sumptuous taste of female upper-class dress. This is a particularly good example of a headdress, which shows clearly the bent wire which holds it in place and on which the veil, which falls down from the back of the head, is fixed. Because Françoise is half turned we can see the flow of her skirt behind her and the generally soft outlines suggestive of continental influence

Above: In this Victorian engraving, Diane de Poitiers wears a dress which is similar to that worn by Anne of Cleves, but the decoration is more ostentatious and her headdress more closely fitting. The square-topped, tight bodice which flattened the bust was an alternative to the 'V' necked version. The strong outline of the cone-shaped skirt suggests Spanish influence, so often seen in the court fashions of this time in northern Europe

Right: The two courtesans shown in this painting by Carpaccio differ greatly from most of the young women shown in available Italian portraiture of the time, but they may give more realistic information about dress than other formally posed commemorative pictures. Their heads are bare with extravagant amounts of false and crimped hair. The casualness of their dress is also suggested by the pair of red shoes abandoned near the peacock. These are a pair of typically fashionable Italian shoes of the time, with high wooden soles to lift the wearer clear of the streets

worn beneath. They were tight-fitting gauntlets frequently decorated with embroidery on the backs and at the cuffs.

These rich garments were, of course, only within the reach of the nobility and wealthy merchant classes. Working women of the late fifteenth and early sixteenth centuries wore a simple coat of the type described earlier. This was worn over a simple chemise and the V-neck was sometimes adopted to display an area of the undergarment. With the coat were worn a large white apron, a linen bonnet, and a white handkerchief tied round the neck. Shoes were of the prevailing style, but they were cruder both in material and construction than those of the nobility.

The Late Sixteenth Century

Costume changed perceptibly both in form and decorative style. The outrageous styles and bright colours inspired by Germanic fashion gave way to the more severe styles of Spain. The massive padded figures of the previous decades were superseded by a more slender, more elongated silhouette. Tiny waists and long legs were the ideal, and clothes were designed to emphasize these qualities. The move from bright colours to blacks and browns, however, does not mark a period of restraint. On the contrary, the clothes of this period were more extravagant than those worn during the first half of the century. Priceless fabrics were decorated all over with precious stones. Necks were encircled by huge ruffs and farthingales exploded around women's hips.

Men's costume

The individual items of clothing during this period differed little from those of previous decades. The shirt, doublet, jerkin, gown, upper- and netherhose all survived, but there was a marked change in their cut and in the way in which they were worn.

The shirt, which was always covered save at the neck and cuffs, resembled that of the previous period: a long-sleeved blouse gathered at the neck with a drawstring. It was this shirring which later developed into the ruff which is so typical of late sixteenth-century costume. Philip Stubbs, the English satirist, complains in *The Anatomie of Abuses* of the widespread extravagance lavished on shirts: 'Their shirts, which all in a manner do wear, for if the nobility or gentry only

did wear them, it were more tolerable, are either of cambric, hollande, lawne, or else of the finest cloth that may be got; and these kind of shirts every one now doth wear alike, so as it may be thought our forefathers have made their bands and ruffs, if they had any at all, of grosser cloth and baser stuff, than the worst of our shirts are made now-a-days.'

The ruff, which developed directly from the neck frill of the early sixteenth-century shirt, emerged about 1555 when it was of comparatively modest proportions. It was not part of the body of the shirt but was tied at the neck with strings and supported with a wire framework. Made of lawn, linen, cambric or lace, it was starched and then crimped with a special poker-shaped iron. By 1580 some ruffs are portrayed as extending up to nine inches from the wearer's neck. These must have been grossly uncomfortable and certainly restricted greatly the wearer's freedom of movement. But it seems that the costume of the leisured classes was supposed to display the fact that they did not need to take strenuous exercise. Narrower ruffs could be up to three inches thick, while the enormous cartwheel ruffs were much thinner and were supported by an underpropper—a yoke made of wood or

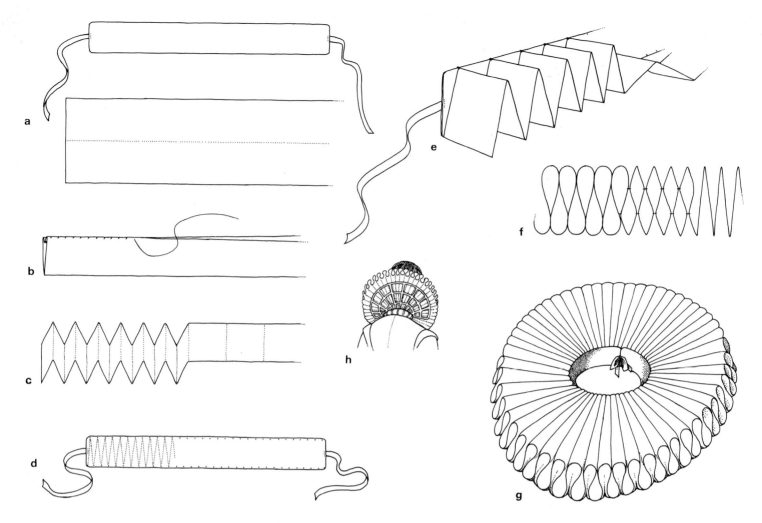

cardboard which was placed on the shoulders and covered with satin.

The size and shape of the fluting varied considerably from a tight honeycomb design to soft curves. While ruffs were generally white in colour, red, green, and blue were also recorded. Smaller versions of the ruff were also worn at the wrists.

Once again Stubbs censures such extravagance of dress. Of the great ruffs of England he says: 'They have great and monstrous ruffs made either of cambric, hollande, lawne, or of some other fine cloth; whereof some be a quarter of a yard deep, some more and very few less: they stand a full quarter of a yard, some more, from their necks, hanging over the shoulder points instead of a pentise; but if it happen that a shower of rain catch them before they can get harbour, then their great ruffs strike sail, and down they fall as dishclouts fluttering in the wind, or like windmill sails. There is a certain liquid matter which they call starch, wherein the devil has learned them to wash and dye their ruffs; which being dry, will then stand stiff and inflexible about their necks: this starch they make of divers substances, sometimes of wheat flour, of bran and of other grains, sometimes

Above: To make a ruff, first a neckband and another strip of material are necessary (a) —the depth of the band will depend upon the depth of ruff required and the length of the strip upon the density of the pleats. The width of the strip should be twice that required for the finished ruff. The strip should first be folded lengthwise and sewn together (b). The folded strip should then be pleated as in (c)—the depth of the pleat being the same as the depth of the band. The band should be marked along each edge indicating the position of the pleats (d). The next illustration (e) shows the strip being sewn on to the band; the strip is stitched at top and bottom of each pleat. The pleats are then sewn and goffered or crimped with a 'poking-iron'. The large cartwheel ruff is shown in (g) and (h) shows the curved wire frame called the underpropper—or supportasse—that had to be worn underneath the cartwheel ruff as a support

Right: This portrait of Robert Dudley, Earl of Leicester, shows the English male fashion of the latter half of the sixteenth century, before its more refined development which is seen in the picture on page 114 (far left). There is a deeper, stiffer ruff, elaborate cuffs and a scalloped edge to the waist. Although the hose, which end sharply above the knee, are padded and their size accentuated by a construction in vertical ridges, the codpiece is almost entirely gone, and the new accent is on the swollen front of the doublet, known as a 'peascod'

113

of roots, and sometimes of other things, of all colours and hues, as white, red, blue, purple and the like.' The dimensions given can probably be taken with a pinch of salt, but he continues to give an accurate description of their method of manufacture and support: 'There is also a certain device made of wires, created for the purpose, and whipped over either with gold, thread, silver or silk; and this is applied round their necks, under the ruff, upon the outside of the band, to bear up the whole frame and body of the ruff from falling or hanging down. Almost none is without them; for everyone, no matter howsoever mean or simple they be otherwise, will have of them three or four a-piece for failing.'

One of the few new items of dress adopted by men during this period was the waistcoat. This was worn immediately over the shirt and appears to have been an unpadded jacket either with or without sleeves. Like the shirt, it was always concealed in contemporary portraits for a doublet was invariably worn over it. The doublet varied considerably from the early sixteenth century. It was now sometimes fitted with a *peplum* and sometimes not. The waistband reached the hips and was pointed in the middle, terminating at the crotch. The sleeves

were detachable and often of a different material from the bodice, but they were not as heavily padded as before.

This early style did not last, however, and by 1575 the 'peascod-bellied' doublet had come into fashion. This garment had a stiff lining to pinch the waist at the sides, and the belly was padded out at the front, giving an extraordinary pigeon-chested, pot-bellied effect. This effeminate and uncomfortable outfit was not only adopted by dandies, for it is also shown on many of the great men such as Drake and Raleigh. The restrictions on movement placed upon the wearer by the peascod-bellied doublet are commented on by Philip Stubbs, and from this it can be assumed that it was only worn at court or at least abandoned on active service.

The doublet was worn alone or with a small loose cape. The jerkin of the late sixteenth century could be either skirted or not according to the wearer's fancy. It was frequently sleeveless, but when sleeves were fitted they were open or hung loose by the sides so that the doublet sleeves were visible. The jerkin was fitted with buttons up the front, but it was frequently buttoned only at the top or left completely open—therefore assuming part of the role of the gown of

the early part of the century.

Although the open gown with square collar and wide revers was fashionable for some time, it had virtually vanished by the 1580s, except for the statesmen and scholars who still wore it. In its place there were a number of other outergarments. The most popular of these was the short cloak or cape which had come back into fashion after a short period. But, Stubbs observes, this was only one of many forms. 'They have cloaks also,' he tells us, 'of white, red tawney, black, green, russet, purple, violet, and infinite other colours; some of cloth, silk, velvet, taffeta and such like, whereof some may be of Spanish, French and Dutch fashions; some short, scarcely reaching to the girdle-stead or waist, some to the knee, and others trailing upon the ground, resembling gowns rather than cloaks; then are they guarded with velvet guards, or else faced with costly lace, either of gold, silver or at least of silk, three or four fringed broad down the back, about the skirts and everywhere else ... some have sleeves,' he continued, 'some have none; some have hoods to pull up over the head, some have none; some are hanged with points and tassles of gold and silver, or silk; some without all this.'

The first true overcoat, as we know it today, appeared at this time. It was widely worn by servants and members of various institutions, such as the boys of Christ's Hospital, who were called blue-coat boys. The coat had a neat fitted body and a calf-length gathered skirt, and it was generally buttoned from neck to waist, from where it fell open to the hem. In the case of the blue coats, these were fitted with a simple white linen collar and cuffs and were tied at the waist with a narrow leather belt.

Despite these long descriptions of upper garments, it was the lower garments which underwent the most obvious transformations during the latter part of the sixteenth century. The distinct division of hose into upper- and netherhosen, established earlier in the century, was consolidated. One of the earliest styles of upper hose was the *French*—or *melon*—*hose*. The latter name describes them admirably since they gave the appearance that the wearer had threaded his legs through two ripe melons. They were very short, reaching less than half-way down the thighs, and enormously padded with wool, rags, tow hair or even bran. Raphael Holinshed, the English chronicler, tells us of a man '. . . who is said to have exhibited

the whole of his bed and table furniture, taken from these extensive receptacles.' French hose were often worn over a second trunk garment, *canions*, which were simple tight-fitting knee breeches.

After about 1570 *Venetians* became very fashionable. These were longer breeches, reaching to the knee. They were less heavily padded than the French hose and in some cases were completely unpadded. Fuller knee breeches appeared which were about half-way between the two types described above. They had a band at the knee but were so full that they puffed over it much in the style of plus-fours. There was also one style which was loose at the knee, like modern cut-off trousers, frequently worn by labourers and farmers in the southern Mediterranean.

Since upper hose were now almost universally worn, tights were no longer necessary, and netherhose consisted of two separate stockings once again. Stockings were now frequently knitted, particularly after 1589 when the stocking frame was invented. Silk stockings, however, remained fashionable for a considerable time. Stockings were generally fastened just above the knee with a garter. But, we are told, some men prided

Above left: This mid-sixteenth century portrait by Sanchez-Coello shows Alexander Farnese in noble Spanish male fashion. His short brocade coat, worn in an affectedly casual way, is bordered with embroidery and lined with ermine. His hat, as well as his hose, is stuffed to make a bulky shape, but it is neatly marked with feathers at the front, creating the distinctively smart silhouette of Spanish fashion of the time

Above: In this painting, known as The Tailor, by Moroni, the tailor shows an example of middle-class male dress from the north of Italy. His hose are heavily padded, stuffed with horse-hair or wool, but this is offset by the small, discreet ruff and cuffs. The subtle shade of the jacket is patterned by quilting and is thickly lined to give it substance

themselves on the shape of their legs and wore them without any form of fastening.

Cross-gartering was also much used. This was not, however, the criss-cross bandaging of medieval times, but a method by which a garter was fixed at the knee. The garter was placed below the knee, passed round to the back, crossed over, brought forward and tied at the front above the knee. Stockings continued to be an expensive and varied item of dress as one can gather from further complaints by Philip Stubbs.

It is quite clear from other reports of the time that stockings could come in any number of colours and they were frequently decorated with embroidered motifs. Elizabeth I is reported to have been given a pair of black knitted silk stockings early in her reign and was so pleased with them that she refused to wear any other style thereafter. This no doubt created a considerable vogue, at least in England.

Round-toed shoes remained popular; actual heels were not introduced until the beginning of the seventeenth century, but the soles were now wedge-shaped—thicker at the heel than at the toe—which thrust the foot forward in much the same way as a heel does. Most

shoes from this period were of leather or heavy velvet and were made in a number of different colours. There was also a fashion for decorating them with ribbon rosettes. For the most part they were simple slip-ons, but some fastened with a lace or buckle at the instep.

Thigh-length leather boots were also fashionable, particularly for soldiers and horsemen. These were generally very tight on the calf but were then ample enough to be folded over in buccaneer fashion above the knee. They were sometimes decorated with punched designs, covered the whole upper leg, and were held in place by suspenders from the doublet.

After about 1550, hair was generally worn fairly short but styles gradually became more flexible. One of the most fashionable, adopted towards the end of the century, was to brush the hair back from the forehead and wear it just reaching the collar. Beards were worn by young and old alike, neatly trimmed, with small moustaches.

The change of emphasis from the horizontal to the vertical which typifies the costume of this period meant that there was no place for the flat caps of the first half of the century. These were, however, retained by the working class:

a situation which was reinforced by legislation in England introduced in 1571, which insisted that all persons over the age of six should wear woollen caps of English manufacture on the Sabbath and Holy days. The nobility and 'persons of degree' were exempt from this, and various more suitable forms of headgear were developed to complete their elegant outfits.

One form was a bonnet with a high crown stiffened with buckram. Others, however, were proper hard hats of the type still worn to this day. They varied considerably in shape, but they all had a high crown and brim. Some had a conical crown, others resembled the present-day bowler, and a third style had parallel sides and a flat top, almost identical to today's topper. Velvet, beaver, felt or leather could be used in the manufacture of all these hats, which were generally decorated with jewels and ostrich feathers and worn at a jaunty angle. Hats were as much a part of indoor dress during this period as they were of outdoor, and there appears to have been a much more flexible attitude towards removing them in the presence of ladies than has been observed in more recent times.

There were a few other accessories

which were deemed necessary for any well-dressed man of the period: belts carried a purse, dagger, lace handkerchief and gloves, which, as before, were of the gauntlet type in elaborately embroidered leather. Men also wore embroidered baldricks or sashes diagonally across their chests, tied in a bow at the right shoulder.

Women's costume

The rigidity and ostentation which dominated men's costume during the late sixteenth century was even more obvious in the dress of their female contemporaries. It must be remembered that Queen Elizabeth I, for much of her reign the most powerful and influential monarch in Europe, had inherited her father's love of display. She was not a lady to be outdone, and it is not surprising that a mode of dress should have emerged which allowed her to outshine the men of the court. Although she succeeded in this, it was at considerable cost both in financial terms and in comfort.

The only modest garment of the period was the chemise, which, though never portrayed in contemporary portraits, is reported to have been of simple linen with long tight sleeves. Over this were

Right: This portrait of Lord Cobham and his family shows that children at this time were dressed as adults from an early age and imitated the deportment of their elders. The three girls wear lavish chains and brooches, although they do not yet wear rings or headdresses, and their stuffed and slashed sleeves are much shorter than those of the women behind them. The father is the least fashionable figure. The rest of his family all wear the tilted ruffs which reach the ears

Circumfusa sedet digna parente cohors
tatis erat quondam patriarchae mensa Iacobi:
Mensa fuit Iobo: sic cumulata pio·
Fac Deus ut multos haec gignat mensa Iolepho
Germinet ut Iobi stirps renouata fuit;
Fercula praeclaro donasti laeta Cobhamo
Haec habeant longos gaudia tanta dies:
Añ Dñ 1567

ÆTATIS SVÆ 5 GEMELLI

ÆTA 4

AETATIS SVAE LVIII
Anno Dñi 1591

Left: In 1591 Sir John Hawkins was painted by Hieronimo Custodis. Soberly dressed, with a thick, high ruff, he has made great use of chain jewellery to display his rank and wealth, and at his left wrist a piece of fine lace is visible. His hat, also expensively but choicely decorated, suggests the changes to come in male headwear during the next century

worn the bodice and skirt which, while frequently of the same material, were cut separately and should therefore not be referred to as a gown or dress.

Tiny waists were the ideal for women of the period and, before discussing the elaborate bodices, one must first consider the various undergarments adopted to maximize this effect. The lengths to which women were prepared to go were almost masochistic: we are told that, towards the end of the century, Catherine de Médicis prescribed the ideal waist measurement as being thirteen inches. She, in fact, is given credit for the introduction of the legendary iron corset—though this may have been a surgical garment never intended for everyday wear. It was an entire bodice of iron bands, like a suit of armour, which was hinged on one side and fastened with a clasp on the other, and some examples still remain. Whatever the true function of this item, other methods of corseting were hardly less extreme. The most common method was to reinforce the back and sides of a linen corset with whalebone or narrow steel bands. The V-shaped opening at the front of the bodice was filled with a *stomacher*—a rigid triangle of material which reached from the chest to end in a sharp point

below the waist, flattening the bust.

The woman's bodice was the equivalent of the man's doublet. It was generally tight-fitting with an open V-front to accommodate the stomacher. The sleeves followed much the same pattern as men's, although puffed sleeves were rather more common than with the doublet. Necklines, however, were considerably more varied and complex. The square-cut décolletage of the preceding period was retained, but, in the 1550s and '60s, the bosom and shoulders were often covered with a *partlet* of a different material.

The question of the neckline posed something of a dilemma. Naturally, women wished to emulate the men by wearing a ruff, which was an important status symbol. But they also wanted an area of décolletage to display their femininity. For a time they opted for the status value and wore high-necked gowns with cartwheel ruffs, but later a compromise was reached. This was achieved firstly by leaving the front of the ruff open and later by the introduction of a completely new kind of ruff. This fanlike arrangement of jewelled gauze and lace framed the face without interfering with the décolletage. Many of these ruffs were so large that they had to

be reinforced by wires to ensure that they fanned out evenly and did not sag. Some portraits of Queen Elizabeth at the end of her long reign show her with a second and even larger lace ruff rising behind the head and shoulders—an arrangement so delicate as to have rendered her almost immobile.

From about 1560, developments in women's skirts produced a garment which was even more extreme and ostentatious than the bodice already described. The desire to accentuate the wasp waist led to the development of the farthingale, perhaps the most cumbersome and uncomfortable device ever incorporated into costume in its entire history.

The first farthingales are considered to have originated in Spain in about 1550 and from there they were introduced to England on the marriage of Philip II of Spain to Mary Tudor. The first farthingale, a comparatively modest garment, was a simple underskirt distended by graduated hoops of whalebone or cane which, when the skirt was draped over it, produced a bell-shaped silhouette not unlike the skirts of the Minoans some 3500 years earlier. As time passed, farthingales expanded, a development which is satirized in a

poem of 1590:

> Alas poor verdingales must lie in
> the streete,
> To house them no doore in the cites
> made meete,
> Syns at our narrow doores they on
> can not win,
> Sende them to Oxford, at Brodegates
> to get in.

In about 1575 an even more outrageous farthingale was introduced. It was known as the *French*, or *wheel*, farthingale and consisted of a huge metal hoop worn round the hips. The fabric of the skirt therefore left the base of the bodice at right angles until it reached the perimeter of the farthingale, from where it fell to the floor. The hoop was tilted slightly forward to accommodate the stomacher, which gave the impression of an even longer and narrower body. The plateau formed by the material between the waistband and the edge of the farthingale was often covered by a pleated ruffle. This extreme fashion soon became popular throughout western Europe, but countries further east had obviously never conceived such a garment, let alone thought of adopting it. We are told that, when Sir Peter Wych visited Constantinople, his wife and her ladies-in-waiting were presented to the

Sultaness. She is reported to have treated them with great respect, but enquired whether their shape was peculiar to the women of England.

The French farthingale was quite obviously suitable only for the leisured classes, but this did not stop the middle classes from imitating it. They generally achieved a similar effect with a contraption known somewhat crudely as a *bum-roll*. This was an enormous padded sausage which was tied round the hips, making the skirt billow out.

All forms of the farthingale had a secondary benefit for the ladies of the late sixteenth century. Since the skirt was stretched fairly tightly over the under-skirt, the embroidery was clearly visible, rather than being broken up in folds. And these skirts were indeed magnificent. They were sometimes closed all round, but they were also frequently slit from waist to hem, revealing an area of the under-garment.

For obvious reasons, outer garments were not practical above these elaborate court dresses. During the earlier part of the period, however, women wore an upper-gown over the skirt and bodice. This was a long gown which fell in folds from fitted shoulders. Some were sleeveless, but most had short, puffed sleeves

Above: This is the Armada portrait of Elizabeth I, painted, it is thought, in 1588. For this commemorative and symbolic portrait, the Queen's costume is rigid and padded, but although dress at court usually changed more slowly than elsewhere, her ruff suggests the evolution of fashion. Whilst still being closed at the front, it is thinner and more frail than it would have been before, and it is sharply tilted. The pointed bodice echoes male dress of the time and the older, denser type of ruff is visible at her wrists. A preponderance of minute detail loads this dress with pearls, emblems, bows and braid, all carefully arranged in a symmetric composition

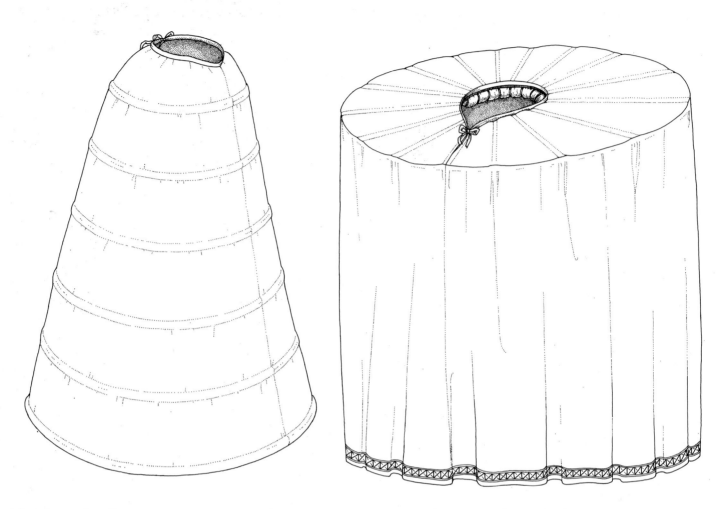

ending above the elbow and revealing the arms of the bodice. Occasionally, long hanging sleeves were used. The upper-gown was generally fitted with buttons from neck to waist, but it was frequently worn completely open or with only the top button fastened. Later, a short jerkin was added to women's wardrobes; it was usually long-sleeved and open at the front, falling to mid-thigh level.

From 1550 ladies' hair continued to be parted in the middle and drawn back over the ears, but later the pulled-back hair was shaped over a support. By the 1590s the front hair was frizzed and a 'high roll' style appeared at the back.
The sheer amount of hair required for this to be achieved satisfactorily, together with the vogue for red and blonde hair, meant that there was a very large demand for false hair pieces and even complete wigs.

Various hats and headdresses were, as in the previous period, very much in evidence. Perhaps the most typical of these was the coif, or close-fitting cap, which could either be worn alone or as a foundation for some larger hat or hood. When worn alone, the coif would be made from a rich fabric embroidered with coloured threads or encrusted with

jewels; worn as an undergarment, however, it would generally be made of plain white linen.

French hoods continued to be worn by the elderly and more conservative throughout the second half of the sixteenth century. These were similar to the hoods of previous decades, though they were sometimes deeper and covered the hair completely. A second type of hood, often associated with Mary Queen of Scots, was really little more than an elaborate coif worn on the back of the head and decorated with a heart-shaped border of wired lace which surrounded the face.

Proper hats were the most important innovation during the latter part of the century and, as with their masculine counterparts, the emphasis switched from the horizontal to the vertical. In fact, women's hats were generally very similar to those of their male contemporaries. They ranged from simple brimless bonnets to highcrowned sugar-loafs. Ladies' hats were usually made from stiffened taffeta, often embroidered and decorated with plumes and fancy hatbands. Women of the lower orders tended to wear the simple linen coif alone and, in the summer, wide-brimmed straw hats.

Above: The Spanish farthingale, shown on the left, was made from circular wooden hoops of graduated widths which were sewn onto a stiff linen underskirt. When the skirt was worn over the structure, it assumed a bell shape. The French 'wheel' farthingale on the right was a later, more exaggerated, version. It consisted of a large metal hoop which was worn round the hips. A 'cushionnet' or 'bum-roll' was worn inside the structure, so that it tipped forward slightly. When the skirt was placed over it, the material spread out horizontally to the edge of the rim and then fell to the ground

Right: This famous Ditchley portrait of Elizabeth I was painted in about 1592 by Gheeraerts the Younger. She stands, symbolically, on a map of her realm, her dress an epitome of Elizabethan taste in courtly style. Coral red used with black and white was a very popular colour combination, but here the Queen's dress is also encrusted with appliquéed gold and pearl decoration. These can be seen most clearly on the edge of her cloak and the hem of her skirt where they stand out in relief. Her ruff is a magnificent example of this impressive fashion. The pale colour of the dress perfectly complements the carefully arranged jewellery, just as the broad skirt counteracts the elongated wasp-like bodice

POTEST NEC VLCISC

DA [...] C [...]XPECTAT

REDDENDO

BVCKINGHAMIA   MIDDELSEXIA

CONFLICT OF THE FAITHS

The Seventeenth Century

The seventeenth century was marked by political stress and turmoil throughout Europe, culminating with civil war in England and the establishment of the Commonwealth under Cromwell, and the independence of Holland from Spain.

Since two of the most influential nations in Europe had adopted the Puritan way of life, it is hardly surprising that there was a rapid change in costume from the exaggerated and elaborate dress of the late Renaissance.

Men's costume

The doublet remained the basic upper garment throughout the first half of the seventeenth century, but it underwent several modifications. By 1630 padding had been eliminated, but the garment was still generally rather stiff and tight-fitting, with a short waist and a peplum which flared at the hips. At the waist there were a number of ribbon bows which held the breeches and doublet together. After 1630 doublets were even higher-waisted, though generally looser, and the peplum was generally constructed from a number of overlapping panels. The habit of slashing the bodice continued, which allowed greater freedom of movement and revealed the shirt underneath.

Sleeves were attached to the bodice with metal-tipped ribbons, the join being concealed by wings or epaulettes. They were much less full than they had been at the beginning of the century and normally tapered towards the wrists. Like the bodice, the sleeves were almost always slashed, sometimes from elbow to wrist and sometimes on the upper arm only. The most significant change to the sleeve, however, was the addition of wide cuffs. These could be up to six inches deep and were often trimmed with lace. They were generally separate from the shirt and turned back to cover the cuff of the doublet.

Only in Holland was the wide cart-wheel ruff retained. Elsewhere the practice of starching collars was generally attacked by moralists as excessive vanity. Instead the wide falling collar, either of plain white linen or lace, was fashionable with the nobility and was periodically adopted in other parts of Europe by the upper classes. The jerkin, which had previously been worn on most occasions, was now considered a dispensable outer garment to be worn only when necessary. It was generally sleeveless, with a long skirt ending at mid-thigh level. Like the doublet, it was generally waisted and

Above: The late sixteenth-century doublet, shown on the left, was padded so that the shape was distended into a 'peascod-belly', and the waist was pinched in at the sides. The second doublet is of the period 1620–30 when, without padding, the doublet takes on a longer, more elegant line, fitted with a peplum from the waist flaring over the hips. The third doublet is of the period 1630–50 when the waist became higher and the doublet more ornate. The peplum waist was cut into panels, and the sleeves and front of the garment were slashed so that the undershirt showed through

Right: Frans Hals captures the gaiety and movement which reappeared in the dress of his time. As if fashion was reacting against the confinement of the styles of the sixteenth century, more florid colours were used and garments were looser. The middle classes had their portraits painted more and more often, and we can see that, although rank was still clearly manifested in dress, this was often achieved in the quality of the fabric, the details and the choice of decoration rather than in different styles

Right: Henry Rich, first Earl of Holland, shows in his expensive dress the evolution of fashion from the stiffly padded styles of the sixteenth century to the much softer outlines prevalent in the seventeenth century. Intricate embroidery was still highly prized, especially for the edging on men's suits and on women's stomachers, and fine lace was still much in fashion. By this time, however, there was a new taste for bolder colour combinations and a growing use of asymmetric decoration

fastened at the front or side with buttons or ties.

Cloaks also continued to be worn by all classes. They were generally a semi-circle and were frequently fitted with a wide, limp collar. The length varied considerably from knee to ankle, according to the choice of the wearer.

From the waist down there were also significant changes. The exaggerated French melon hose with their stuffing had virtually vanished by 1630 and were usually replaced by close-fitting knee-breeches which were fastened just above the knee, either with wide garters tied in a bow or with a number of narrower ribbons. These knee-breeches became increasingly tighter until the 1640s when a totally different style emerged, and there was a fashion for calf-length tubular trousers which were of nearly uniform dimensions and hung loose from the leg. They generally ended about six inches below the knee and were decorated with a fringe. Stockings changed little, being made of cotton for everyday wear, and of silk for formal occasions. Contemporary portraits frequently show the stockings falling into loose folds, which suggests that they might well have been more loose-fitting than before.

Henry Rich Earl of Holland.

The most popular mode of footwear, particularly for the Cavalier, was the riding boot, which was now worn indoors as well as out. It was a wide funnel-type boot with the top turned down, sometimes decorated with a lace fringe. Shoes were often extremely elaborate and costly. They had a long squared-off toe, high heels, and were often decorated with enormous rosettes which concealed the fastening.

The large stiff ruffs of the late-sixteenth century had made short hair a necessity, but, as they went out of fashion, hair was worn longer by all but the Puritans. (It was from the practice of cropping their hair that the Roundheads in England obtained their nickname.) The aristocracy, or Cavaliers, on the other hand, allowed their hair to fall to shoulder length and drew it back from the forehead to emphasize the high brow so much admired by their predecessors. Nowhere was there a more obvious difference in dress between the Puritans and the Cavaliers than in their choice of headgear. The Puritans preferred a high-domed, stiff-brimmed hat decorated with a simple hatband and silver buckle. The Cavaliers, however, adopted low-crowned hats with wide brims, decorated with

jewelled hatbands and flowing ostrich plumes.

There were several other items which were considered essential accessories for the well-dressed man during the first half of the seventeenth century: gloves were of the gauntlet type, often richly decorated with embroidery; belts were usually fitted with a leather purse; and walking sticks became very popular during the 1630s. Daggers, which had been worn during the previous centuries by civilians, went out of fashion, but both soldiers and civilians frequently wore a dress sword on formal occasions.

Women's costume

Changes in women's fashions during the first half of the seventeenth century were even more dramatic than those of their male contemporaries. The severe styles of the late Renaissance persisted until about 1625, but after that date women began to prefer lighter and freer fashions, which of course demanded other materials. The stiff brocades of the Elizabethan period gave way to light silks, and strong contrasting colours were softened. At about the same time the farthingale diminished, and full skirts were supported by petticoats.

Above: Dirk Jacobs and his family wear styles which differ considerably from those of the previous century, for although the older couple adhere to the original closed stiff ruff, the others wear the fallen collar and dresses or suits which emphasize the slope of the shoulders. The long wasp-waist is now replaced with a higher one for both men and women

Right: Charles I, although king of England, is seen in this famous portrait in dress which is typical of that worn by the nobility at the time. The shiny high-waisted jacket, and the rakish hat and high boots may be seen on any gentleman of fashion at this date

130

Left: William and Mary in this double portrait affect the same silhouette in their dress. William wears the emblem of his rank on his sleeve, traditionally the place to display badges of allegiance. At this time the popular long hair was probably always natural, although Mary's tight and carefully placed curls suggest a little artifice. The shiny fabric of her dress is typical of the time. William's boots have become very exaggerated: the practical use of cloth to bind the leg above the boot has now degenerated into an entirely decorative feature, even inhibiting movement

Right: In this portrait Princess Mathilda Sybil of Spain wears a dress which has entirely smoothed-down shoulders, contained in this position by the bloated sleeves which are elaborately puffed and tied

The basic forms, however, remained virtually the same. The overall costume was made in two parts, the bodice and the skirt being made separately, although frequently of the same material. The bodice was still designed to emphasize a small waist, although the means employed to achieve this result were much less severe. The overall appearance was that of a considerably shorter waist. The stomacher of the undergown was still partially visible, but the bodice of the upper gown was usually laced over it. High necklines and plaited neck ruffs also survived until about 1625, but then this trend reversed to allow the introduction of a very low, square-cut décolletage. The Puritan element, needless to say, disapproved of such immodesty, and there was a vogue for covering the shoulders and bosom with folds of sheer lawn and lace. More daring ladies supported this fashion, but adapted it to allow this cape—fastened at the throat—to fall apart in an inverted V, thus displaying a handsome area of cleavage. Puritan women of the period wore a similar cape, but of stout opaque linen securely fastened across the bust.

Women also displayed part of their arms for the first time in centuries.

From about 1625 onwards their sleeves generally ended a few inches below the elbow, although Puritans once again scorned such immodesty and retained the wrist-length style. These new shorter sleeves were still full, though rarely padded, and were sometimes divided into two halves by a ribbon on the upper arm. After about 1630 they became less full and little wider at any point than at the armseye. Women's sleeves, like those of their male contemporaries, invariably ended with some form of contrasting cuff. The long Puritan sleeve was trimmed with a simple turn-back cuff of plain white linen, the more extravagant with a lace cuff similar to the male version. The small ruff at the wrist was still worn occasionally until the 1640s.

The farthingale was retained only in Spain where it had originated. Else where it had been discarded by 1630, but skirts were still anything but light. Yards and yards of material were employed to fill out the skirts in an attempt to emphasize the smallness of the waist. The Renaissance fashion of a split overskirt, falling apart to reveal a triangle of petticoat, persisted until about 1630. Women, however, still contrived to display the magnificence of

their undergowns by holding up their long skirts while walking.

We are considering a period of comparative restraint in women's costume, but this did not prevent the Puritanical critics of the day from launching into tirades about their ostentation and extravagance. Bulwer, for instance, writing in the mid-seventeenth century, tells us: 'Their gowns be no less famous than the rest; for, some are of silk, some of velvet, some of grosgrain, some of taffeta, some of scarlet, and some of fine cloth of ten, twenty or forty shillings a yard; but, if the whole garment be not of silk or velvet, then the same must be layed with lace two or three fingers broad all over the gown, or else the most part; or, if it be not so, as lace is not fine enough, now and then it must be garded with great gards of velvet, every gard four or five fingers broad at the least, and edged with costly lace . . . Then they have petticoats of the best cloth that can be bought, and of the finest die that can be made; and, sometimes they are not of cloth neither, for that is thought too base, but of scarlet, grosgrain, taffeta, silk, and such like, fringed about the skirts with silk fringe of changeable colour. But, what is more vain, of whatever the petticoat

Left: Mrs Tradescant and her son wear the middle-class fashions of the mid-seventeenth century and, although deceptively plain, her dress shows details of the future evolution. The skirt is intentionally pulled back to reveal a pretty petticoat, and this anticipates the later prominence given to the underskirt. Still favouring the long wide collar and cuffs, Mrs Tradescant and her son, however, wear their sleeves looser and wider, anticipating yet another change

Above: This picture from late seventeenth-century Holland shows the fullness of women's sleeves and the use of the stomacher. The courtier wears his hair typically long and full, together with the fashionable looser jacket and petticoat breeches over stockings. He also carries the indispensable wide-brimmed hat

Right: Margaret Bromsen's dress of 1626 shows how the cuff became looser, and the whole outline of the figure wider. The ruff followed this trend by broadening, and was lowered so that the neck and chin were clearly visible. The popular apron is another example of a once-practical garment being taken up by high fashion and so highly ornamented and decorated that it became impracticable

Left: Samuel Pepys wears a loose necktie and casually folded cuffs in this portrait. Many features of dress at this time showed this taste for studied relaxation—for an apparently careless display of what were nevertheless quite generous amounts of fabric and fur. Even for the softness of outline and a cascading effect, great skill in tailoring was required

may be, yet must they have kirtles, for so they call them, of silk, velvet, grosgrain, taffeta, satten, or scarlet, bordered with gards, lace, fringe and I cannot tell what.'

Bulwer goes on to describe in equally derogatory terms women's stockings and shoes which, because skirts were so long, are seldom shown in contemporary portraits: 'Then their nether-stocks, or stockings, in like manner, are either of silk, jarnsey, worsted, cruel, or, at least, of fine yarn, thread, or cloth as is possible to be had; yes, they are not ashamed to wear hose of all kinds of changeable colours, as green, red, white, russet, tawney, and else what not?'

The exaggerated high coiffures which typified the late sixteenth century remained fashionable for a decade but changed well before other Renaissance fashions. The ideal outline for the head was now oval rather than pointed, and the hair was arranged accordingly. Women's hair was generally drawn straight back from the forehead and crimped or frizzed at the sides before being tied into a high flat bun at the back. After about 1625 the style became more elaborate and, while the hair was still drawn straight back and tied into a bun, the sides hung in neatly dressed

Below left: The ubiquitous ruff finds even more variations in the seventeenth century: on this dress it is still closed but concedes to the new wish to reveal more of the shape of the chest, and so a secondary flattened collar is included below. The cuffs, too, on this dress are particularly fine and ornate. Even with a liking for dark or plain colours, a woman could display wealth and taste with her choice of elaborate lacework

MARGRETA BRÖMSEN
NATA Aº 1626. 30. NOVEMB:
NVPTA Aº 1641. 20. NOVEMB:
MORTVA Aº 1642. 16. APRIL:

ringlets. Later still, a portion of the hair was drawn forward and arranged across the forehead in tight curls.

The French hood of the late sixteenth century soon went out of fashion, except with the very conservative, but seventeenth-century women adapted other Renaissance styles to their new way of dress. The simple linen coif which had previously been worn either as an under-headdress, or as a single garment by the lower classes, continued to be worn during the period by those of Puritan tastes. It altered slightly in form, with a small pouch being added to the back to accommodate the bun which was an essential element of the coiffure for all classes. More fashionable ladies wore hoods of fur during the winter, frequently with a mask of black velvet or satin which, it is generally considered, was intended more to protect the complexion from the elements than to disguise the features.

Women's hats of the period barely differed from those of their male contemporaries. There were two basic forms: the high-crowned sugarloaf and the low-crowned, wide-brimmed Cavalier style. The demarcation between the two, however, was not as clearly defined. Many fashionable ladies preferred

to wear the sugarloaf made from rich fabrics, but they were just as likely to opt for the Cavalier style, similarly decorated with an ostrich plume.

Jewels and accessories

Apart from the mask, there were several other accessories widely adopted by fashionable ladies of the period. Perhaps the most important of these was the muff. This was mentioned towards the end of the sixteenth century, but now it became virtually indispensable, more as an item of fashion than as a protection against the cold: women are shown in portraits of the period in décolleté dresses with no outer-garment, yet carrying a muff. It was almost always of fur and was, by the 1640s, widely adopted by men.

Fans were also fashionable and these were sometimes seen carried at the same time as a muff, another indication of the decorative nature of each accessory.

The new shorter sleeve gave ladies more scope for gloves and they introduced an elbow-length glove, similar to a contemporary evening glove, generally of soft leather without any form of embroidery or decoration. Aprons, which had previously been used only by the lower classes, now became an element of fashionable costume. The Puritans continued to wear them in plain linen, but the fashionably-dressed are frequently portrayed wearing aprons either entirely made from, or at least trimmed with, costly lace.

FROM 1650 TO 1700

The restoration of the English monarchy in 1660 and the coming of age of France's Sun King in 1661 brought about a complete change in attitudes in both countries. In France these changes came with the rise of Louis XIV's powerful and dazzling court and in England with the start of the self-indulgent rule of Charles II. Both countries had seen enough of Puritan ideals. In France the situation was exaggerated by the persecution of the Huguenots, who had represented the staid middle classes. They were forced to leave the country in their thousands, going mainly to Holland and America where their Protestant religion and Puritan ideals were sure of a more sympathetic reception. It was in these two countries that Puritan costume survived as everyday wear. On either side of the English Channel these changes were clearly reflected in the costume of both sexes. Gone are the subdued fashions of the Puritans: we enter an era of ostentation equal to, if not in excess of, the high Renaissance.

Men's costume

The basic forms of male costume, the doublet and breeches, continued from the first half of the century. But their cut changed considerably. The doublet worn between 1650 and 1660 was generally called a cassock and was much longer than the earlier version, frequently reaching to the knee. It had a lower waistline, a flared skirt, and could be worn with or without a belt. This was generally worn over a loose white skirt with a detachable collar. Cassock sleeves were considerably shorter than on any earlier doublet, ending half-way up the forearm and fitted with a turned-back cuff. After about 1660 this rather plain and austere garment was worn only by more conservative members of the community, particularly clergymen, who of course retain the style to the present day. But after this date other more foppish garments were adopted, which were more in keeping with Restoration tastes.

As early as 1650 courtiers were wearing the short doublet. This was extremely short, similar to a bolero top, and

137

frequently exposed an area of shirt between the hem and the top of the breeches. Sleeves, either of the same or contrasting material, were sewn in at the armseye and could vary in length from a few inches to full length. The whole garment was generally made from a richly embroidered satin of a pale colour, decorated with bunches of ribbons. The neckline was concealed by the spreading shirt collar, but all the other edges were trimmed with lace or braid. The shirt collar was, more often than not, open at the throat and this gap was frequently filled with a richly coloured handkerchief, the forerunner of the cravat which will be seen to typify the mode of the last two decades of this century.

From about 1670 another coat, or vest as it was often called, found favour in the courts of Europe. This is generally thought to have been of Persian origin. Certainly contemporary diarists refer to it in this connection. Evelyn, writing in October 1666, comments on the dress of Charles II: 'To the court, it being the first time his Majesty put himself solemnly into the Eastern fashion of the vest, changing doublet, stiff collar, bands and cloak, into a comely dress after the Persian mode, with girdles or

straps, and shoe strings and garters into buckles, of which some were set with precious stones, resolving never to alter it, and to leave the French mode, which had hitherto obtained to our great expense and reproach.'

The actual garment mentioned was, in fact, so similar to the cassock described above that one wonders why its origins were credited so far afield. When it was first introduced, the Persian coat was fairly long, reaching to about mid-thigh, but as time passed it became even longer, falling to knee-level and covering the breeches entirely. It was comparatively loose-fitting, collarless, and it was fitted with close-set buttons from throat to hem.

Later, the coat had a tighter fitting body and a more defined flare in the skirt; it was also slit from waist to hem at the back and sides, which accommodated the sword as well as making it more convenient for riding. These vents were often trimmed with buttons and false button-holes, much in the manner of a twentieth-century overcoat.

Pockets were always fitted. Initially these were very near the hem of the coat, but as the garment became longer they were set rather higher. They were horizontally cut into the garment, as

Above: This illustration shows what the people—rather than the nobility—were wearing at this time. Trimmings such as bows and lace were omitted and collars were smaller. The men here wear short doublets, revealing part of the shirt underneath, straight breeches and high-crowned felt hats with fox-tail plumes

Above right: These very interesting examples of Dutch middle-class dress show how the fallen collar of previous years has developed into a distinctive cape-like part of the dress. Sleeves, too, have become shorter and, when looked at as part of an overall evolution, can be seen as another example of an increasing revelation of various parts of the body, which in women's dress reaches unparalleled extremes at the end of the next century. In this case, wrists and foreheads are exposed in a way previously considered immodest

138

opposed to patch pockets, and were usually fitted with a flap which could be buttoned down.

Coat sleeves were at first elbow-length but became longer towards the end of the century. They were fairly tight and were often fitted with a turned-back cuff.

In the late 1660s and early 1670s the coat was generally worn over a shirt of the type described earlier. But later the waistcoat was introduced, and we see the first true forerunner of contemporary male costume. The waistcoat was a similar garment to the overcoat, a few inches shorter and tighter both in the body and sleeves. After it was introduced it was common practice to wear the overcoat partially or completely unbuttoned, revealing an area of the waistcoat, which was generally made from much more ornate fabrics. The waistcoat cuffs were also often folded back over those of the top coat, these again being of richer fabric. Many experts believe, however, that only the visible area was made from the richly embroidered cloth and that the sleeves and back were generally made from cheaper stuff—a practice which has persisted in the manufacture of waistcoats to this day.

With the introduction of the coat and waistcoat, the cravat came into its own. It started as a simple band of linen which was either knotted in a bow or tied beneath the chin with a cravat string. Later, the fashion was for lace cravats, and the accounts of Charles II tell us that he paid over twenty pounds for a new cravat, an enormous sum of money. With the advent of this new and more substantial mode of dress, over-garments were seldom necessary. In very cold weather, cloaks with collars were worn similar to those favoured at the beginning of the century. But they were no longer considered an item of fashion and were instead relegated to a purely functional role.

During the 1650s and 1660s, while the short doublet was in fashion, a new style of breeches came into use. These were generally known as petticoat-breeches, and they originated in France. They were very full, and, while they were often divided into two sections, they were also made as pleated skirts. Like the doublet, they were invariably decorated all over with bunches of ribbons.

Under the cassock a rather less ornate version of the petticoat breeches was generally worn, and, after the coat and waistcoat were introduced, a completely new type of breeches appeared. These were seldom visible because of the length of the coat, but they are described as being tight-fitting, knee-length breeches which fastened with either buttons or a buckle. Tight stockings were generally pulled up over the breeches and fastened with either a garter or eyelets. Sometimes this garter was decorated with a bunch of ribbons. A second pair of hose with ornamental tops was also sometimes worn over the first pair, with a lace cuff falling over the garter.

The big wide-topped Cavalier boots of the previous period went out of fashion as court dress, and, although they were retained by soldiers for a while, even they soon adopted a tighter and lighter style. Shoes had slender squared-off toes. Generally of black leather with high red heels, they were often open-sided, and the huge rosettes of the previous period were replaced with ribbon bows of varying sizes. After about 1680 they were also fitted with large square tongues in front.

Nothing characterizes the overall appearance of a late seventeenth-century gentleman more than the full-bottomed wig. Long hair had been made possible

Left: Men's fashion had by this stage completely developed the earlier sloping shape, and now, with the addition of the tall hat, an almost perfectly conical outline was achieved. This bulky and dark figure is strangely serious, but the squared toes and draped rosettes of his shoes and the lacing at his wrist add a more frivolous note

Right: This dancing Dutch lady wears a variation on the entirely straightfronted bodice. It has a break near the natural waist and a pointed section reminiscent of the earlier stomacher. Her feet are invisible, and a less modest display of her wrists and neck is allowed. The cuffs of the man's suit have changed in a similar way, and the skirt of his jacket is longer

Far right: The 1670s saw the introduction of a distinctive headdress, named after one of Louis XIV's mistresses, Mlle Fontanges. The Fontanges consisted of a stiffly wired frill of lace, mounted on a lace cap base. This portrait of the Queen of Denmark, Charlotte, also typifies female court dress of the period, with swept back skirts, stiffly padded bodice-front softened by a lace trim, and wrist-length sleeves, equally softened by falls of lace. The bunched back of the skirt creates a bustle effect

earlier in the century when the rigid ruff was abandoned. At the beginning of this period, the lower ranks continued to wear their hair straight, falling to their shoulders. But the aristocracy preferred to crop their hair and wear wigs. These initially looked quite natural, but by the end of the 1660s any pretence of reality had been abandoned and the periwig, or full-bottomed wig, became one of the most impressive items of male costume. They were, however, seldom powdered before the end of the century.

At the start of this period there were two distinct types of headgear for men: the sugarloaf with its narrow brim and high crown, and the Cavalier with its low crown and wide brim. These two styles survived for some considerable time, but by the 1670s it was fashionable to wear the Cavalier style with a rather higher crown and with the brim cocked—that is, with the brim turned up on one or two sides. By the 1690s all three sides of the hat were cocked, forming the tricorne hat which was to become the only acceptable form of fashionable headgear for more than a hundred years.

Whatever the station or beliefs of the wearer, hats were invariably black and made from felt or beaver. But while the wide uncocked brim remained, courtiers

embellished their hats with ostrich plumes or bunches of ribbons, whereas Puritans and the lower classes left their hats unadorned. After the full-bottomed wig became fashionable men frequently carried their hats, rather than wearing them, but they remained indispensable accessories both indoors and out. It was not, however, that etiquette restricted their being worn—in fact it was quite acceptable to wear them even at dinner, except in the presence of royalty.

The close-cropped head, necessary to those who wore wigs, led to a fashion for a simple cap, similar to a nightcap, on informal occasions—to protect the wearer from the cold.

There was also a considerable change in the minor accessories carried by fashionable men. Gloves, for instance, were no longer generally worn, but there was a considerable increase in the vogue for muffs, which were suspended on a ribbon round the wearer's neck. With the advent of the coat with pockets, the belt pouch was no longer necessary and these pockets would generally contain a large handkerchief, a comb and a snuff box. The whole outfit was generally rounded off with a tall walking stick and, by the end of the century, a slender dress sword which hung under the top coat.

Women's costume

In both France and England, and thence throughout the rest of Western Europe, women's costume showed the same renewed freedom after the accession of the Sun King and the restoration of the English monarchy. It had a studied negligence which attracted the praise of some and the scorn of others. The overall effect was of an increasing freedom, but women were still constricted by stays or a boned bodice. These were longer now than earlier in the century, reaching from beneath the arms to the waist, emphasizing the more pointed and longer waistline which was once again the desired shape.

The bodice of women's dresses was still generally cut separately from the skirt. At the beginning of the period, the bodice was usually fitted with a short peplum or a number of tabs. But after about 1670 these were generally omitted as the bodice became tighter and more pointed, frequently at the back as well as at the front. It was fastened in a number of ways, with lacing, ribbons or brooches, usually at the front. Sometimes this was done down the back, however, with the material stretched tight across the front. Fashionable ladies still preferred a décolleté neckline cut straight across in the same manner as before. More modest ladies had their bodices similarly cut, but covered up the shoulders and bust in a number of ways. The most common of these was a soft scarf draped over the shoulders and tucked inside the bodice top. Sleeves were generally elbow-length or a little longer. On simpler dresses these were of the same material as the bodice and were sewn in at the armseye. In France there was a fashion for a sleeveless bodice which exposed the plain white chemise sleeve.

Women also adopted various forms of jackets, which both provided a little extra modesty and a genuine protection against the climate. One style, particularly fashionable in Holland, was a

simple hip-length loose jacket of plain velvet, lined and trimmed with fur and fitted with sensible wrist-length sleeves, also faced with fur. A more ornamental and less functional jacket, known as a night-rail, was a short shoulder-cape, made usually of muslin, trimmed with lace, which fastened down the front and generally covered no more than the shoulders and upper arms.

Skirts were once again full and reached the ground. In court dress they were generally split at the front and were held open to reveal a rich petticoat, and this, according to Samuel Pepys, was an expensive item of dress. Writing in 1660, he tells us, 'Towards Westminster by water. I landed my wife at Whitefriars . . . to buy a petticoat, and my father persuaded her to buy a most fine cloth, of twenty-six shillings a yard, and a rich lace . . .'

The skirt of the gown was generally made of the same material as the bodice and, as the period progressed, they were more often sewn together. More and more elaborate methods were devised by which the material of the overskirt could be held back to make the most of the more ornate petticoat. At its most extreme it was bunched at the back like a simple bustle and held in place by a ribbon

looped under the material and attached to the shoulders of the bodice. When this elaborate arrangement was employed, the skirt was generally very long and fell in a train behind. Less fashionable ladies once again preferred skirts which were sewn all round. But even they devised methods of tucking up the material when engaged in active pursuits, thus exposing the more modest petticoats beneath their skirts.

Aprons, which became fashionable earlier in the century, took on even more importance. They were now an essential part of the wardrobe of the bourgeoisie and even figured in court costume. Once again of the finest materials trimmed with lace, they were generally short, seldom reaching below the knee. Housewives and country women, however, continued to wear a large apron of stout material, for protection rather than decoration.

Because of the length of skirts, women's shoes are seldom visible in contemporary portraits, but they were similar in style to those of their male contemporaries. They were more colourful, however, and were made from lighter and more feminine materials, especially satin-embroidered silk.

Women's hairstyles showed little

Above: This painting by Mignard is of Mlle de Lavallière with her children dated about 1672. It shows how similar children's clothes were to their elders' and that they were without doubt very restrictive. The boy is dressed in a jacket and beneath that a type of blouse worn by small boys of the time over breeches and square-toed doeskin shoes. Mlle Lavallière's daughter wears a copy of the adult fashion of the day with her sash tied in a large, loose bow. Mlle Lavallière herself wears a low-cut, deep-waisted, blue-grey dress which is cut very closely to the figure. The sleeves are bound just above the elbow where they flare again to reveal a pink silk lining and undersleeves

Below: The bodice of the early seventeenth
century was elaborately boned with either
strips of wood or whalebone and then
covered with linen or damask. The boning
gave the impression that the wearer had a
low and narrow waistline. It laced up at the
back and could be adjusted by means of tabs
on the peplum

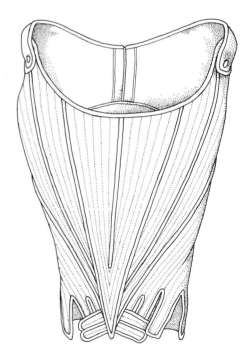

basic change from the first half of the
century until about 1690. The hair was
still drawn back from the forehead and
tied into a high flat bun at the back of the
head. The small curls over the forehead
were generally abandoned. The ringlets
at the side were rather longer, more
self-consciously arranged, and, for a
while, wired to stand away from the
head. The overall profile, however, was
the same. The use of hair-dye and false
hair once again became fashionable.

By 1680, centre partings came into
fashion, with masses of curls on either
side and, as time passed, they were
dressed higher and higher, gradually
changing the outline of the face from
horizontal to vertical. By 1690 hair was
being piled high in front and was often
arranged over a wire known as a
palisade. Artificial curls were sometimes
added to increase the height, and this
arrangement could be elaborated with a
number of ribbon bows.

Towards 1678 a most unusual form
of headdress was introduced to the
French court. It was called the Fontanges,
after Mlle Fontanges, a mistress of
Louis XIV. This was a complex arrangement based on a simple lawn cap with
long side-lappets. Above the cap there
was a high structure of stiffly starched

and wired lawn or lace. This was fluted
and formed a tower of up to eight inches
above the top of the head. This arrangement was sometimes made even more
elaborate by the addition of large black
ribbons.

This was not, however, a good time
for women's headdresses. The very
nature of their coiffure made headdresses both unnecessary and, in many
cases, impractical. Puritans on both
sides of the Atlantic continued to wear
coifs of the type described in the
previous section, but more fashionable
women relied on the addition of bows
and decorated their curls by inter-
weaving strings of pearls. In general, a
softer, more naturalistic way of hairdressing was beginning to emerge.

Jewels and accessories

Accessories in the second half of the
seventeenth century differed little from
those of the first half. Fans were an indispensable item of formal dress. Muffs
continued to be carried, but were by
this time so small that they could be
pushed up over one wrist. Elbow-
length gloves continued to be worn
both indoors and out, and masks lent
an air of mystery as well as offering
protection against the elements.

THE AGE OF ELEGANCE
The Eighteenth Century

The early part of the eighteenth century still saw the domination of the Court of Versailles in all matters of taste and fashion for the European aristocracy, but at the same time the middle classes experienced a steadily increasing prosperity. The English colonies in North America and the East Indies, and the Spanish colonies in South America produced more revenues. England itself saw tremendous advances in technical achievements, not only those in clothing manufacture such as John Kay's 'Flying Shuttle' invented in 1733, and James Hargreaves' 'Spinning Jenny' of 1764. These inventions, together with vastly increased supplies of cheap cotton from India and the New World, brought about a revolution in textile manufacture. England, with her technical and colonial advantages, dominated the world market. Centres emerged throughout the country noted for individual fabrics: Manchester for cotton, Norwich for wool and Coventry for silk. Improved, wash-proof dyes were also developed at the beginning of the century, and an important new industry emerged, manufacturing block-printed cottons which brought attractive, coloured fabrics within the reach of a mass market for the first time.

All these new conditions, together with the emergence of a true middle class, narrowed the gap between the fashion of the aristocracy and the general public. For the first time in Europe we can talk about fashion in terms of a majority rather than a tiny minority.

The basic costume forms of the eighteenth century were already established in the last two decades of the seventeenth and, for the first fifteen years of this period, changes in dress were quite minimal. The eighteenth century, therefore, can be considered from the fashion historian's point of view as starting in 1715 and ending in 1789 with the French Revolution, when changes in fashion were so dramatic that they must be considered in a separate chapter.

Men's costume
Even after 1715, the basic forms of dress worn by men did not change. They continued to wear a coat, waistcoat and breeches, but all these garments underwent continuous modification during the ensuing decades. The cut of the coat continued to develop along similar lines. It was close-fitting to the waist; the knee-length skirt now had a definite flare and was cut with a straight vent

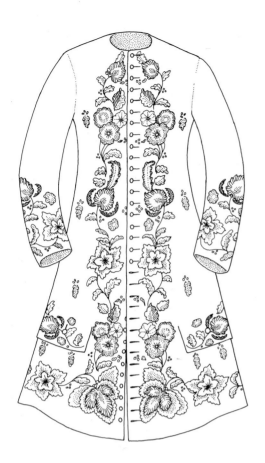

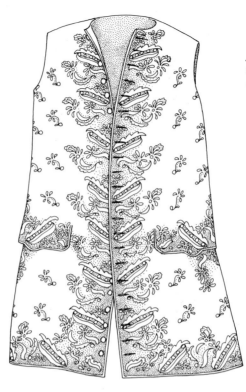

Left: The coat and waistcoat on the left show the cut before 1760. Both flare slightly from the waist, and both are buttoned from top to bottom and have round, collarless necklines. After 1760 coats and waistcoats were cut away at the front, so that there was far more fullness in the back of the garment, making the front appear quite skimpy by contrast

in the back, and a pleated vent in either side. It was generally collarless but was sometimes finished with a narrow, stand-up band. The front of the coat was still fitted from neck to hem with buttons, but these were seldom all fastened. With this in mind, tailors omitted buttonholes in the section where they were not required, although the sections of buttons which were to be fastened varied from year to year. The position of the pockets also varied from just below the waist to just above the hem. At the beginning of the period sleeves had enormous button-back cuffs which sometimes reached the elbow but, as time progressed, these became smaller and smaller.

A waistcoat or vest continued to be worn under the topcoat and, though slightly shorter than those of the late seventeenth century, it was seldom more than a couple of inches shorter than the coat. The vest's construction was similar to that of the outergarment, tight fitting and buttoned from neck to hem with a flared skirt. The front was frequently decorated with elaborate embroidery, but the back of the garment continued to be made in some inexpensive lining material. Under the waistcoat, shirts were made from either cambric or muslin according to the means of the wearer. The full sleeves ended in ruffles of lace or cambric which always showed beyond the coat sleeve. Collars were narrow and turned over, although they were seldom visible since they were almost always hidden beneath some form of neck-cloth. The cravat remained fashionable until about 1710 when well-dressed young men adopted the neck-stock. This was a broad band of linen or cambric, sometimes stiffened with cardboard, which was buckled round the neck. A narrow black tie, called a 'solitaire', was often worn with the stock.

Knee-breeches continued to be worn throughout the eighteenth century and later. In the first decades of the century they were generally of black velvet, but later satin breeches in lighter colours became fashionable. They were quite full but fitted over the hips and needed neither belt nor braces to support them. They fastened just below the knee with a row of three or four buttons. Until 1730, stockings were usually pulled up over the bottom of the breeches, but after that date the breeches were generally more often fastened over the stockings and the buttons were replaced by a buckle.

Right: Sir John Stanley, painted by Romney, wears a much shorter wig, with two tight curls at each side. This is much closer to the natural shape of the head than in previous years. When the wig finally disappeared, so too did the 'peacock' imagery of men, and the slimmer, darker outline which we see today then came into being. The fashionable silhouettes of men and women at this stage were just beginning to differ substantially

147

In 1760 there was an important development in the cut of men's coats and waistcoats. Top-coats began to be cut away at the front, the first step towards the tail-coat of the next period. They were also fitted with a fairly high standing collar, and they were seldom buttoned at all. In fact the buttons were frequently omitted altogether, and the jacket cut so skimpily that the material would not meet across the chest. At the same time, vests became much shorter and began to resemble the waistcoats of today, ending at the waist or a little below. Coat sleeves remained at wrist length, revealing the shirt ruffle, but turned-back cuffs fell from favour. The three buttons, which had originally held cuffs in place, were often retained for purely decorative purposes, another feature which lives with us to this day.

Stocks, by the 1760s, were the universally accepted neckwear, with the cravat retained only for casual dress for country and sports wear.

Men's accessories

The full-bottomed wig was well established before the end of the seventeenth century and continued to be the most fashionable headdress for some considerable time.

Most of these wigs were immensely elaborate and obviously impractical for anyone involved in any active pursuit. This led to a range of more reasonable and practical wigs, most of which were pioneered by the military. The most common was known as a combat wig which was fairly long, but the hair was arranged in three locks, one at the back and one at each side, tied at the end with knots. Another was the Ramillies, named after the Duke of Marlborough's defeat of the French in 1706, which had the hair dragged back into a single plaited pigtail which was held in place by two black ribbon bows. Another wig, fashionable with civilians, was the bagwig. With this, the pigtail was enclosed in a black silk bag which not only kept the hair in place but also prevented the wig powder from falling onto the collar or the jacket.

Tricorne hats were the standard headgear for men throughout the eighteenth century, with the exception of clergymen and some workers who wore their hats uncocked. Crowns were generally a little higher than those of seventeenth-century hats, and they were decorated rather more liberally with gold braid, feathers, brooches or ribbon bows. They continued to be made from beaver or, for the less affluent, rabbit was used.

Many different types of cloak and cape survived from the seventeenth century but they were, to a great extent, abandoned in favour of the greatcoat. These were cut much in the manner of the coat but were longer and fuller. At the beginning of the century they were single breasted, without a collar and with cuffs turned back to the elbow; by 1770, however, they were generally double-breasted with a high standing collar, and the cuffs had gone.

Shoes were long and slender, as they had been during the seventeenth century, but with a rather rounder toe. Other accessories carried by men changed little, although gloves and handkerchiefs had ceased to be decorative and were now purely functional. Canes with round silver knobs were carried, and ornamental dress swords protruded through the side vents of their coats.

Women's costume

Women's costume during the eighteenth century showed an inexplicable change of direction, unlike its male counterpart which developed along the lines established in the preceding era.

back of the neck, and it had loose elbow-length sleeves pleated into the bodice. It is not known exactly how the gown was cut, but it may have been made in one piece without any shoulder seam. It was almost certainly worn over a number of heavy starched petticoats and a tight underbodice. The sack was short-lived as high fashion, and by 1730 it had been virtually abandoned in favour of the open gown with hoops. The introduction of the hoop was one of the oddest developments in eighteenth-century costume. Initially it was merely a petticoat reinforced with graduated hoops of either whalebone or cane which gave a rather more defined bell-shape to the skirt than starched petticoats had done.

The hoop rapidly developed into a range of contraptions similar to those of the farthingale, but by 1735 the bell-shape was becoming less popular. The new silhouette was a skirt with wide hips but flat at the front and back. This shape could not be achieved with the hooped skirt and a new undergarment was introduced, which consisted of two baskets of whalebone or cane slung at either hip. These were called paniers after the side-slung baskets carried by donkeys, a similarity not unnoticed by contemporary satirists.

Throughout the seventeenth century women had moved steadily away from the extremes of Renaissance dress towards greater freedom and comfort. Indeed this is a trend which continued until about 1725 when, for no obvious reason, there appears to have been a complete *volte-face*, with a return to the exaggerated and contrived silhouettes of the late sixteenth century. Before discussing this phenomenon, however, it is worth considering the ten years from 1715 when one new mode emerged which was a continuation of the fashion trends of the late seventeenth century.

In about 1715 the sack, Watteau gown or mantua first appeared. It was called the Watteau gown because Watteau's portraits of society ladies are the best surviving representations of this particular mode. It may have been derived from eastern fashions for loose robes or kaftans, which could have been brought to Europe through trade contacts with Islam, for example. The gown was a rather shapeless garment, and very full and loose. The back was set with deep box pleats which gathered to a yoke at the

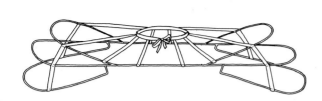

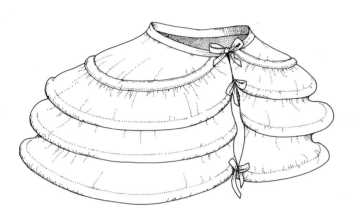

Above left: On the left, paniers, the undergarment which extended the hips but made the front and back appear flat. The basic item (top) comprised loops of wire secured at the waist with tapes, while below is a more luxurious version. The hooped petticoat (right), made of whalebone hoops, gave the overskirt a bell shape

Below left: The back of the dress on the right shows the long, gathered piece which fell from the low neck, and is an example of the loose, sack style. Chinese silks and Italian brocades came into favour and were shown off in these wide-skirted dresses by building them up underneath with hooped petticoats and heavily quilted underskirts. The men's coats are also wide and much embroidered

Above: Mr and Mrs Andrews, seated in their country park, show mid-eighteenth century English dress at its most popular and informal. The hoops of Mrs Andrews' skirt have risen up as she sat down. Her tiny shoes are backless, and covered in silk, not leather. Her husband wears a typical three-cornered hat. His coat is closed by only one button, and is pushed back to show his shirt and belt, echoing the high-fashion silhouette. His wig is by now very slight and reduced to two stiffened side-curls

By the 1750s skirts were reaching absurd widths. This girth obviously presented severe practical problems. It was impossible for two women to sit on the same settee or pass through a door side by side. The problem faced by the theatres is illustrated by this extract from *Faulkner's Journal*, published in 1742 in Dublin to announce the first performance of Handel's *Messiah*: 'The Stewards of the Charitable Musical Society request the favour of the ladies not to come with hoops this day to the Musick Hall in Fishamble Street.' Travelling in carriages also presented its problems. One ingenious solution was illustrated in a satirical print of the 1760s; it shows a coach with a removable roof and a frame fitted with pulleys by

Left: Female aristocratic dress was still much the same for children as for adults. A new taste appears here for broad and bold stripes. Silk was still a very popular fabric and London was famous for its Spitalfields silk. These side-views of fashionable dresses show that, although the front was still held in a tight line by the corset beneath, the back was full and fell quite freely from the neck. Hair was built up with plaiting and entwined with ribbons and flowers. It was quite as elaborate at the back as at the front

Right: Hogarth painted the Graham children in 1742. Even the smallest child wears the straightfronted bodice and is allowed the fashionable plain silk for her dress. The other two girls wear white aprons and floral caps —part of a frivolous 'shepherdess' craze. The little boy, even at play, wears an exact replica of his father's suit

which ladies might be lowered into the coach from above without disarranging their gowns.

By 1770 costume designers had devised a method whereby width and mobility could be achieved together. The whalebone paniers were replaced by two hinged paniers of iron which could · be lifted up when the wearer approached a narrow entrance. This marked the beginning of the end for paniers. The sheer inconvenience had killed the fashion.

While the skirt shape was continually changing throughout the eighteenth century, the outline for the bodice remained static. The slim, long waisted look, which had prevailed at the end

of the sixteenth and seventeenth centuries, was still preferred. The waist invariably ended in a sharp point at the front, but not at the back as it had at the end of the previous century. This tiny waist was achieved once again with stays, many examples of which have survived. They were far from being a new concept but, of course, they became more sophisticated and elaborate with each decade. They were usually constructed from heavy linen or cotton, closely stitched from top to bottom and reinforced with row upon row of whalebone or cane. In some cases these strips were so close to one another that the material resembled a coarse twill. The stays were carefully tailored to the

individual figure, rising to the bosom in front and to the shoulder blades behind; they fastened at the back with criss-cross lacing and were held in place with shoulder straps. Expensive stays were manufactured in bright colours or covered with embroidered silk. In some cases, the stays served as the gown bodice: they were then covered with the same material as the skirt, sleeves were laced into the shoulder straps and a stomacher was attached to the front.

The gowns which covered these elaborate undergarments were no less remarkable. They were immaculately tailored in rich silks and brocades, often embroidered with floral motifs which were so typical of the Rococo style. They

were usually what we would now call 'open gowns', although the term was not used at that time. A V-shaped panel was omitted from the front which was filled with a decorative stomacher. This was balanced by an inverted V taken out of the skirt which displayed a large area of petticoat, a garment which was frequently even more elaborate than the gown itself. A description of such a petticoat can be found in the pages of Mrs Delany, an English courtier and prolific writer on eighteenth-century fashion: 'The Duchess of Queensberry's clothes pleased me best; they were white satin embroidered—the bottom of the petticoat brown hills covered with all sorts of weeds, and every breadth had an old stump of a tree that ran up almost to the top of the petticoat, broken and ragged and worked with brown chenille, round which twined nastersians, ivy, honeysuckles, periwinkles, convolvuluses, and all sorts of twining flowers, which spread and covered the petticoat; vines with leaves variegating as you have seen them by the sun, all rather smaller than nature, which makes them look very light; the robings and facings were little green banks with all sorts of weeds; and the sleeves and the rest of the gown loose, twining branches of the same sort as those on the petticoat. Many of the leaves were finished with gold, and part of the stumps of the trees looked like the gilding of the sun.'

The open robe with paniers was fashionable for thirty years and its style during that period altered very little, except where the sheer dimensions of the undergarment made a change of shape inevitable. Sleeves were always about elbow-length with the frilly cuffs of the chemise protruding. Stomachers were usually decorated with ribbon bows of diminishing size from top to bottom, a style which, because it resembled a ladder, became known as *échelles*. The only other addition to the gown which enjoyed periodic favour was a modesty-piece, a chiffon scarf which covered the décolletage.

In about 1780, there was a complete and sudden change, with a return to the

gowns of the late seventeenth century. Instead of paniers, gowns once again had bunched fabric at the back. The bustle-look which typified dresses of the 1680s was once again in vogue. Its arrival is reported in the *Ladies Magazine* of April 1782: 'The Queen of France has appeared at Versailles in a morning dress that has totally eclipsed the levée robe, and is said to be the universal rage. The robe is made of plain satin, chiefly white worn without a hoop, round, and a long train. It is drawn up in the front on one side, and fastened with tassels of silver, gold, or silk, according to the taste of the wearer; and this discloses a puckered petticoat of gauze or sarsenet, of a different colour. The sleeves are wide and short, drawn up near the shoulder with small tassels, or knots of diamonds; . . . the sleeves of the finest cambric, full plaited, and trimmed at the elbow with Brussels or point, give infinite charms to the whole. The fastening of the waist is not straight down the stays, but generally swerved, and trimmed with narrow fur, as is the bottom of the robe.'

The new style appears to have been adopted simultaneously by both the French and English courts and remained in favour for about ten years. It enjoyed

several names but perhaps the commonest was the *Polonaise*: it had a long, boned bodice with a low, square or rounded neckline, usually edged with pleats, and the décolletage filled with a square of muslin. The sleeves remained at elbow-length but were rather more tight-fitting and finished with a frill rather than the cuff of the chemise. The skirt returned to the bell-shape: the skirt of the gown was open at the front and tied back with bows, revealing almost all the material of the petticoat skirt which could either be of the same or of contrasting material. For the first time skirts were two or three inches from the ground, revealing a daring area of ankle.

After about 1785 the bustle look was taken a stage further, with a temporary return to artificial padding. The most common form of gown was the *levite*, which was a logical development from the Polonaise but with several important differences. The skirt of the overgown was still open at the front, revealing the petticoat, but it was no longer tied up to form a bustle at the back. This was now achieved with either a bum-roll or extra starched petticoats. Skirts once again fell to the floor and formed a train at the back. The bodice was still

Above: Upper-class female dress at this date was often very densely frilled and ruched. In this case the children wear simpler garments than their parents, and this was part of the new trend towards simplicity and naturalness. Their father's wig is short and has the fashionable tailpiece tied behind

Right: The 1780s saw the introduction of a very flattering fashion for women's travelling and riding clothes, to emulate the cut of men's fashions. Hip-length jackets and waistcoats were teamed with high-tied cravats. Cocked hats, trimmed with feathers or ornate satin bows, completed a rakish but feminine vogue

Far right: This was a popular hat, with a turned-up brim usually held in place with a decorative item. The muff is a common feature too. As often happens in pictures of this time, the figure turns to show her back—for dresses were designed with copious ornate detail on the back as well as the front

tight but much shorter-waisted and girded with a broad sash. Sleeves were close-fitting, reached several inches below the elbow and were decorated with short muslin frills. The modesty piece, which had been a feature of gowns since low necklines had become fashionable, had now become a sort of stole. A large piece of muslin was draped round the shoulders, crossed over the bosom and tied at the small of the back, giving a full pouter-pigeon look. Muslin, in fact, was one of the most fashionable materials of the 1780s, particularly for petticoats. For the overgown, velvet ousted brocades were used, which meant that the contrast between the gown and petticoat was much more pronounced both in colour and texture than it had been in previous decades.

At about the same time as the Polonaise became fashionable, we see an interesting development in women's riding and travelling dress. These were based on the male fashions of the day. For riding, ladies wore a hip-length jacket and short waistcoat, both with wide turned-back collars. A cravat was tied at the throat with a bow and on the head a typically masculine cocked hat with a plume was worn. All this was worn above a many-petticoated, bell-shaped skirt which fell to the ankle. For travelling, women adopted the redingote which was based on the male great-coat. It was a full-length gown, cut like an open gown, but fitted with a shoulder cape and buttoned at the breast. It was generally worn over a white shirt and short waistcoat giving a rather masculine but elegant look. The outfit was saved from severity by the very feminine accessories which accompanied it.

Hair styles and hats

The change from moderation to extremity in mid-eighteenth century costume is reflected in the development of coiffures. After about 1717, the high Fontanges of the late seventeenth century went out of fashion and a lower, more natural style was adopted. There were several different styles, but they

were generally variations on one theme: the hair was scraped straight back from the forehead and fastened in a bun high at the back of the head. This style tended to look rather severe, and it was quite customary to soften the look by the addition of bows or jewels.

In the late 1760s ladies' hairdressing changed dramatically. In complete contrast to the moderate and even austere hairstyles of the previous four decades, we see more exaggerated arrangements than ever before. Height was the order of the day, with hair arrangements towering above the wearer's head, sometimes in excess of three feet. This colossal height was achieved by building the hair over a 'pad' which was a cushion stuffed with tow or horsehair; to this arrangement false hair was added. The basic style was of stiff curls rising to a peak. When the hair had been satisfactorily arranged, it was plastered with pomatum and powdered white. So elaborate and time-consuming were these hairstyles that they were left intact for several weeks. The inevitable result of this was that they became a sanctuary for parasites. It was to relieve the itching caused by these insects that the fork-like implement—now called a 'back-scratcher'—was invented.

After 1750 there was a general move towards more natural, less elaborate hairstyles which was accentuated by the gradual abandonment of the habit of hair powdering. Around 1780 there was a brief vogue for very frizzed hair, with the emphasis on width rather than height, but this lasted a comparatively short time and did not influence the main trend towards simplicity.

Women's hats during the eighteenth century were as varied as their coiffure. The Fontanges vanished at the beginning of the century and, with the lower and more restrained hairstyles, a simple linen mob-cap was worn, either alone or under a hat. The most fashionable hat style was a simple, low-crowned, wide-brimmed affair which could be made of a number of different materials, including straw, and generally tied under the chin with a ribbon. Hoods also enjoyed a brief return to popularity during the 1720s and 1730s. These were of the 'Little Red Riding Hood' style, but they were almost invariably made up of black silk or wool. These too were frequently worn over a linen cap.

As hairstyles became more elaborate in the 1760s, headgear changed completely. The most unusual style to emerge was the *calash* which was a form

157

of hood made from fine silk and shirred onto cane hoops; the whole contraption folded in concertina-fashion, like a carriage hood. A small, wide-brimmed hat with virtually no crown was also worn with the high hairstyles. This tilted forward at an almost perpendicular angle with the brim shielding the forehead.

In the 1780s, as coiffure became lower and wider, some of the most amazing hats ever seen were produced. Huge low-crowned picture hats of velvet, beaver or straw were festooned with ostrich plumes; steeple crowned hats similar to those of the mid-seventeenth century Puritans were now decked with feathers, ribbon bows and ornamental buckles. The most original form to emerge during the 1780s, however, was definitely the balloon hat or Lunardi, inspired by Vincenzo Lunardi, the celebrated Italian balloonist who made his first flight in England in 1784. These hats were made in fine silk or gauze, with a huge puffed-up crown and a wide brim and frequently decorated with feathers or ribbon bows.

Women's accessories
Shoes were one of the few items of feminine costume which remained much the same for the whole of this period. Women's shoes were very similar to those worn by men. They had a long vamp and a French heel. The long tongue vanished in about 1715 and shoes were decorated with an ornamental buckle. For formal occasions, shoes were made from satin or brocade, but everyday shoes were generally of plain leather. Mules and clogs were also worn. Clogs were wooden soles strapped onto the shoe for outdoor wear to prevent slipping on cobbled streets and to protect the delicate fabrics from mud.

Other seventeenth-century accessories continued to be worn throughout the eighteenth. Muffs of a moderate size were always fashionable, as were pomanders and elbow-length gloves. Fans entered a period of unparalleled splendour and became a high art form. Magnificent landscapes and figure compositions were painted onto the fine silk, a new area of self-expression enjoyed by several major artists of the day.

Aprons, which had been an item of fashion in the seventeenth century, were relegated once again to their purely functional role. The one new accessory was the parasol, which was introduced at the beginning of the century from China.

LIBERTY, EQUALITY, FRATERNITY

The French Revolution

Left: The spirit of the French Revolution is epitomized in this painting by Boilly of the actor Chénard in the role of a revolutionary, a sansculotte. Gone were the Court breeches and instead loose, baggy trousers were worn. There is still a waistcoat, but it is of plain material and double-breasted, and a short-sleeved jacket replaces the fitted brocade coat of the hated 'aristo'. The hair is no longer pomaded but worn loose, with a shapeless 'phrygian' cap instead of the trim tricorne

After the French Revolution of 1789, we see for the first time a complete change in both the form and the general attitude towards clothes, occurring in a dramatic and rapid way, the effects of which were felt throughout Europe and far beyond. Paris was the arbiter of fashion for the Western world and changes there were reflected everywhere.

Men's clothes changed in emphasis, while women's changed in both emphasis and form. Both sexes moved towards greater simplicity—understandably considering the political and social climate after the fall of the Bastille. During the Terror anything that smacked of ostentation, privilege or wealth was an invitation to a swift end.

The discovery of Pompeii and Herculaneum, earlier in the century, was one of the factors that had fostered a growing interest in things Classical and it was in the styles of Ancient Greece and Rome that French women sought their inspiration. Men, rather less ambitiously, looked across the Channel to the English aristocracy, whose country clothes were, in fact, only simplifications of French eighteenth-century modes.

Women no longer wore the extravagant paniers, corsets, wigs, plumage, and rich fabrics of the earlier part of the century. In their place came simple, flimsy muslin gowns and even simpler sandals. Men no longer wore rich embroidery, powdered periwigs or ornate dress-swords. Instead, they had sturdy woollen fabrics, tousled hair and, for self-protection, sword-sticks disguised inside plain-topped, walking canes.

In France these changes had come about in the cause of self-preservation, but they were immediately imitated elsewhere in countries where there was no such pressure towards moderation. Initially, the fashions of Paris were rather more severe than those of her followers but, by 1800, the French modified their attitudes, whereas the rest of the world had become more extreme.

Men's costume

Overall changes in men's fashion after the French Revolution were far less dramatic than those in women's costume during the same period. There was a move towards simpler fabrics, with less embroidery and trimmings, but the overall forms were a logical development from the previous decade.

Left: The fashionable shape is now much
less exuberant and sharp, and it has toned
down into softer more natural lines. The
man's dress here has arrived at the three-
piece suit of garments which men wear
today

163

Above: The flimsy chemise dress of transparent muslin required great stamina of its wearers and was the cause of much illness. The lady in Boilly's picture appears to be dressed for a very different climate to that for which the costume of the gentleman is suited. This includes an enveloping neck-cloth, shirt, waist-coat, knee-length coat and half-length boots, whereas the poor lady in her thin, white chemise has bare arms, bare neck, bare feet, no hat and nothing but a blue ribbon to comfort her

The frock or tail-coat, cut away at the front, had been introduced on a limited scale about ten years before the Revolution: now it was universally worn throughout Europe and America for both formal and informal wear.

Tail-coats fell into two basic categories: those which were cut straight across at the waist, in the style of present-day 'tails', and those which were cut away at an angle from a very high waist, like today's morning suit. In the early 1790s the most fashionable coat was of the square-cut type, single-breasted with wide revers. Towards the end of the decade these were largely replaced by double-breasted coats of the same family which could be worn one of two ways: either they could be buttoned to the neck with the fabric lying flat across the chest, or only the bottom two buttons were fastened and the material at the top folded back to form revers. The coat was sometimes left completely unbuttoned, exposing the waistcoat. In the mid-1790s tails were often very long, falling to calf level but, after the turn of the century, they seldom reached below the back of the knee. They were generally cut with two pleats, each decorated at the top with a large flat button. Sleeves were wrist-length and quite tight-fitting, although some room was allowed for mobility at the armseye. The wide, turned-back cuffs popular in the mid-seventeenth century were abandoned, but the buttons remained. Most coats were fitted with two cut-in pockets with flaps which were generally situated at waist level on either side.

Tail-coats of the second category were originally designed for riding, but shortly after the turn of the century they were adapted for town wear, being made in finer fabrics. In fact it was this style which was destined to become the court costume of both Napoleon and George III.

Both styles of coat lasted well into the nineteenth century and, in about 1810, they were joined by the bob-tailed coat. This is thought to have been of American origin. It was cut in exactly the same way as the square-cut tail-coat but with the points of the tail cut off in a straight line just below the buttocks. This was the first garment to resemble the contemporary suit jacket, but it was several decades before the fashion was consolidated.

Waistcoats could be either single- or double-breasted and were generally cut straight across at the waist level.

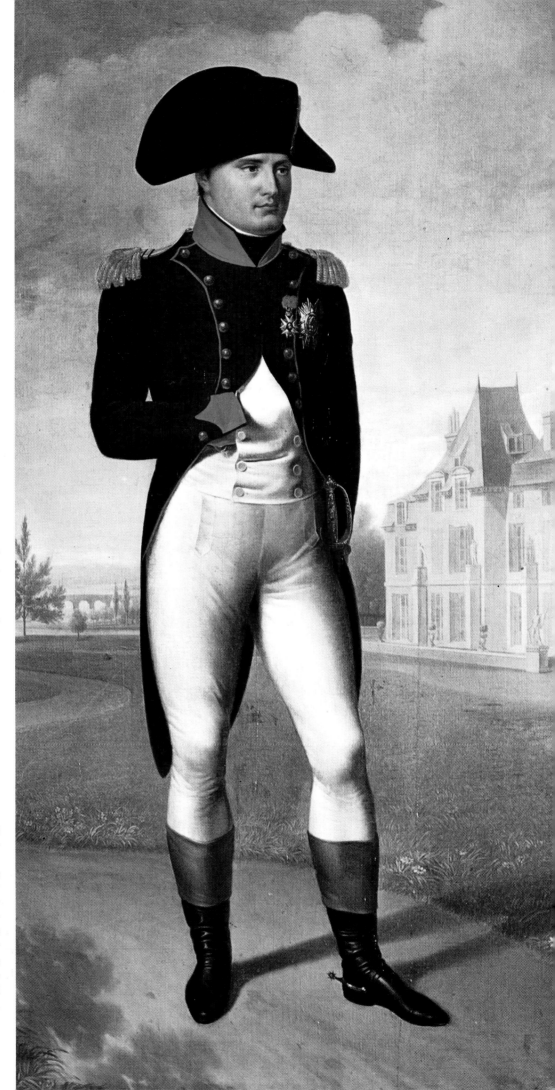

Right: Napoleon was a perfectionist, not only in military and political affairs but also in all sartorial matters. He minimized his lack of height by creating a silhouette so personal that it has impressed itself on every generation since his time, and the epaulettes which give size to his shoulders, his dark felt hat turned down in front and up at the back, together with the characteristic left hand tucked into his waistcoat, have become part of his image. In this portrait by Gérard, he wears a long tail-coat cut away over the hips, mid-calf boots of soft leather and his customary tight, white breeches

Occasionally, they were slightly longer so that, when the coat was buttoned, a small area of waistcoat was still visible. When worn with the cut-away coat, they were sometimes cut in a double V in front, very much in the fashion of most contemporary waistcoats. Double-breasted waistcoats could be buttoned to the neck, or, like the coat, the upper material could be turned back to form revers which were often worn outside the collar of the coat itself. Although the rich brocades and embroidery of the mid-eighteenth century had vanished from waistcoats, they were as a rule rather less austere than coats, frequently being decorated, for example, with a stripe.

When the waistcoat was turned back, it revealed the frilled front of the shirt underneath. Above the shirt, neck-stocks continued to be fashionable; some of these were stiff, as before, but many men achieved the same effect by wrapping a white cravat round their necks and tying it in a soft falling bow at the throat. The *Incroyables*, the dandies of late eighteenth-century France, wore enormous neckcloths which often engulfed the chin and sometimes even covered the mouth. In all cases, the stiff shirt collar was turned

up inside the cravat, and its points were always visible against the jaw-line.

Breeches, normally of white satin, continued to be worn for formal dress throughout this period. They were skin-tight and fastened just below the knee with a simple row of buttons. For normal wear, however, they were abandoned in favour of pantaloons which were, if anything, even tighter and finished just below the calf. After the turn of the century they became full-length and gradually less tight. Unlike breeches, they were generally made of a kind of jersey which allowed greater mobility and did not wrinkle. They were cut quite high, and the waistband was generally covered by the bottom of the waistcoat. Most were fitted with two small fob-pockets at the waist.

Both breeches and pantaloons were worn indoors with tight stockings, either white or patterned, and soft heel-less, black leather pumps, decorated either with a simple silver buckle or a small ribbon bow. Sometimes a calf-length gaiter was worn over the top of the foot and the lower leg. For outdoor wear, boots were generally worn until the end of the century. These were short, seldom rising above the calf, with the top cut at an angle and decorated with

braid or tassels. After 1800, however, longer and tighter-fitting boots came into fashion, similar to those of the mid-eighteenth century, with a turned-over top.

Although capes were still worn after the Revolution, the great-coat had finally established itself as the most fashionable outer-garment for men. Great-coats were cut in a very similar way to those of the preceding period, although the skirt was rather shorter, and they were more often single- than double-breasted. Most were fitted with a small turned-over collar and several overlapping shoulder capes, a style which offered admirable protection against the rain and survived as the coachman's box coat for several decades after it had ceased to be fashionable town-wear.

Perhaps the most immediately notice-able area of change in men's costume after 1790 was in hairstyles and hats. A few diehards continued to powder their hair and wear wigs, although these were of modest dimensions compared with the elaborate arrangements of the preceding decade. Hair was now worn in its natural state and cut quite short. There was no particular style in the 1790s, but the general effect was one

of studied disorder. After 1800, however, the 'Brutus' cut became fashionable. Whether or not it was pioneered by Napoleon is uncertain, but it is with him that it is most readily identified. With its short curls brushed forward over the forehead, it was perhaps the only neo-classical element in male costume, a style which—on the other hand—dominated the fashions of their female contemporaries.

After more than a century as the only headwear for men, the tricorne hat finally went out of fashion. Even the most conservative seem to have dropped it without question. It was replaced by one of two styles: for formal occasions there was the bicorne, again associated with Napoleon. This was a wide-brimmed, black hat cocked on two sides, sometimes decorated with feathers or some other ornament, but more often left totally plain. The other style, which was used for everyday wear, was the forerunner of the top-hat. Until 1800 it had a narrow, slightly curled brim and a crown which tapered towards the top. At the base of the crown it was decorated with a hat band and buckle, and it was in fact very similar to the Puritan hat of the seventeenth century. After 1800, the sides of the crown became almost

parallel and the buckle was abandoned. Other accessories were virtually the same as they had been earlier in the century. Gloves were made from soft kid and fitted very closely. The only real change was the disappearance of dress swords and these were replaced by sword-sticks which were cunningly disguised as simple walking canes.

Women's costume

After the Revolution, women's costume in France moved towards simplicity and freedom from both moral and physical restrictions. The new mode was pioneered by Mesdames Récamier and Tallien who were the leaders of the new Parisian social set known as *les Merveilleuses*. These ladies' clothes showed a much more definite break with the past than did those of their male counterparts, *les Incroyables*. Paniers, bum-rolls, corsets and even petticoats were abandoned completely. From 1790 to the turn of the century, women wore a style known as *robe en chemise* which, as the name suggests, resembled the undergarment of the previous century. Never since ancient Egypt had society ladies been seen in such a state of undress. So sheer was the material used for these gowns that, for the sake of decency, they were sometimes worn with flesh-coloured tights. The robe en chemise worn with open sandals was an attempt by Parisian ladies to copy the costume of ancient Greece.

They looked towards Greece not only for aesthetic inspiration but also for a philosophy upon which to base their new Republic. In fact this outfit bore only the most superficial resemblance to the Greek chiton. No self-respecting Greek woman would ever have appeared in public in this state of near nudity. During the early 1790s the gown was at its very simplest, a slender shift of sheer muslin, gathered at the neck and under the breasts which gave it an extremely short waist, in contrast to the elongated waists of the previous decade. This became a feature of the more sophisticated empire gowns of the early nineteenth century which, together with the sheerness of the fabric, led to the famous couplet:

Shepherds, I have lost my waist;
Have ye seen my body.

Necklines varied considerably but, at their most extreme, these early gowns certainly revealed more of the breasts than they concealed. The modesty-pieces, which had covered the décolletage during the 1780s, were no longer

Above: A lively scene on the Boulevard des Italiens shows ladies in light trailing dresses, sometimes held up to reveal legs tied with the laces of a Greek-style sandal known as a cothurne. They have wide scarves and a variety of headgear. The men are all in dark clothes of plain cloth, for to be dressed in brocade or embroidered satin would be to denounce oneself as an emigré

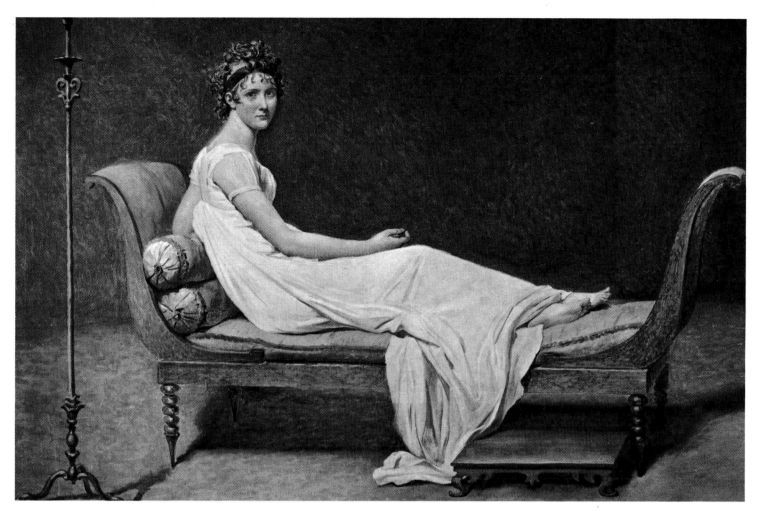

Above: Madame Récamier, the loveliest and most elegant woman of her time, was the declared enemy of Napoleon and his circle. She refused to be dressed by the fashionable couturier of the day, Leroy, who designed the wardrobes of the Empress and the Emperor's sisters, and her love of simplicity, her loose robes of white muslin and the perfection of her rooms made her a striking exception to the ostentation of the new Emperor's court

any aid to modesty. They were smaller and became a neckcloth similar to a man's stock. Most sleeves were very short and puffed, but others, in an attempt to copy the chiton, had open sleeves fastened with a row of small brooches. The same purists insisted on wearing open sandals with criss-cross ribbons extending up the lower leg. Skirts were generally very long, and the excess material from the hem was loosely draped over the forearm, effectively exposing the lower leg.

The whole outfit was obviously quite unsuitable for the northern climate, a situation which was aggravated by the practice of dampening the gown so that the material would cling more closely to the body. Carlyle described a lady of the time thus: 'Behold her, that beautiful citoyenne, in costume of the ancient Greeks, such Greek as painter David could teach; her sweeping tresses snooded by antique fillet; bright dyed tunic of the Greek woman; her little feet naked as in antique statues, with mere sandals and winding strings of riband—defying the frost.'

The fashion was not, of course, peculiar to Paris or even France. Rose Betin, the Parisian dress designer, fled from Paris during the Terror and intro-

duced it to London where it became all the rage. From there it spread elsewhere in Europe and indeed to America.

After 1800 the vogue for these extremely flimsy outfits began to wane. Some dresses were still made from muslin and other diaphanous materials, but court gowns reverted to traditional fabrics such as satin and velvet; gowns for the less wealthy and more conservative were once again made from printed calico or linen. The basic silhouette remained the same with its high waist, but the cut was considerably more sophisticated—the gown was now neatly tailored over the bust. The early gowns had been cut from a single piece of material, but now dressmakers reverted to the practice of cutting the bodice and skirts separately and then joining them together into a single garment.

Necklines were still generally cut low and square. The skirts of court gowns were long, reaching the ground at the front and forming a train behind, but for daytime wear they were about ankle-length or a couple of inches shorter, and were rather more flared than they had previously been. Borders and hems were often embroidered, and skirts were sometimes flounced. Sleeves

were again short and puffed, and they usually ended half-way down the upper arm.

Even before the turn of the century some women, particularly those who needed them, had returned to corsets. As fabrics became less transparent there was a universal return to underwear of all types, but there was nothing noticeably new about their form or design. Corsets stretched from hip level to below the bust, pushing the breasts upwards. Chemises were much in the style of those of the mid-eighteenth century, and the only new arrival to this area of dress was drawers. This was the first time that trouser-type underwear had ever been worn by women in western Europe and, despite the fact that they undoubtedly offered more protection against exposure, they were frowned upon as being immodest. Drawers developed into pantaloons, which were quite tight-fitting undergarments fastening just below the knee. Later, presumably as a concession to femininity, the name was changed to pantalettes.

Some women remained rigidly faithful to the neo-classical mode well into the nineteenth century with the result that sandals were still in evidence. The most

170

popular mode for footwear after 1800, however, was a simple low-sided, heelless slipper in either satin or soft leather. It had a short, rounded toe which was often decorated with either a small ribbon bow or a panel of embroidery.

During the 1790s, outer garments were more necessary than ever before, with gowns offering no protection against the elements. A number of different styles emerged. There was a great vogue for Cashmere shawls but, as war made trade routes with the East increasingly hazardous, imitations were produced on a large scale both in France and in Scotland. The pelisse was a totally new outdoor garment which was cut as a coat-gown, usually about three-quarter-length with raglan sleeves and lined with fur. Women also wore a version of the male great-coat, the redingote, which was fitted with two or more overlapping shoulder capes and afforded considerable protection in wet weather. For less extreme conditions, the Spencer was very fashionable. This was a very short, single-breasted jacket, originally from England, which covered the bodice of the gown. Some of these jackets were sleeveless, others were fitted with tight, wrist-length sleeves, but all were fitted with buttons from neckline to hem, although they were usually worn unfastened. Other even smaller outer garments included the pelerine, a cape which covered the shoulders, scarves and fur boas.

Hair, hats and accessories
After 1790 the wide frizzed hairstyles of the previous period vanished, as did powder and wigs. In their place came several different styles. There were a number of pseudo-classical coiffures which consisted of masses of ringlets held in place with a bandeau. This in itself was a reasonable approximation to some ancient Greek styles, but the effect was ruined by a huge vertical plume which invariably accompanied it. During the Terror there was a vogue for cutting the hair very short in a style called *à la victime*. This style emulated victims of the guillotine, whose hair was cut away from the nape of the neck to ensure that the head would be severed cleanly. With this somewhat ironically macabre style people appropriately wore a narrow red ribbon round their necks.

Towards the turn of the century a new variety of neo-classical hairstyle appeared which was, judging from con-

temporary portraits, slightly more like the Greek original. A portion of the hair was brushed forward over the forehead and the rest scraped back and tied into a chignon of curls. The similarity was strengthened by the addition of various Greek-inspired hair ornaments.

During this period of 25 years, women adopted a wide range of headwear. Mob caps, which had first appeared in the mid-eighteenth century, were made in silk trimmed with ribbons and were still very fashionable for daytime wear. For evening wear, they were largely replaced by turbans, which were often made in patterned fabric to match either the gown or shawl and, like the early hairstyles, were usually decorated with a plume or aigrette.

The wide-brimmed picture hats of the 1780s vanished with the broad hairstyles, and the high-crowned hat of the same period was now worn only as part of the riding habit. In their place came a wide range of bonnets, predominantly of straw. Most were of moderate proportions and tied under the chin with a coloured ribbon, but *les Merveilleuses* adopted a most extraordinary line of headwear known as a poke or poking-hat. This was a form of bonnet, but it had an enormous brim which extended far beyond the wearer's face.

Perhaps the most important accessory adopted by women during this period was the reticule—or 'ridicule' as it was known by the cynics of the day. This was a small handbag used to carry money, handkerchiefs and other small personal effects. It was first carried in the early 1790s with the *mode à la grecque* which had no room for belt-purses or any other similar containers. Reticules were made in a wide variety of materials and varied in size from a small purse to that of an average twentieth-century handbag.

Parasols continued to be fashionable; some were short and carried on a strap round the wrist, others were longer and doubled as walking sticks. They were usually made in cane covered with either glazed paper or embroidered silk. Gloves were another important accessory throughout the period. They were long, elbow-length or even longer, reaching to within about two inches of the short puff sleeves of the gown. White was the favourite colour, but gloves were sometimes decorated with embroidery on the back of the hand and at the top of the sleeve section. Muffs were still carried and they were even larger than they had been earlier in the century. Most were of fur, but some were made in a combination of fur and shirred silk. Folding fans of richly decorated silk were similar to those carried in the previous period.

During the Terror jewels were most definitely out of favour. They, above all else, represented the ostentation so much despised by the new régime. Even a simple silver shoe buckle invited trouble. There were three or four exceptions which were regarded as symbols of loyalty rather than jewels as we understand them today. The cropped hairstyles left the ears exposed, and there was a vogue for earrings made from various base metals in the form of guillotines. A special finger ring, called a *bague à la Marat*, was also permissible. These rings were made in copper and carried three plaques representing the martyrs of liberty: Marat, le Pellier de St Fargeau and Chaliér.

When Napoleon provided France with a court once again, attitudes changed completely. The Emperor himself and his wife were inordinately fond of jewels and spent vast sums on them. Napoleon recovered almost all the stones from the old French crown jewels and had them re-set for Josephine.

Left: A wide variety of hats were worn in the early nineteenth century, and they were all very feminine and rather fussily decorated. The mob cap (top row, right) was very popular for daytime wear. An innovation in headwear was the poke or poking-hat (see second row centre, second row right, bottom row left and centre). Bonnets also had a projecting brim but not as extreme as that of the poking hat; four variations are shown of this style, and each is made of muslin stretched over a wire frame. In that shown top left, the muslin is ruched, and the edge is decorated with scalloped ribbon, while the bonnet, top row centre, has a serrated ribbon edge, and both tie under the chin. The bonnet, second row left, fits closely to the head, and the bunch of flowers accentuates the forward tilt of the brim. The bonnet, bottom row right, would be worn on the back of the head with the brim shading the face

Right: Napoleon commissioned the artist Isabey to design the costumes for his Coronation, which were carried out with great éclat by the couturier, Leroy. Marie-Julie, Queen of Spain, was painted by Lefèvre in the gown she wore for this ceremony, which was a more elaborate, heavier version of the classical tunic-dress. Rich satin is used in place of flimsy muslin; Greek motifs inspire the gold embroidery and the design of the jewels. The curls arranged flat on the face and the jewelled bandeau complete the Grecian theme

THE ROMANTIC PERIOD
From 1815 to 1850

Left: A precursor of the fancifully dressed, long-haired young men of today was the 'poodle' of 1827. With his white, baggy trousers gathered on the hips, his waisted tail-coat with its high collar, his striped shirt and his top-hat perched at a strange angle on his exuberant locks, he presented the height of romanticism and foppishness achieved in this era

The political and economic climate in Europe changed radically after 1815. Throughout the West there was a universal disillusionment with war. The Industrial Revolution was now in full swing, and most people were more interested in making profits than capturing territory or embarking on nationalistic crusades. Wealth rather than birth was now the measure of a man. The middle classes, who had started to influence fashion in the mid-eighteenth century, were increasing in numbers and wealth. Fashion was no longer dictated by the nobility as it had been for centuries. Despite the restoration of a French monarchy, the French court never regained its position as the arbiter of public taste either at home or abroad.

After 1825 Classicism was on the wane, and there was a general move towards Romanticism. Throughout Europe, the middle classes identified with the work of English Romantic poets and novelists such as Scott, Keats, Shelley and, of course, Byron, who epitomized the movement with his untimely death while supporting the Greek insurgents.

The savage commercial rivalry which developed between the countries of Western Europe gradually displaced the military conflicts; nowhere was this fiercer than in the textile industry. Economic and technical developments completely changed the structure of the industry in the years after 1815. The most important change was brought about by the vastly increased cotton production in America, which now rivalled India as a source of raw material. Between 1815 and 1830 the American cotton trade grew by more than one thousand per cent.

The new rivalry in the cotton trade brought the prices down in the textile industry, as did new labour-saving devices. More and more sophisticated machinery was introduced to textile manufacture during the early decades of the nineteenth century. The most important innovation, however, affected the manufacture of garments rather than the production of textiles: this was the invention of the sewing machine. The first man to use a machine commercially was a Frenchman, Barthélemy Thimmonier, but the man who made an international success of the idea was the American, Isaac Merrit Singer.

The whole structure of the trade underwent a complete change, with the emergence of specialist companies. Exporters, importers and wholesalers all

Above: Not since the Minoan civilization, which was not to become known to the Western world until the next century, had the smallness of men's waists been so important. From this cartoon it is clear that the Dandies of 1819 were concerned with corseting and diminishing the size of their waists while the Dandizettes were more occupied in developing and exposing their bosoms. But in the excesses of their coiffures they were as one

appeared for the first time. Department stores sprang up in all the major cities, which offered a bespoke service, and retail shops selling 'off the peg' clothes appeared for the first time.

The basic forms of costume for both sexes were well established by the beginning of the nineteenth century: gowns for ladies, and jackets and trousers for men. Changes in costume from then until today are, therefore, concerned with cut, fabric, decoration and accessories rather than form.

After 1815 Anglomania hit Western Europe once again. Britain had never lost its hold over male fashion. The reason for this was twofold: firstly, British tailors were accepted throughout Europe and America as the finest cutters of woollen fabrics, now used almost exclusively for men's clothes; secondly, English dandies were accepted as the most elegant of the day. Now English taste started to invade female fashion, a fact which is well illustrated by this scathing extract from *La France* by Lady Morgan: 'Everything English is now in Fashion in Paris and is reputed to be romantic. So we have romantic tailors, romantic milliners, romantic pastry-cooks and even romantic doctors and apothecaries.'

Men's costume

For about the first ten years of the period, men's costume remained virtually the same as it was during the first fifteen years of the century. After 1825 there was a definite move towards Romanticism. The French poet, Chateaubriand, writing in that year describes the desired appearance of a fashionable young man. 'He had to appear ill at first glance . . . he must have something neglected about his person, neither clean shaven nor fully bearded, but as if his beard had grown without warning in a moment of despair; locks of wind-blown hair, a piercing gaze, sublime, wandering, faded eyes, lips puckering in disdain for the human species, a bored Byronic heart, drowned in disgust and mystery of being.'

Between 1813 and 1825, the cut-away coat continued to be fashionable both for evening- and for day-wear, but it was gradually replaced by the double-breasted tail-coat which, unlike earlier versions, had a low waistline and tails which curved back well over the hips and were cut straight across a few inches above the back of the knees. Men attempted to acquire the same silhouette as women with a narrow waist and wide hips. This shape was achieved in

Right: To the elegant costume of dark frock-coat and trousers so tight that Jane Carlyle referred to them as 'invisible inexpressables' was added a single-breasted waistcoat which had a small pocket to hold a fob and a watch. For travelling, a supremely chic great-coat of green and black checked wool with a shoulder cape was worn

Above: As the 1820s ended, it was recognized that no fashionable man could be seen in any public gathering except in the uniform of top-hat, tailed coat and striped trousers

Right: The dandies of the Romantic Age had no reason to fear the cold. For the evening a long cloak inspired by the Italian opera cape was carried out in brown wool with a pink satin lining and a shoulder cape and high upstanding collar were added for extra warmth. For day-wear a single-breasted ankle-length great coat had a high collar, and was accompanied by a top-hat

two ways: the bodice tapered to a tight waist and the tails, cut separately from the bodice, were pleated and flared out over the hips. The narrow waist was further accentuated by the use of corsets or a back-laced waistcoat. When cuffless, the coat sleeves were made longer, almost covering the hand.

After 1825 the frock-coat came into fashion for daytime wear with tails retained for evening dress. This new garment was generally single-breasted with a full skirt. The coat was open down the front and fitted with half a dozen large buttons from neck to waist. Like the tailcoat it had a fitted waist, and the skirt section flared to a hem which ended two or three inches above the knee. There was, however, a shorter version of the frock-coat which was worn for riding.

The bob-tailed coat, which made a brief appearance during the previous period, was still not considered an item of fashion and was worn only by young boys and lower grades of white-collar workers.

Waistcoats were, once again, the one area where a little flamboyance was considered in good taste. The most fashionable materials were velvet, satin and cashmere and, while black or white were considered proper for formal occasions, all manner of colours were adopted for everyday wear. Apart from being tighter fitting, their cut was little changed.

Breeches were now never worn for everyday wear. They were retained solely for court dress and, as such, rate more as ceremonial dress than as typical male costume of the period. In their place, pantaloons were worn by all classes throughout Europe. They varied considerably in cut and length according to the requirements of the wearer. For evening dress they normally reached to about two inches above the ankle, were open seamed from the calf down and fastened with a row of gold or pinchbeck buttons. For daytime wear they were usually full length and strapped under the foot in the same way as contemporary ski-pants. The shortest version, known as smalls, were worn for riding and reached to the top of the calf-length boots. All pantaloons were cut quite fully over the thigh and were tight from the knee down. Materials varied considerably, again depending on their use. Day trousers were normally of a stretchy jersey fabric and, for riding, corduroy, twill or doeskin were used. In the evening pantaloons were

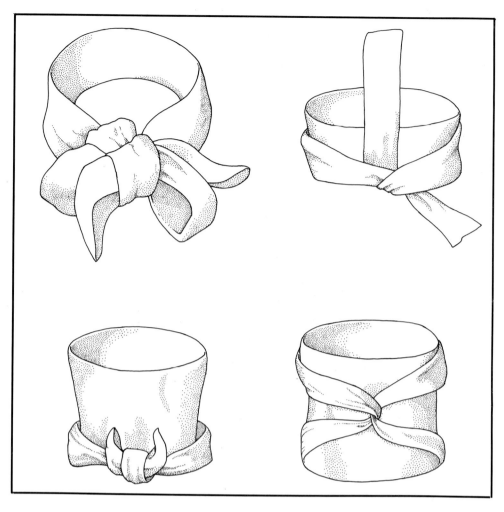

worn with black silk socks and soft black leather pumps, decorated with a small bow or buckle. During the day striped socks were most common, and they were worn with short boots. These were generally of black leather with a low heel and a squared-off, pointed toe.

Men's accessories

Neck-wear was the most important feature of male costume in the Romantic period. It was elevated to a considerable art form and often credited to the king of the dandies, Beau Brummell. It is reported that a caller visited him one day in the middle of the morning to find him with his valet standing in the middle of a large pile of crumpled cravats. When the visitor enquired about these, the valet replied, 'Sir, those are our failures'. In 1828 H. Le Blanc published the definitive work on the cravat entitled *The Art of Tying the Cravat*. This gave step-by-step instructions for thirty-two different methods of tying a cravat, illustrated by portraits of the author. The introduction is certainly worth quoting if only to demonstrate the snobbery attached to this feature of male fashion.

'When a man of rank makes his *entrée* into a circle distinguished for taste and elegance, and the usual compliments have passed on both sides, he will discover that his coat will attract only a slight degree of attention, but that the most critical and scrutinising examination will be made on the *set* of his Cravat. Should this unfortunately not be correctly and elegantly put on— no further notice will be taken of him; whether his coat be of the reigning fashion or not will be unnoticed by the assembly—all eyes will be occupied in examining the folds of the fatal Cravat.'

Outer garments varied during the Romantic period according to the time of day. For evening wear, with tail-coats, a calf-length cloak was the most popular. These were usually made in a dark blue woollen fabric lined with a contrasting silk and fitted with a velvet collar. Up to about 1830 the great-coat with shoulder capes, of the type described in the previous chapter, was worn for everyday wear. After that date, however, it was retained only by coachmen and travellers. In its place a waisted, knee-length overcoat came into fashion. This was generally double-breasted and made in a heavy woollen fabric with a black velvet collar.

Hairstyles were similar to those of the previous decade but rather neater. Part-

ings, either central or to one side, came into fashion after 1825, as did side-boards and pencil moustaches. The top-hat was the only form of head-gear which was worn throughout the whole Romantic period. Its shape changed slightly: initially, the crown tapered a little towards the top but, by 1825, the sides were parallel or even splayed slightly outwards. A novelty, designed for wear at the theatre, was the opera-hat or *gibus*, named after its inventor. This was a spring-loaded, silk topper with a collapsible crown.

Ruffles were no longer worn at the wrist and gloves came into fashion for men once again. They were wrist-length and tight-fitting, usually made in soft leather. Other accessories included a silver-topped cane and a quizzing glass. This was a small rectangular magnifying glass with a handle used to examine objects at arm's length.

Women's costume

The real change in women's fashion, the move from the Classical to the Romantic, occurred between 1820 and 1822. The waist, which had been high for more than a quarter of a century, returned to its natural level and became much tighter and reminiscent of the

1828 (2655)

Estd 1847 HOARE & SONS Estd 1847

THE 1847 FASHIONS

Above: By the mid-1840s the flamboyant elegance of the dandies was forgotten and businessmen were more admired than fops. Day-time wear demanded knee-length frock-coats with a choice between a waisted or a straight skirt. For evening there were tail-coats, uniformly black, which displayed a large expanse of starched white shirt, white waistcoat and white tie, and a splendid fur-trimmed great-coat replaced the picturesque opera-cloak. For travelling or country wear there were caped coats with matching tweed caps, otherwise the top-hat was the only possible headgear

late eighteenth century. The corset, which had been abandoned, except by those with fuller figures, was by now universally adopted once again. These corsets were full length, stiffened with whalebone or steel and were worn even by young girls. Exaggerated, small waists are always emphasized by the fullness of the skirt, and the gowns of this period were no exception. Skirts were swelled by anything up to ten starched petticoats.

Despite the change in silhouette, the gowns of the Romantic period owed much to those of the previous quarter of a century. The low neckline, so typical of the first decade of the nineteenth century, was still widely fashionable. It was, however, now frowned upon by more moralistic members of society and the *fichu* was re-introduced to fulfil its original function as a modesty-piece rather than the decorative scarf which it had recently become. The gown bodice fitted closely over the corset, demanding a much higher standard of dressmaking than had recently been necessary. It was drop-shouldered, narrow-backed, and the small waist was often highlighted by the addition of a wide belt with a large buckle.

There were two totally different styles

of sleeve during this period. Until 1820 the short puffed sleeve, typical of the neo-classical style, was very fashionable, particularly for evening wear. Puffed sleeves existed as well as simple, wrist-length tubular sleeves. Sometimes the two styles were worn together with a puffed sleeve worn over a long sleeve made in a contrasting material. After 1820, the puff sleeve became much fuller and often extended to elbow level. At about the same time a leg-o'mutton sleeve, very full at the armseye, became fashionable for morning dresses in place of the fitted tubular style.

Skirts, which had fallen straight from a high waist at the beginning of the century, were already fuller at the bottom by 1815; and the width increased gradually throughout this period. At first the fullness was purely at the hem but, by the early 1820s, more fullness was introduced at the hips, emphasizing the narrow waist. The general outline was bell-shaped, and it paved the way for the crinoline of the next period.

Fabrics used for gowns were usually quite plain, the only form of decoration being horizontal bands of patterned material sewn at intervals from waist to hem. Later these bands were replaced

Right : Two novel items became essential to the wardrobe of a woman in the 1820s—the parasol and the large-brimmed hat. Ruching was one of the favourite trimmings and forms the ornamentation of the bodice, sleeves, cuffs and skirt of this white dress

Above: After 1820 new silhouettes were devised for women's fashions, the most obvious of which was the introduction of the leg-o'mutton sleeve. The fullness often extended as low as the elbow, becoming tightened to the wrist. In keeping with a new mood of modesty, the once ample neckline was covered with a fichu. The waist continued to be exaggerated, prefiguring the crinoline of the next period

by proper flounces. This horizontal striped effect was another method of emphasizing the fullness of the skirt and thus the smallness of the waist. The most noticeable feature of skirts of the Romantic period, however, was neither their width nor their decoration but their length. Never before in Western society had women's gowns been so short. They varied in length from ankle to instep, and some extremists went so far as to wear them at calf-length, which gave a most unflattering outline. This shorter skirt meant that footwear was now quite unusually conspicuous. Until 1820, women generally wore soft, flat-heeled slippers for all occasions but, after that date, shoes or ankle boots were widely favoured for outdoor wear.

Over the gown, women wore a number of different outer-garments, all based on earlier styles. The Spencer, the

small tight jacket described in the previous chapter, continued to be fashionable, but it was now rather more robust and reserved almost exclusively for outdoor wear. It was often accompanied by a pelerine, the short fur shoulder cape also described in the previous chapter. The other outergarment was a *pelisse* which was also seen before 1815; this was virtually a second gown, open down the front, revealing an area of the gown proper; after 1825 it was usually fitted with very full leg-o'mutton sleeves and one or more shoulder capes, in the style of a man's overcoat of the period.

Hair, hats and accessories

Some women remained faithful to the curls of the previous period well into the 1820s. Others adopted a new style with the hair parted in the middle and scraped flat across the top of the head with the sides arranged in falling ringlets. After 1820, however, hairstyles became gradually higher. The height was achieved in a number of ways, but it was generally with some form of top-knot. By 1830 these arrangements had reached absurd proportions, with one style appropriately dubbed *à la girafe*. These very high arrangements were supported by wire frames and held in place by ornamental pins and further decorated with feathers, ribbons or flowers. This extreme mode of coiffure, however, was quite shortlived. By 1835 hairstyles were already becoming lower, although they were of the same basic construction. The elaborate top-knot was changed into a braided knot worn high at the back of the head, the hair was once again centre-parted, and the sides were dressed in neat ringlets.

As always, hats and other headwear had to reflect the hairstyles they were required to cover. Between 1815 and 1820 caps and turbans continued to be elongated but, as hairstyles became higher, so the crowns of both were enlarged to accommodate them. A distinction was made, as it had been at the beginning of the century, between caps used for informal day-wear and turbans which were usually worn in the evening.

Bonnets continued to be fashionable, but here again their form changed during the late 1820s to accommodate the higher hairstyles. During the early 1830s they were at their most extreme, with large, high crowns and huge sweeping brims stiffened with whalebone, and they were usually lavishly decorated with large wired ribbons.

Left: This Parisian walking costume of 1822 consisted of a buff-coloured, ankle-length pelisse fastened with decorative, braided loops and buttons known as Brandenburgs. In imitation of men's overcoats, it was common to add one or more shoulder capes, which relieved the utilitarian style of the coat. After 1825 pelisses often had leg-o' mutton sleeves

Above: The two ladies of a later date show the change of fashion at the end of the 1820s which emphasized the width of the shoulders by ballooning sleeves which were balanced by a wider skirt and a tightly pulled-in waist

Left: In this portrait of the lovely Duchesse d'Aumale, painted by Winterhalter, her blonde hair is parted in the centre and smoothly brushed forwards into ringlets which reach her shoulders, with a pink rose poised on one side

Far left: By the mid-nineteenth century the skirts were billowing out, supported by many starched petticoats and over these, as the full-length pelisse would be too heavy over such bulk, the mid-length, waisted wrap appeared. This was fur trimmed and fitted into the waist with loose, wide armholes and loose sleeves. Wide hems were counter-balanced by wide-brimmed bonnets

187

Left: The prim figure of the mid-1840s showed a small waist and a full skirt which reached the ground. There were only two ways of wearing the hair, both of which covered the ears: either smoothly brushed bands or a cascade of ringlets. Modesty and softness were the qualities most sought after in fabric and decoration

Right: For a time in the mid-1840s it seemed that dress was almost reasonable. The bodice was fitted by means of darts stitched from the bust to a small, but not exaggeratedly tight, waist. The sleeves were round but no longer balloons, and the full skirt was short enough for easy walking. The colours, too, were delightful. With her beige dress, this lady wears a small hat trimmed with a feather and her only jewellery is a gold cross on a chain. All is moderation—but not for long

Developments in hat design were exactly parallel with those for bonnets, the crown gradually becoming higher in the 1820s. Hats were made from straw with wide brims and decorated with plumes, ribbons and flowers.

Gloves once again were an essential item of female dress. These varied in style to suit the different types of gown sleeve. Wrist-length gloves were worn with long tubular and leg-o' mutton sleeves, and elbow-length gloves were worn with the short puffed sleeves.

Fans, both folding and rigid, parasols and muffs continued to be carried, apparently more for decorative than practical reasons. Handbags, which had made their first appearance just before the turn of the century, were now made in every conceivable style ranging from soft leather purses with draw-strings to rigid handbags with flaps and buckles.

With the return of belts, many women wore decorative watches and chains at the waist, and sometimes the belt buckle itself was decorated with semi-precious stones. Machine-stamped jewellery, which was invented at the beginning of the nineteenth century, was now quite cheap, and this, together with other semi-precious materials, catered for the expanding middle-class market.

VICTORIAN VIRTUE
From 1850 to 1870

Left: The Great Exhibition of 1851 was a turning point in English industrial and commercial life. The ladies, floating in their wide skirts, shawls draped over their shoulders and their bonnets tied close beneath their chins, were amazed at the possibilities offered by the new technological era and soon their homes, as well as their persons, would be examples of that conspicuous consumption which was the mainstay of commerce

Overleaf: W. P. Frith was the supreme artist-showman of his time and his pictures give as clear and detailed a record of the pastimes and clothes of his generation as could be obtained by any snapshot. Derby Day of 1858 shows clearly who is a gentleman and who is not, for all the upper classes wear the inevitable topper, while lower members of society sport caps. The women, rich or poor, wear large, hooped skirts, bonnets and shawls

Despite the political upheavals which dogged both Europe and America, industrial development continued unabated throughout the Western world. The two arbiters of fashion, France and England, were both deeply involved in this development. In France the Third Empire was backed by bankers and industrialists and, in England, the young Queen Victoria and her Consort celebrated the wonders of technology with the Great Exhibition at Crystal Palace.

This was a period of unprecedented prosperity for an enormous number of people. The middle classes, as a direct product of economic development, were increasing in number and were already creating an élite of their own. From now on fashion is dictated by them. In the last chapter we saw the emergence of the rag trade, but in the 1850s we see an even more significant development, the emergence of haute couture. Individual dressmakers have been mentioned from the eighteenth century onwards, but this was the first time that a 'house' was established. Ironically it was an Englishman, Charles Frederick Worth, who made this breakthrough. He was the undisputed giant of the international fashion world.

After moving to Paris and working as an assistant in Gagelin and Opigez, the leading fashion fabric retailers of the day, he went into business as a 'couturier' in partnership with a wealthy Swede, Otto Boberg. Starting in 1858 with a total staff of twenty and premises in the rue de la Paix, he set about revolutionizing the fashion business. He was the first man to introduce the now celebrated mannequins to Paris fashion. He also decorated and lit his salon to simulate the conditions in which a gown would eventually be seen.

For several years, however, his main clientele came from the lower end of the middle class whose budgets did not allow the magnificent fabrics which Worth best understood. Worth wanted the *crème de la crème* as his clientele and he knew that if he could once make a gown for the Empress he would never look back. To this end he went to great and devious lengths. He finally saw his opportunity when Prince Metternich was appointed as the new Austrian Ambassador to Paris. Madame Worth called on the Princess at the Embassy and showed her some of Worth's drawings. The Princess was impressed by the designs and by the price. Worth was offering to make them at roughly half the normal rate. She ordered two gowns

*Above: These three models show some of
the exquisite creations from Worth's
Collection of 1865. Each of them displays a
similarity in the use of fitted waists,
luxurious fabrics and elegant trains*

and was further impressed when they
arrived at her home, a perfect fit, after
only one fitting as opposed to the six
or seven which were considered necessary by other dressmakers of the day.
Worth's plan worked to the letter. The
Princess wore one of the gowns at the
next ball at the Tuileries.

Worth's fame rapidly spread outside
France, and this set a precedent for international individualism in couture.
By 1865 he was dressing the nobility
and royal families of Russia, Austria,
Spain and Italy. In England they were
particularly proud of Worth who, as an
Englishman, had taken the fashion
capital by storm. Even Queen Victoria is
reported to have purchased several of
his gowns.

Soon his reputation had reached
America and a stop at his *Maison*
became one of the features of the Grand
Tour. Edith Wharton, writing in the
1860s, tells us that every wealthy
American lady visiting Paris would buy
a trunk full of Worth dresses which,
because Paris fashions were at least a
season ahead of America, they would
store and then become the first to display the new mode.

By 1867, when the great Paris Exhibition was held, Worth had at least

1200 employees and was exporting his
gowns to every corner of the world.
But by the end of this period, the
Franco-Prussian War forced many of
Worth's richest customers abroad and,
although his business continued to
prosper, he never regained the suprem-
acy of the 1860s. His example, however,
was an inspiration to others, and it was
he who set the precedent for the great
couture houses of today.

Despite his enormous reputation, it
is doubtful whether Worth had any
revolutionary influence on costume
forms. He certainly did not invent the
crinoline, which was the only truly
dramatic development in women's costume during the period, and of course
later he claimed to have been responsible
for ousting it.

Worth's outstanding contribution was
in the field of marketing. Ladies' dress-
making in workrooms was now a
thing of the past. In its place were
beautifully furnished, luxurious salons
with all the trappings they have to this
day.

While Worth was struggling for recognition in Paris, many technical innovations were invading the production
both of textiles and finished garments.
By 1850, Britain had already established

herself as the world leader in mass-produced fabrics. In the 1850s, there were 750,000 powered looms working in the country.

After 1851, as the Emperor encouraged greater luxury, mechanization was gradually introduced to France on a wider scale, and the price of richer fabrics dropped considerably. This brought fashionable garments within the reach of ordinary people, and they were no longer restricted to the upper, or even the middle, classes. Surtees, writing in 1853, bemoans this development: 'The housemaid now dresses better, finer at all events—than her mistress did twenty years ago, and it is almost impossible to recognize working people when they are in their Sunday dresses.'

The variety of fabrics worn by women was as wide as ever. Cottons held their popularity even for evening dresses, and young girls used muslin and lawn for the same type of gown. For summer dresses, gingham decorated with checks or stripes was widely favoured, together with a wide range of printed calicos. For winter dresses a variety of soft woven woollen fabrics were used, including flannel, serge and broadcloth. Silk, satin, velvet and taffeta continued to be worn by the very wealthy for

formal evening wear, and lace and rich furs were used for trimming. Men's costume was now made exclusively from a variety of woollen fabric with the single exception of silk, which was used for facings and waistcoats.

Changes in form for both sexes were comparatively subtle. In men's costume, new cuts for jackets and trousers appeared, but they often existed alongside older styles without either being considered eccentric. The overall feeling for both sexes was one of greater comfort and relaxation.

Men's costume
Without undergoing any dramatic changes, male costume of the 1850s and 1860s showed all the characteristics which were to dominate it for the remainder of the nineteenth century. The two basic forms of coat survived, the frock-coat for day-time wear and the tail-coat for evenings. The frock-coat was no longer nipped in at the waist but fell to just above the knee. It continued to be standard wear for gentlemen on both sides of the Atlantic with very little change until the First World War. It was, however, destined to be replaced for less formal occasions by a number of other types of coat. One of these was the

Above: Eugénie de Montijo, is exquisitely portrayed here by that arch-flatterer, Winterhalter, calm in her unsurpassed loveliness. Her fashionable sloping shoulders are exposed by her dress of palest satin and lace. The gowns of her ladies-in-waiting play variations on the theme of off-shoulder bodices, full spreading skirts of white, blue and rose flounced with tulle and lace. Ringlets fall on their necks, some tied with black ribbons, others encircled with jewelled necklaces

LE MONITEUR DE LA MODE.
Journal du Monde Élégant

morning-coat, which developed from the cut-away riding coat of the 1840s. The sack-coat also made its first appearance as fashionable dress during the 1850s. This was a short suit-jacket which had previously been worn exclusively by young boys and workers. It was now perfectly acceptable but was produced in rough woven materials and considered as a casual garment, much in the fashion of a twentieth-century sports jacket. The relative importance of these four jacket forms fluctuated from year to year, but their shape remained virtually unaltered. Slight changes were witnessed, such as the position of the pockets, the width and height of the collar and the fit of the sleeve, but these were minimal.

Waistcoats varied considerably according to the coat with which they were to be worn. The double-breasted style of the previous decade was still worn, particularly with sports clothes. Evening dress waistcoats were single-breasted and had the deep neckline that remains to this day. For day-time wear they were also generally single-breasted with a rolled-over collar and were usually of a fabric which either matched the jacket, trousers or both. Rich fabrics, however, were retained, but after 1855 embroidery was considered rather flashy, and display was restricted to checks or plaids in woollen fabrics.

Knee-breeches were now totally obsolete, except in certain ceremonial costume and that of specialist roles such as coachmen and footmen. Peg-top trousers of the previous decade also virtually disappeared, and the tubular trousers which have survived to this day were left. They were generally a little tighter than those worn in the twentieth century and were neither creased nor fitted with turn-ups. In the 1850s they were still strapped under the foot but, by 1860, the strap was used only on formal evening dress, and the leg had increased in length to cover the shoe.

Footwear was again the precursor of today's. Short, elastic-sided boots were worn inside trousers and, in the 1860s, lace-up shoes were introduced.

For outdoor wear during the day, loose-fitting overcoats with quilted linings were one of the most fashionable forms of outer-garment. For formal evening wear, capes continued to be the

122

most fashionable mode, but overcoats were now quite acceptable for this purpose. The stock and standing collar gradually went out of fashion during the 1840s as comfort replaced elegance as a priority in masculine dress, and, by 1860, the turn-over collar was almost universally worn either with a cravat, or a bow-tie, for informal wear. The standing starched collar was still worn with an evening tail-coat throughout this period.

Men were more aware of their hair than they had been for several decades. Both straight and curly hair was fashionable parted to one side, falling to the collar at the back and covering the ears. To control these rather unruly styles men wore a variety of hair oils, ranging from tallow to perfumed macassar oil (hence the antimacassars on the

back of chairs) according to the individual's means. Facial hair also enjoyed a new wave of popularity. This took a wide variety of forms: sideboards, mutton chop whiskers, beards with moustaches, beards without moustaches and moustaches without beards, all were common during this period.

For formal wear the top-hat remained the only fashion universally accepted but, for less formal occasions, a number of other styles were common, including a form of bowler, the cap and the soft, slop hat.

Other accessories of male costume included the monocle, which evolved from the earlier quizzing glass. Walking-canes were carried outdoors, and light-coloured gloves were worn at all times, even with formal evening dress. Men's

jewellery, with the exception of finger rings, was restricted to practical areas such as cuff links, collar studs, tie pins, and watch chains. All of these were generally made from gold and, in some cases, were set with gems.

Women's costume

Women's gowns of the 1850s and 1860s developed logically from those of the preceding decade. The bell-shaped skirts of the 1840s were supported by multiple, starched petticoats. This arrangement was now considered cumbersome and uncomfortable. At the same time, wide skirts still provided the desired outline. The answer to the problem came with the introduction of the crinoline or hooped petticoat.

The idea of having skirts expanded

Above and left: Fashions recorded by the new technique of photography differ from fashion-plates and give two quite different aspects of the same style. All the men in the photographs above wear variations of the frock-coat

Above right: One exasperated wearer of a crinoline wrote: 'Men should wear women's clothes for a day—for only one day—and then something would be done about clothing.' Here a cartoon shows a man enclosed in the cage of a crinoline, which is just how many women felt all the time. The surrounding females lift up their skirts to reveal the ankle-high bottines which replaced the flat slipper towards the middle of the century and some of the would-be reformers wear hats, not bonnets

by a rigid undergarment was not of course new. The farthingale of the sixteenth and early seventeenth centuries and the paniers of the eighteenth century had already been in and out of fashion. The difference was that the crinoline was a genuine move towards freedom. Nineteenth-century technology allowed the production of extremely lightweight flexible steel bands which were sewn into a single petticoat. Inside this light steel cage a woman could move much more freely than she had done when surrounded by layer upon layer of starched petticoats.

The danger with this new garment was that, in high winds, they were inclined to blow inside out like an umbrella. Legs were still taboo and, to protect a lady's modesty in these unfortunate circumstances, pantaloons were always worn beneath the crinoline. These were made in the same way as those described in the previous chapter and were usually of linen and trimmed with lace. Skirts were still worn a couple of inches from the ground, and it was quite proper for the bottom of the pantaloons to be clearly visible beneath the hem.

By 1860 these crinolines had reached enormous proportions which gave rise to all the problems previously associated with the paniers of the eighteenth century. Passing through doors, sitting on sofas, and getting in and out of carriages presented the familiar difficulties. Needless to say crinolines attracted their share of ridicule. *Punch*, the satirical voice of the middle class, launched a campaign against the fashion which provides good reading but did little or nothing to change the public's attitude to the crinoline. One particularly amusing article of 1860 outlined a possible use of the garment: 'Among the million objections to the use of the wide petticoats, not the least well-founded is the fact that they are used for the purposes of shop-lifting. This has many times been proved at the bar of the police courts, and we wonder that more notice has not been attracted to it. For ourselves, the fact is so impressed upon our mind, that when we ever come into contact with a Crinoline which seems more than usually wide, we immediately put down the wearer as a pickpocket, and prepare ourselves at once to see her taken up.'

A more practical attempt to curb the extremes of the crinoline came from America in the person of Mrs Amelia Bloomer. She sponsored a mode which

THE FASHIONS Expressly designed and prepared for the Englishwoman's Domestic Magazine.

APRIL 1862

Above: The fashionably-dressed women of the mid-Victorian era were encumbered by enormous skirts which swept the ground and sometimes formed a train behind, which inevitably swept up the dirt of the streets and carried it into the house. Nor could the heavy silks and velvets of the garments be washed. 'Dry' cleaning was embryonic and so the ladies were as unhygienic as they were uncomfortable

Left: Amelia Bloomer is rightly credited with promoting the bifurcated garment which bears her name but, by her own account, she was not the inventor. When it appeared in London, mysteriously called the Camilla costume, English ladies refused to tolerate it, though Mrs Bloomer pertinently asked why they were so offended since they did not mind some of their men in Scotland wearing skirts

Above right: An idyllic vision by John Ritchie of London's Hyde Park in 1858 shows the newly-rich middle classes enjoying a holiday in the sunshine. All the gentlemen, except the boatman who sports a straw sailor, wear top-hats and the little girl, as well as all the women, wears stiffened-out skirts

comprised a knee-length skirt worn over baggy trousers. It was not a particularly striking outfit, but it was not unfeminine, and was certainly much more practical than the crinoline for everyday wear. Her attempts to introduce the fashion to Europe, however, were met not only with ridicule but with considerable hostility. This hostility came not from the ladies but from their menfolk, who suspected a sexual revolution. *Punch* once again was their spokesman:

As the husband, shall the wife be;
he will have to wear a gown
If he does not quickly make her
put her Bloomer short-coats down

Mrs Bloomer had to wait until the end of the century for the style to catch on and even then it was as a cycling outfit.

Above the waist, women's silhouettes remained virtually unchanged. Corsets had returned to general use in the previous period and, while they served an identical purpose, they were now probably more comfortable than they had been at any previous time. They were made from lighter materials and were usually pre-formed to the desired shape, which made the extremely tight lacing unnecessary.

The gowns which covered this elaborate underwear were in themselves unremarkable, except for the quantity of material and the standard of cutting needed to make them. Bodices were still low-waisted and necklines continued to vary enormously. There appears to have been no relation between the height of the neckline and the occasion on which the gown was to be worn: evening dresses are seen with high necks and summer frocks with a deep décolletage.

During the late 1840s and early 1850s the full leg-o'mutton sleeves nearly disappeared. In their place came a close-fitting sleeve which reached either to the mid-forearm or completely to the wrist. Evening dresses usually had a similar sleeve, ending just below the elbow. Gradually, after 1855, fuller sleeves came back into fashion, but the fullness was now at the wrist rather than at the armseye.

Skirts and bodices were made separately with the skirt pleated into the waistband. They were often of contrasting material, the bodice generally being lighter than the skirt, rather than the reverse arrangement which was true of earlier contrasting gowns. Some bodices were separate blouses which buttoned up the front and were tucked into the waistband. These were called *garibaldis* after the red shirts worn by the followers of the Italian patriot and were considered suitable for casual summer wear.

Skirts in the early 1850s were usually quite plain for day-time, but evening dresses were often decorated with flounces or festoons which, once again, added to the impression of width. In the late 1850s and 1860s, however, horizontal bands of velvet were often sewn onto the skirts of street dresses.

Skirts at the beginning of this period were about two inches from the ground but, during the 1850s, they gradually became longer until they once again reached the instep. The soft slippers described in the last chapter continued to be worn indoors, but ankle-length boots were considered more suitable for outdoor wear. These, like the slippers, were originally flat, but a heel was soon added. In the mid-1860s, the fullness of the skirt came to be gathered more to the back so that the crinoline shape was more oval, with a train, than completely round. This shape led to the bustle of the following decade.

By far the most fashionable outergarment was the shawl. These were rather larger than they were earlier in

the century and were sometimes partly
shaped and fitted with a collar. The
range of materials used was also extended to include cashmere, wool, silk
or lace and each one was selected to
suit the occasion. Larger wraps much
in the style of a man's cloak were also
worn for evening wear.

Hair, hats and accessories
The previous decade saw a complete
transformation in women's coiffure from
the exaggerated top-knot to the flat-
topped arrangement with a bun and
ringlets at the side. This style continued
to be fashionable until the mid 1850s
when the hanging ringlets gradually
went out of fashion, and the bun moved
downwards to the nape of the neck and
was contained in black silk. The hair
was either drawn back smoothly over
the ears or arranged in a series of plaits
which were tied back into the bun or
encircled it. All these styles could be
decorated with gems or flowers.

Caps were no longer worn by the
young except as night caps, but they
were retained by the middle-aged for
outdoor wear. They were simple, following the contours of the hairstyle, and
were made from lawn or muslin trimmed with lace. Turbans were also worn

exclusively by the elderly for evening
dress. Bonnets continued to be fashionable, particularly with younger women.
Again, these altered shape to suit the
changing hairstyles. The exceptionally
high crown of the earlier style had already vanished by 1850 and, as the
bun was worn further down the neck,
bonnets became smaller and were worn
further back on the head. They were
made in a variety of different fabrics;
straw was a favourite for summer,
velvet for winter and, for dress wear,
silk trimmed with lace. All bonnets were
decorated with ribbons or flowers which
tended to be bunched to one side, and
sometimes the main fabric of the bonnet
was covered with a sheer lace veil.

There were also a number of different
hat styles which became fashionable
between 1850 and 1870. Until 1860 they
were generally of straw with wide
sweeping brims, similar to those described in the previous chapter. After
that date, as the low bun came into
fashion, small pillbox or pork-pie hats
became fashionable. They were worn
tilted forward over the forehead and
trimmed with a small tuft of feathers.
For evening-wear women often covered
their head with a rich scarf of silk or
lace, arranged to frame the face.

Aprons, which had been reduced to
a purely functional role for generations,
once again became part of a lady's
wardrobe. They were not as much a
part of high fashion as they had been
during the early seventeenth century
but were worn for such tasks as sewing
and embroidery. They were delicate
little garments made in silk with patched
pockets and trimmed with lace.

Dainty parasols were fashionable, but
they were rather shorter than before
and usually decorated with a small
fringe. Proper umbrellas, however,
which were also introduced during this
period were more robust and designed
for protection rather than decoration.
Muffs and handbags were fashionable
accessories, too, but again these were
rather smaller than they had been in the
first half of the century.

Mechanization, which had already
invaded the production of jewellery, was
now starting to affect its design. Filigree, which had been so popular, presented considerable production problems when mass-produced, and it was
widely replaced by foliated designs
pressed from a single sheet of metal.
Gold, for the wealthy, and pinchbeck
were used for these items and set with a
variety of semi-precious stones.

FIN DE SIECLE
From 1870 to 1900

During the late 1860s the expansion of world trade encouraged by international exhibitions and the growing wealth of the middle classes had conspired to create an era of apparently endless prosperity. This euphoria was rudely shattered in France by the outbreak of the Franco-Prussian war and the disastrous French defeat at Sedan in September 1870. The brilliant court at the Tuileries became a memory and the Empress Eugénie a refugee in England, the House of Worth was closed and the premises used as a hospital. The European scene was changing, the beautiful Empress Elizabeth of Austria-Hungary was a sad world-wanderer, England was ruled by a widow in seclusion, fashion was in the doldrums, and Western women were to rival their recently discovered Hottentot sisters in the size of their buttocks.

By 1870 skirts were flat in front with the fullness drawn back over a pouf formed by several frills of horsehair or a small, saddle-like cushion. The skirt reached the ground in front, continued into a small train at the back and, allied to a trim waist and fitted bodice, composed a figure of great charm.

Soon the bustle increased in size and, to support the complicated arrangements of two or three different materials trimmed with a medley of folds, frills and pleats, several new types of demi-crinoline were devised. The most popular was composed of curved steel bands at the back which ceased at the hips and were fastened in front with tapes so that the wearer could place the framework behind her and tie it in front, instead of stepping into the circular frame of a complete crinoline. Although Worth, and possibly the public too, was heartily tired of the crinoline, this grotesque figure was hardly a happy replacement.

For these increasingly complex designs such trimmings as buttons, fringes, braids and ribbons became ever more and more important, and the manufacturers concentrated on producing a vast selection of trimmings for dresses which used almost as much yardage as the spreading crinolines and required a far greater variety of fabrics. St Etienne did a thriving trade with its ribbons, and the Lyons mills turned out an endless stream of novelties in colours and weaves, plain and watered Jacquard silks, fine satins, brocades and velvets. In England, Spitalfields brought out fewer novelties but many silks of exquisite design. The woollen mills of Northern France began to equal the

English products, but Nottingham pro-
ducts replaced the hand-made laces of
Valenciennes and Flanders.

In the middle of the 1870s the
bustle deflated, but the new silhouette
was far from giving more freedom of
movement to the wearer. The closely-
fitted bodice continued into a point
on the stomach or reached the hips
beneath which a sheath skirt was
decorated with a mass of draperies and
frills which fell to the ground and
continued into a train. The French
aptly termed this figure *la femme
ligotée* for women's legs were wrapped
in folds resembling those of the swadd-
ling bands of a medieval infant or the
cere cloths of an Egyptian mummy.
There was no sign of the feet and
women appeared to move as if pro-
pelled by some invisible machinery.

A variation of the long tunic dress
with hip draperies pulled to the back
was the Polonaise which presented the
entire torso from shoulder to knee
defined as clearly as if in a body-
stocking. To attain the right proportions
for this demanding silhouette, innumerable artifices were incorporated into the
body of the gown: busts were built out,
waists pulled in, hips constricted or
padded and the bodice seamed and

Page 208 left and right, this page left:
During the 1870s the bustle varied greatly in shape and construction, sometimes high, sometimes low, with the skirt looped up over the protuberance, revealing an underskirt, like Corot's Lady in Blue (p. 208 right). This dress was a novelty in its time for it had no shoulder frills or embryo sleeves to soften the upper arm and conceal the armhole. Sometimes the bustle jutted out over the buttocks as in the picture on this page, or was tied back behind the knees, as in the fashion plate (far left)

Below left: Bustles for sale!

Left: The hideous fashions of the 1880s included both long basques and princess backs onto which a series of gathers, ruffles or folds were superimposed, but they did have the advantage of shorter skirts

darted until the correct shape was achieved.

Women have always had the capacity of changing their shape to agree with the current mode, and in 1878 Degas complained that the sloping shoulders, once *de rigeur* with the wide décolletage of the crinoline, had disappeared, and he considered the broader shoulders of the new style a sign of decadence.

Unsupported skirts were not a success and it was realized that a mass of material hanging limply round the legs was not only less attractive but also as hampering as when held out by artificial means. In the 1880s the bustle re-appeared in what became known in England as the 'upholstered' style because it concentrated on a woman's body a wealth of draperies more suited to furnishing a room than trimming a dress.

Only one good word can be said for the fashions of the 1880s, surely the most hideous ever conceived. The skirt was sufficiently short for the feet to be visible and for the wearer to walk in comparative comfort, except in the evening when trains were worn. It allied elaborate, frilly skirts draped over huge bustles to mannish jackets, which were sometimes buttoned down the entire front from high collar to hip, or

sometimes opened over a waistcoat or vest. This was not the first time that women had adopted a quasi-masculine garment and, in the eighteenth century, they had delighted to add manly riding jackets to paniered skirts.

Beneath the ambivalent outer wear of the 1880s all was one hundred per cent feminine. Over the corset were large open pantaloons embroidered and ribbon-threaded, a chemise and a corset bodice similarly trimmed, and one or more petticoats. These latter were close fitting in front and buttoned down the back as far as the knees where a full panel, edged and covered with frills, was inserted to support the back draperies. These were sometimes made with detachable portions which could be buttoned on to the daytime version and so give sufficient volume to the train of an evening gown.

Women's clothes were as colourful as a parrot's plumage. Men's were the exact opposite. Colour had almost disappeared from the male wardrobe, successful industrialists, not dashing military men, were the ideal. Sobriety was the paramount characteristic of a gentleman's costume which had to be of excellent cloth and cut, but in black or dark muted shades. Even light-

coloured trousers were rarely seen, and the elegant opera cloak only occasionally revealed a coloured lining. Men wore tail-coats in the morning, in a plain light wool material, the style being known as a morning-coat; this shape remained unchanged for evening wear, except that only black with a white satin waistcoat was permissible. Together with overcoats and possibly a looser fitting jacket for the country or for sports, this remained the full range of men's wear for about fifty years.

A variation on the sack coat or paletot appeared in the 1860s, forerunner of the lounge suit, which reached the hips and was fastened by three buttons with only the top one done up, usually accompanied by check trousers. Collars could be upright and stiff, or soft and turned down and the tie either knotted and held in place by a pearl or solitaire pin, or tied in a bow.

The opera hat, invented by the ingenious Mr Gibus in 1823, remained an essential item in every man's evening equipment until the First World War. The top-hat was so popular that it was worn by the house-painter, the butcher, the postman, the city merchant, the country squire, as well as the gentleman in town or by the seaside. The frock-coat

was equally ubiquitous, although the 'bliaus' of the Saxons persisted in one form or another in France where the 'blouse', always of blue denim, continued to be worn by workers of all trades well into this century. The democratic cap, symbol of the working man, began to be adopted by the sporting man and to replace the topper on the cricket field or when boating on the river, now a favourite pastime. On such informal occasions, a discreet note of colour could be allowed the feet, and tan and white shoes were considered smart, but rather 'fast'. Sporting clothes also showed little variation from daytime clothes, except for riding when tight breeches and boots were worn with a top-hat.

The insistence with which Queen Victoria continued to wear mourning gave a great impetus to this gloomy fashion and brought into being a whole new department of dress. Some houses specialized in mourning only, and assured their clients that suitably sombre garments to fit all the members of their family and staff could be despatched immediately to any part of the country.

New ranges of materials and accessories were created to satisfy this demand of which crêpe and jet were the main items. Crêpe, a gauzy stuff with a crinkly surface which quickly lost its gleaming coal-black lustre, became synonymous with grief, and long veils of it were worn by the widowed. Caps and toques were draped with it, and crêpe trimmed the revers and bustles of black mourning dresses. Black velvet was widely used for the first evening gown permitted a woman in mourning, for whom whole parures made of jet were devised.

The small toques of folded crêpe which topped the muffled figures of the female mourners were sometimes tied beneath the chin, but, in the home, caps of crêpe or lace were worn in imitation of the ageing Queen, who continued to favour the tiny cap of white crêpe which became an inseparable part of the Royal portraits familiar to her peoples all over the world.

Striped materials, with the stripes used in different ways, were extremely popular, partly owing to the influence of the great French actess Réjane who appeared in *Décoré!* in a striped silk travelling dress, a creation of Jacques Doucet.

For evening the oval off-shoulder décolletage was discarded in favour of a square which widened slightly as it descended to the bosom and, edged with frills, made an enchanting frame to the face and neck around which a black velvet ribbon with a locket hanging from it was often worn.

Alexandra, Princess of Wales, was responsible for yet another new fashion. This was a full-length pelisse, double-breasted and buttoned to the hem, with long plain sleeves, the first really practical day-coat suited to the English weather but which at first was not a success, though it fathered a fashion which lasted until the 'garçonnes' shortened their skirts in 1924, and various versions are still with us. An alternative was a full-length, high-collared cloak with curved back and side-seams to allow for the exigencies of full sleeves and skirt draperies.

The excess of tight-lacing, the weight of petticoats, flounces and draperies at last brought about a rebellion. Already the aesthetes of the pre-Raphaelite era had refused to be encased in a crinoline cage but had had little influence outside a limited circle. In 1881 Liberty offered gowns 'à la Tadema', loose flowing robes, but these were only popular within a limited circle.

Unfortunately the designs for Rational Dress were on the whole aesthetically

Left: The trim figures of the women with their waisted jackets fitting closely over their moderate bustles, their short skirts and high hats clearly show that La Grande Jatte by Seurat was painted in the 1880s. Note that the little girl wears a looser garment—the beginning of separate styling for children to suit their lives and figures

Right: Les Parapluies by Renoir shows several interesting details of daily life in the 1880s. The bare-headed messenger girl is delivering her goods in a wooden box. The little girl has a wooden hoop such as children bowled in the streets until the last war, and she wears an elaborate lace-trimmed velvet coat and feathered hat

deplorable and the movement did not succeed. Some of the dresses were still floor-length and therefore as unhygienic as the fashionable variety. Sleeves were long and collars high, and it was only the rejection of the dreaded corset that could offer some hope of easier breathing and less painful movement.

In London the Rational Dress Society convened a meeting in 1883 chaired by the only man present: Oscar Wilde. Sketches of possible costumes were judged and the first prize given to a woman shown riding a tricycle in a close-fitting dress with a high-collared bodice fastened by smart brandenburgs, long sleeves and a mid-calf, straight skirt which revealed ankle-length trousers, a general outline not far from the modern maxi-coat over trousers. Worth designed a special costume for Mrs King which was far more feminine and, minus its very short over-skirt, faintly resembled the Saint Laurent 'hot-pants' suits which were the news of 1968. The dress showed a neck-high bodice with an embroidered yoke, long full sleeves gathered into a frill at the wrists, knickerbockers fastened just below the knees edged with frills, and, over them, a tiny, frilled mini-skirt bordered with lace. Mrs Oscar Wilde contented herself

Above: Men's dark clothes were allowed the licence of striped trousers and fancy linings to the cape-coat which was fashionable for evening wear. Top-hats were universally worn. Queen Victoria's predilection for Balmoral and all things Scottish resulted in plaid trousers for men, and little boys wearing kilts, Highland shawls and bonnets just like the boys of the Royal family

Right: In a typically mid-Victorian gown the Queen who gave her name to the period was photographed wearing a rich, black crinoline with a becoming off-shoulder bodice and short, loose sleeves edged with ermine tails

with dispensing with a bustle and was criticized by some relatives for appearing in limp white muslin without any whalebone support. The Americans devised a relatively short Princess dress with a comfortable back pleat and small bolero worn with matching leggings and neat shoes.

The fashionable world paid no attention to the fulminations of the Rational Dress movement, and women continued to load their bodies with masses of material which now ballooned out in a different place. The extension of the hips and buttocks gave place to that of the shoulders, and leg-o'mutton sleeves of enormous proportions jutted out from the shoulders in huge puffs to just above the elbows where they were joined to long tight sleeves.

The hip-length basque was replaced by waist-length bodices which ended in a point on the stomach, and the skirt fell from flat pleats or godets which increased in fullness at the back. Hems continued to reach the ground and feet to be invisible except when the wearer was obliged to raise her skirt when mounting stairs or crossing a dirty street.

In the evening the full panoply of irrational dress continued to be worn.

Above: Photography began to rival painting, but in a far less flattering manner, in recording daily happenings. In a family group of 1885 the mother is certainly a widow since she wears the small white cap adopted by Queen Victoria since the death of the Prince Consort, but the two girls are obviously emancipated for they are shown with their tennis rackets

Right: The actresses of the fin de siècle in Paris had great influence on the fashions of their day. Réjane, Sarah Bernhardt and Eleonora Duse were dressed either by Worth, Redfern or Jacques Doucet, with whom Duse had a particularly close association. Here Réjane is wearing one of the all-lace costumes then so popular

Far right: Robert de Montesquieu was one of the greatest dandies of the fin de siècle in Paris. Boldini painted him in 1897 with his famous cane, into which he had inserted a jewel once belonging to Louis XIV, wearing a dove-grey morning suit

213

Tight bodices were still draped with tulle or lace, skirts had overskirts of similar materials often edged with artificial flowers and long trains fell from a low waistline at the back creating an utterly artificial figure which could, however, be extremely elegant.

Two young Englishmen in Paris helped to launch the 'tailor-made' for women. Redfern, whose real name was Charles Poynter, came to Paris as a representative of the firm of Redfern (founded in 1842), which numbered Queen Victoria among its clients. He opened a branch in the rue de Rivoli and created a great sensation by his tailor-mades, an innovation often and incorrectly attributed to Paul Poiret. These consisted of slightly feminized male jackets, braid-trimmed and buttoned down the front, allied to plain skirts flat in front but with sufficient flare at the back to allow for easy walking, carried out in sensible serge, preferably navy blue. The success of *le trotteur* began a way of dressing which ceased only with the disappearance of formal man-tailored suits during the last two decades.

Another Englishman who at the same period made an impact on Parisian society was the tailor Creed, first

Left: The two young girls in blue and white muslin dresses have adopted the new style of sailor hats, very daring but very appropriate to nautical festivities. The striped silk of the girl on the left was an extremely popular style, after the costumes of the actress Réjane. This record of a summer day was painted by Tissot in 1874

Below left: The new craze for bicycling brought with it a novel garment and bloomers were worn by both men and women in Paris, but these girls in Battersea Park in 1895 still managed to cycle in skirts, leg-o'mutton sleeves and feather-trimmed hats

Above right: This illustration taken from the Ladies Magazine shows the latest French fashions for the end of the nineteenth century. After the very full styles of previous decades, the elegant lady on the left wears a day dress which is very tight and constricting. Her companion on the right wears a dress with a short ruched, silk train. High necklines, small hats, tight sleeves and wide cuffs were characteristic of the day

Right: How surprised the ladies of the Dress Society would be to find that their revolutionary costume of 1896 would cause no comment in the 1970s. This sketch was intended as an unkind caricature of emancipated womanhood, but it is the fashionable dress of the period which would be a subject for derision today

Far right: Madame Paquin excelled in creating sumptuous evening ensembles, and this evening wrap with its upstanding collar, ruched lining and embroidered panels is typical of her taste

WELDON'S LADIES' JOURNAL

18071 18072 18073 18074 18075 18076 18077

WELDON'S LATEST NOVELTIES FOR NOVEMBER.

Flat patterns of Costumes 6d. untrimmed 3/-. Flat pattern of Mantle 6d. untrimmed 1/6.

(COPYRIGHT) DESIGNED BY WELDONS, LIMITED. FASHION AND PAPER PATTERN PUBLISHERS, 30 & 31. SOUTHAMPTON STREET, STRAND, LONDON. (PRINTED IN NUREMBERG.)

Above: By the turn of the century the bustle had been forgotten, skirts flared out below the knees and reached the ground, but there were few trains. Jackets were manly with squared shoulders, tight sleeves and high collars. The waistline sloped lower in front and hair was worn in a pompadour with a knot on the top

recommended by Queen Victoria to Empress Eugénie as a maker of riding habits. Eugénie de Montijo was a magnificent horsewoman, and it was on horse-back that the Emperor first saw and fell in love with the young Spaniard. Her choice of Creed as her tailor made his fortune, and the house he founded in the rue de la Paix continued until the last war, when his great-grandson Charles Creed came to London and opened a house which continued until his death in 1966.

A totally new influence now entered the world of fashion. Hitherto, riding had been the only active sport in which women could indulge, with archery and croquet as fringe exercises. Now a craze for sport launched a wholly novel costume for both men and women. Cycling became the rage of the Nineties, and to indulge in this pastime both sexes adopted the rational costume of knickerbockers, Norfolk jacket, sailor hats, woollen stockings and flat-heeled shoes. The only difference between the sexes was that women's knickerbockers were somewhat more voluminous than men's.

In England the knickerbockers of the first enthusiasts were soon replaced by navy serge skirts which also did duty

for another newcomer into women's sporting life. Tennis became popular and, undeterred by long skirts and petticoats, girls donned a mannish shirt-blouse, attached a sailor hat by an elastic band and learnt to volley back at their brothers on the courts whose white markings were beginning to disfigure most suburban lawns. Women in England even began to play cricket, and for this game they adopted a loose shirt-blouse which continued to the hips and was tied round the waist by a sash, teamed with plain or striped cotton skirts. Golf too was attempted by the female sex, and for this a costume was evolved which included a neat serge coat and skirt of indeterminate colour, brown ankle boots and a Tam o' Shanter, possibly of tartan design, or a Homburg hat, with a matching tweed cape.

While women were rebelling against their over-feminine furbelows and stealing from the masculine wardrobe, men were in revolt against male anonymity. The aesthetes, led by Oscar Wilde, attempted to bring some colour and ornamentation into their drab costumes and appeared in velvet jackets, flowing ties and fancy waistcoats, together with jewelled watch chains and flower buttonholes.

Above: During the last decades of the nineteenth century a great many women began to play active sports. Some of the costumes suggested for these new pastimes were equally novel. The 'Moorish' outfit for a tennis player of 1880 appears to be based on a costume worn by Mrs Amelia Bloomer. The archer of 1895 in her wide trousers and shirt blouse looks remarkably modern, only her head-gear giving the date away

Left: Oscar Wilde posed for the photographer wearing silk stockings and satin knee-breeches similar to those suggested by the Rational Dress movement as suitable for women. His tight-fitting jacket has quilted silk revers and cuffs of a contrasting colour

EDWARDIAN OPULENCE
From 1900 to 1920

1900 was the year of the Great Universal Exhibition in Paris when the Palais de l'Electricité astounded everyone and gave rise to the legend of the *Ville Lumière*. The public which thronged through the fantastic gateway, a horrendous Art Nouveau construction, was uniformly dressed, the men in frockcoats and toppers, the women in tiny fitted boleros or jackets and sweeping skirts which fitted smoothly over the hips and buttocks but were enlarged at the back by *godets*—shaped or triangular panels—and so long that the owner was obliged to lift them up when crossing streets. Smallish hats, flower-trimmed and veiled, were perched on high coiffures and a tall, slim umbrella was universal.

The fashion section was one of the most important in the Exhibition, for Paris remained incontestably the world's fashion centre. The *grand seigneur* of the mode was Jacques Doucet, a man of great culture and impeccable taste who made an exquisite collection of eighteenth-century furniture and paintings (though later he sold these and became one of the first patrons of Picasso, Matisse and their followers), but the president of the fashion section was Madame Paquin. She was the first

Left: The luxurious salons of the Maison Paquin were a favourite rendezvous of smart Parisiennes, who gathered to be shown the new models and materials. They all wear the typical bonnets and hats richly decorated with ribbons and feathers. Madame Paquin was considered one of the most elegant women of her time, and her taste both in clothes and décor was much admired. This animated scene, 5 o'clock chez Paquin, was recorded in 1906 by N. Gervex

Below right: The favourite materials for race dresses were lace and muslin mounted over rustling, silk petticoats. In 1901 they showed small waists sloping down in front and skirts smoothly fitting over the hips but becoming fuller and longer at the back. The forward movement of the bust and backward thrust of the buttocks were often maintained with the aid of a tall Regency beau's stick

Right: Wishful thinking could hardly be more clearly expressed than in this corset advertisement which suggests that a particular make of corset could reverse the basic facts that a woman's hips are larger than her waist

woman to achieve eminence in French fashion since Rose Bertin more than a century earlier; she was particularly known for her blue serge *tailleurs*, but equally famous for her shimmering gold and silver evening gowns which the jealous attributed to her Levantine origin. The committee included Doucet, Cheruit, Dœuillet, the three Callot sisters and the two Worth brothers. Jean and Gaston Worth wanted to show their models on life-like wax figures in realistic scenes, but this was considered too extreme, and the Worths ended by leasing a small pavilion where their clothes were shown in everyday settings. Madame Paquin's display consisted of a beautifully attired figure of herself sitting at her own silver-adorned dressing table. She was a woman of great administrative ability (with a banker husband to advise her) and was the first *couturière* to found houses abroad, opening one in London and others in Madrid and Buenos Aires.

Two other feminine firms greatly influenced fashion in Paris during the first decade of this century, the Soeurs Callot and Madame Cheruit, who was known for her personal elegance, remarkable for its simplicity at a time when too much was never enough.

Lingerie was immensely important and underwear formed a large part of every bride's trousseau. One dozen of 'each' was the minimum and included chemises, corset-bodices, camisoles, drawers, petticoats and nightgowns, all hand sewn, monogrammed, edged with lace and trimmed with broderie anglaise and Valenciennes insertions threaded with pink or blue 'baby' ribbons.

Boudoir caps, introduced to cover up the hair before the complicated coiffures were properly arranged, were also made of ribbon-threaded, lace-edged muslin. When skirts were raised, the contrast between the snowy frills revealed and the black stockings and shoes was considered immensely piquant.

In Montmartre, the apotheosis of these *dessous*, only furtively glimpsed in respectable circles, was more generously disclosed in the popular can-can dance, and drawers, about which there had been so much discussion during the nineteenth century, became at last part of every woman's wardrobe. The dancers held up their flounced muslin petticoats and swayed them from side to side to disclose their knee-length drawers ending in frills above black silk stockings and black court shoes with pointed toes and low Louis heels.

The most important item and the foundation of all these undergarments was of course the corset, which was considered essential even for very young girls. It was an immensely complicated construction of either cotton or satin composed of insets, gussets and bands, some reinforced by whalebones, with straight steel busks in front and laces at the back. The cuirass rose up to the height of the bust and descended well over the hips to ensure a smoothly fitting skirt, and the tiny waist sloped lower in front so that the bust appeared as if it were actually overhanging the stomach.

The passion for lingerie finally came out into the open in the early years of the century, and the partly openwork muslin known as broderie anglaise, made in Switzerland, became a popular fabric for blouses described as 'peek-a-boo'. Much protest against their immodesty was made by the press and in the pulpit, yet all these early see-through models revealed was a corset-bodice of lawn edged with ribbon-threaded, lace insertions, edged with lace frills. With these blouses, dark skirts of navy serge were worn, fitting closely over the hips but flaring into fullness at the back and firmly secured round the waist by a belt fastened with a silver buckle, or composed of pierced silver plaques which were shaped to fit the figure.

Whole dresses and even coats were made of lingerie materials, such as fine embroidered lawn heavily encrusted with lace or Irish crochet, and hats and parasols were trimmed with lace flounces until a woman dressed for Ascot or a garden party appeared as a monument of lace and lingerie. The famous actress, *la divine* Bartet, appeared in a simple dress of openwork Cluny lace with a little vest of *taffetas à fleurs*, trimmed with *galon d'or*. Few, however, could afford real lace on such a scale and the factories of Nottingham flourished.

The movement known as Art Nouveau, which so greatly influenced the decoration of rooms, the construction of furniture and most of the decorative arts, was never as popular in England as on the Continent, except perhaps in the field of textiles where the work of Annesley Voysey and the fabrics designed by Butterfield and Napper, both followers of William Morris, were much admired, and were available at such stores as Liberty's. But it was in jewellery that Art Nouveau found its most success-ful expression, particularly in the work of René Lalique. He created a fairy world with representations of insects and butterflies, and the occasional woman's head in carved crystal.

Alexandra, the Princess of Wales, launched the fashion for a fringe which became known as an 'Alexandra' and most fashionable women wore one, though the accompanying coiffures varied. Not all these fringes were real however, more often consisting of a row of small flat curls mounted on a wire which could be pushed through the hair at the front—arranged in the pompadour style—and fixed by a pin.

Another fashion for which Princess Alexandra was responsible was the high 'dog-collar' necklace of jewels, often replaced by a wide band of black velvet fastened by a brooch or clasp.

The Edwardian era rivalled the 1860s in extravagant display and silks rustled in ever larger skirts flowing out from stiffly boned bodices whose amazingly low décolletages somehow managed to maintain a single curve and ignore the cleavage between the breasts. Shoulders were once more exposed as lavishly as in the days when Winterhalter painted Eugénie and her ladies but were no longer sloping and delicate but were

Above left: During the brief Edwardian era it was the King and Queen themselves who were the leaders of fashion: Edward introduced the soft Homburg hat—an idea borrowed from his German relatives—as an alternative to the hard-blocked bowler. Alexandra launched the high dog-collar of pearls held in place by diamond bars, and also the curled fringe

Above: Echoes of Maeterlinck's poetry and Klimt's pictures are to be found in this picture entitled L'Eau Mystérieuse by the Swiss painter Ernst Bieler, in which the young women are dressed in floral patterned and striped dresses. In France, even more than in England, this style of patterning, known as Art Nouveau, became popular

Above right: The shoes with straps which criss-crossed around the ankles, known as tango shoes after the new dance recently imported from South America, were exposed by skirts draped or slit at the front. Osprey plumes were much worn as head ornaments

Right: The most popular exponent of the 'Gibson Girl' in England—so called after its creator, Charles Dana Gibson—was Camille Clifford, whose mono-bosom and opulent S-shaped figure with its tiny waist was the ideal of the pre-war years

sumptuous and well covered. To have a fine pair of shoulders was among the first requirements of the 'stunner', as the Edwardian beauty was aptly called.

This admired figure became epitomized in the 'Gibson Girl', the creation of Charles Dana Gibson, an American who took for his models the three lovely Langhorne sisters, one of whom became Lady Astor. On the stage, Camille Clifford represented the English version of this curvaceous charmer, and photographs of her S-shaped figure clothed in black velvet, her mono-bosom overhanging her tiny waist, her behind well stuck out and her waved pompadour overhanging her forehead, were among the most popular postcards of the prewar era.

On the padded pompadours of the coiffure were balanced hats as large as that of Betsy Sheridan, younger sister of Richard Brinsley Sheridan who, 150 years earlier, recounted that her new hat was as large as her new tea-table of which the present owner (a descendant) states this is twenty nine and a half inches across. Most of its Edwardian successors were not perched sideways, as Reynolds and Hoppner depicted the 'picture' hats of their sitters, but placed straight on top like a carefully laden

Left: A jewelled bandeau plus an osprey feather were not considered excessive for evening wear in 1911. In this model the waist is slightly raised and the line of the body obscured by a tunic which continues into a train—and over this is worn a fur-edged mantle. It was against such a contradictory accumulation of detail that Poiret campaigned

Right: A young couple are shown on holiday in 1912 in this picture by William Strang. The man's neat bowler with its rolled brim contrasts to its advantage with the girl's shapeless hat of gathered velvet and its disproportionately wide head-fitting

Far right: The women in Corporation Street, Birmingham, England, in the spring of 1914, painted here by Joseph Edward Southall, were wearing hobble skirts, ankle boots and long, fur stoles. One carries a large, flat muff. Note the difference of styling for the little girl, whose coat and spats are practical and becoming

Below right: A new genre of fashion illustration appeared just before the First World War in the Gazette du Bon Ton, edited by the brilliant Lucien Vogel, which aimed to tell a story in contemporary costume

tray with ostrich feathers or flowers. Some even increased their weight and size with a fur border. Hats were of such importance that women wore them in their own homes.

In place of these monstrous constructions Paul Poiret suggested draped turbans. He had been fascinated by some Indian turbans he had seen in the Victoria and Albert Museum when on a visit to London, and he launched this new fashion with great success. Many of these turbans, including the one worn by his wife to his famous Arabian Nights party, were trimmed with the plumage of osprey. There were then no wild-life sanctions, and it was many years before laws were passed which prevented these feathers being torn from the beautiful birds.

In 1912 fashion recalled a dozen styles from the past rather than any conviction about the present. Models were said to be inspired by Oriental, antique and medieval styles and, though few of the results would have been recognized by the originals, there were two obvious thefts from other continents, one from the Middle East and one from the Far East.

From the Middle East came the so-called 'Turkish' or harem trousers,

sponsored by Poiret, which had their fullness gathered around the ankles and were grotesquely allied to bodices of Western style. French women went to Longchamps in 1912 wearing bifurcated garments which the emancipated English were not permitted to wear at Ascot until 1969. However, the fashion was not a success, and half a century had to elapse before the sight of trousered females striding gaily down city streets became quite acceptable.

Japanese culture, which had been brought to the notice of the Western art world in the 1890s by the dealer Samuel Bing and by the artist Whistler and his followers, eventually reached the fashionable world. Instead of teagowns women wore kimonos made of fine silk, hand embroidered with showers of wistaria, bunches of paeonies or the branches of flowering cherries. Among other *Japonaiseries* was the wide, straight 'kimono sleeve' set into a large low armhole which became a constant theme in the construction of full-length coats. These cumbersome garments, cluttered with collar and cuffs of fur in winter or of lace in summer were partnered by immense hats loaded with trimmings and in winter by huge 'pillow' muffs, and the whole composed

Above left: This illustration taken from Bon Ton, of January 1914, is called Robe de Réveiller de Dœuillet. The lady is dressed in a becoming pale pink silk dress with a deep cut, V-neckline. This line is enhanced by loose, short sleeves. The long, narrow skirt is tiered, falling from a high, well-defined waist line

Above right: The stiffened minaret over-skirt, much liked by Poiret, was inspired by Bakst's designs for the ballet Scheherezade

Left: This is another illustration from Bon Ton, of March 1914. The model's dress is a Worth design in a very pale shade of mauve with white. The cross-over bodice has a low, square neckline and is high-waisted. A small train falls gracefully from the skirt

Above right: The gaiety—and the sorrows—of Bank Holiday on Hampstead Heath were recorded with vigour by the famous cartoonist Phil May in 1902. The feather-trimmed hats of the Cockney girls, their trim waists, full skirts and boots are typical of the fashions of the time translated into a form acceptable to the working-class

an exceptionally cluttered and clumsy figure.

Poiret's revolt against this overladen, tasteless fashion was far more successful than either bloomers in America or the efforts of the Rational Dress Association in England had been, though he was not to be fully recognized for the genius he was until after the First World War. He had early decided to enter the fashion world but could not persuade Madame Cheruit to take him on her staff, and his brief periods with Worth and Jacques Doucet were fruitless. Eventually, he borrowed some money from his mother and opened a small house which soon made news, for it was the first to show windows attractively dressed— of course by young Paul himself. He had a remarkable sense of colour, greatly influenced by the *Ballet Russe* which had been seen for the first time in Europe in Paris in 1908, and he was responsible for replacing the half-shades of mauve and blue then fashionable, with the clashing pinks, scarlets and apple-greens of Bakst's décors. He permitted no petticoats or corsets, and his early models have a simplicity which relates them both to classical styles and to the long, flowing evening gowns which are popular today.

In 1912, Poiret was the first couturier to substitute the living for the doll mannequin as a foreign ambassadress of fashion, and in 1912 he set out with a team of nine mannequins to visit the capitals of Europe. All nine were dressed alike in blue serge tailor-mades, comfortable cloaks of reversible beige plaid and oilcloth hats with an embroidered P in front.

A pre-First World War fashion which offered the extreme opposite to the freedom of movement brought by Turkish trousers was the hobble skirt. Although this prevented women from walking except by short, shuffling steps, it was universally accepted for both day and evening wear. With it were worn shoes with ribbons laced round the ankles known as 'tango shoes', after the craze for a new dance recently introduced from South America.

The second decade of the twentieth century saw a considerable simplification in female dress. Hair pads and pompadours were discarded, and the Gibson Girl figure vanished completely. The slim Poiret line grew in favour and, though lace continued to be popular for evening gowns, plain fabrics with strong colour contrasts and straight simple lines began to predominate.

The display of the neck was important. Instead of the high, boned collar with the frill just beneath the chin which had been *de rigueur* for so long, day dresses favoured a low-cut neckline, called the 'Gretchen' since it resembled a collarless peasant's blouse. This brought with it the fashion for a necklace of graduated pearls to lie on the newly revealed flesh.

Dinner gowns took a look back at the past and 'Medici' collars of wire-stiffened lace, reminiscent of the sixteenth century, rose on the shoulders across the back of the neck.

Feather boas became too common to be considered chic, and long stoles of fabric or flat fur, ermine or seal, trimmed with tails or fringes, took their place.

Before the 1914 war there was no question as to what a well-dressed man should wear on any given occasion; each dictated its special uniform and no deviations were possible. Gentlemen went to work in striped trousers, morning-coats and top-hats. For more formal events the morning-coat was replaced by a frock-coat. The top-hat was no longer a funnel shape, it now had a slight inward curve and the brim also curved slightly. Boni de Castellane

favoured quite a low 'topper' with a brim which curled up on either side, and he wore this with a very waisted mid-calf length coat when he went to the races. Grey trousers and grey top-hats were necessary for Ascot, but tan and white shoes could be worn at Goodwood or at summer resorts. Lounge suits were considered suitable only for informal day wear. In the country, tweed jackets and plus-fours were essential, and on the river a striped blazer and white flannels were accompanied either by a cap or a straw sailor. Dinner jackets were worn every evening except for formal occasions when tail-coats, starched shirts, white waistcoats and white gloves were required. When and what to wear was so exactly prescribed that a course to instruct visiting foreigners in the peculiarities of English etiquette was organized in the summer of 1913 by the University of London and was well attended.

With the outbreak of the war, the fashion market was brought almost to a standstill. In Paris the new young designer, Jean Patou, who had intended to show his first collection in August, 1914, enlisted, and in London 'Lucile's' brilliant young assistant, Edward Molyneux, left for the army to become a

Captain and was called 'the Captain' in the fashion world for the rest of his life.

In the middle of the war years, fashion made a sudden *volte-face* and soldiers coming home on leave were astonished to find their women-folk, whom they had left hobbled in long tight skirts, wearing full skirts which barely reached the tops of their boots. 'Lucile', one of the most famous dressmakers in London, in private life Lady Duff Gordon, startled everyone by appearing in red 'Russian' boots, that is with soft uppers and no fastenings.

The shorter skirts brought with them an increased demand for silk stockings, still objects of luxury, which were uniformly black with embroidered 'clocks' on the insteps but no longer decorated with lace insets or fancy patterns. Far greater attention was paid to footwear: the 'tango' shoes continued to be popular, and buckles of paste or cut steel became increasingly important. Although women simplified their clothes, they did not attempt either the trousers advocated by the Rational Dress movement or the harem trousers suggested by Poiret. Only on horseback was the skirt beginning to be discarded, and the end of the war saw the gradual disappearance of the long-skirted 'Amazon' and the emergence of the breeched riding habit.

Corsets did not cease to be worn, but, as more and more women led active lives and there were fewer social occasions, the desire for tight-lacing was considerably less. A slender figure became increasingly admired, voluptuous curves were discouraged, and the comfortable elasticized pull-on girdle and separate brassière made their appearance.

The immediate post-war period was a time of indecision. Some couturiers—and their clients—looked back to the pre-war days of elaborate toilettes, others forward to a new world where women would be less hampered by their clothes. Skirts varied and showed several lengths; for daytime they reached just to the ankles but in the evening some extended into pointed fish-trains, and others were slit almost to the knees on one side. The 'minaret' skirt never became a universal favourite, and an alternative was found in a rounded silhouette achieved by tiny frills called *ron-flon-flons* which made the otherwise straight skirt stand away from the hips. Waists were equally uncertain, but most tended to be slightly higher in front. Real pearls lost their snob-appeal after the production of the perfect 'Tecla' pearls which made them available to affluent middle-class women, and the modest pearls considered suitable for wartime were replaced by flashing stones and long, pendant chains of beads. Diamonds once more sparkled in tiaras, necklaces, bracelets and in long, dangling earrings.

Evening gowns still had embryo sleeves but of the flimsiest chiffon or tulle, and the narrow shoulder straps were more suited to support a spray of flowers than to conceal the limbs. Décolletages were generous but were either square or a deep oval which revealed a satin underbodice.

Hair was parted in the centre and waved into two curtains which partly covered the forehead. Eugène and Nestlé, well-known hairdressers, began to advertise the convenience and attraction of a 'permanent wave', and straight hair suddenly became no longer permissible.

The suffragettes had won their battle, and women were given the vote. They were also being given jobs hitherto exclusively undertaken by men, but, though their clothes were simpler than those of the pre-war era, they were still far from functional.

THE JAZZ AGE
The Twenties and Thirties

At the same time as the emergence of emancipated women, a quite different version of femininity appeared. The 'vamp' was a product of the cinema and its two outstanding exponents were Theda Bara and Pola Negri, whose large dark eyes, rimmed with kohl, looked out beneath turbans which bound their foreheads and reached their brows. Eyes became the focal point of make-up, surrounded by dark lines and with eye-lashes emphasized by mascara, but with the eyebrows either ignored or concealed. Hair was demoted and some of the younger beauties, Paula Casa-Maury and Iris Tree among them, cut theirs into a short 'bob', and both followed the prevailing preference for hiding the forehead, either with a ribbon band or a long thick fringe. Hats were similarly used to conceal any expanse of brow and were as firmly jammed down on the head as formerly they had been precariously perched on top.

All was 'flou' and flowing, dresses were of fluttering crêpe de Chine or chiffon with floating panels which just reached the ankles. Sleeves were long and full, bodices bloused loosely over a lowered waistline, a scarf was often slung across the shoulders, tassels hung

Right: Three years after the end of the war young women tended to look extremely girlish and, in 1921, wore dresses of soft materials with a fluid, vague silhouette and skirts short enough to reveal unbecoming strap shoes. They also favoured sashes, bows and picture hats

Left: In total contrast, the 'Vamp' appeared, dark-eyed and intensely dramatic, and the chief exponent was the film actress Pola Negri. Whatever else she exposed, her forehead was never seen, for she always covered it with bandeaux or turbans which reached her eyebrows. She and Theda Bara, another vamp, launched the fashion for eye make-up and their darkened eye-lids and lashes laden with mascara caused much comment

Robe 3228
Broderie 10917

Robe 3244
Broderie 10914

Robe 3248
Broderie 10806

3246

3259

from the end of sleeves or skirt panels and long earrings dangled either side of the face. There were no more boned corsets, fitted bodices or petticoats and a mere 'step-in' did duty for both petticoats and drawers.

The girls dressed in these soft, limp dresses had a new scene in which to display them. One of the most striking phenomena of post-war life was the craze for dancing: the original Dixieland Jazz Band drew all London to the Hammersmith Palais de Danse; *thés dansants* took place every afternoon in most of the big hotels and nightclubs where the men returning from the army and waiting for jobs spent much of their time. Their only rivals were the gigolos—usually dark young men with a South American background, whose best assets were their thorough knowledge of the tango, their sleek black hair and immaculate costume of tails and well-pressed trousers. This was the last sartorial flicker of the idle man-about-town who was about to be superseded by a figure conspicuous for his casual appearance. The most important item of the new style was the width of the grey flannel trousers, or 'Oxford bags' as these large garments were called since they had been launched by some

undergraduates of Oxford university.

Another fast vanishing way of dressing was that of the tea-gown which lingered on as part of a hostess's or guest's wardrobe in country houses but was rarely seen in town. These negligées, made of rich materials, loose, voluminous and elaborately trimmed, were made to be worn after a woman had taken off her day clothes and corset and was resting before she dressed for the evening. They were a speciality of 'Lucile', but two other London Houses, Dove and Ospovat, deserve to be recalled for the lovely models, usually of an Oriental character, which they created. With the disappearance of the boned corset, the need for negligées lessened, and tea, though still dispensed with elegance in some houses, was not taken by the younger generation who thought more of the cocktail shaker than the tea-urn. This habit brought with it a newcomer to the fashion field and 'le cocktail dress' appeared in some of the more up-to-date Paris collections. As all women's dresses were still nearly ankle-length, there was no problem as to whether they should be long or short, and in the main the early cocktail dresses turned out to be an unpleasant hybrid between the outline of a day-dress and the fabric of an evening gown, often with lace as an intermediary.

In 1923 Lady Elizabeth Bowes-Lyon married George, Duke of York, and gave definite evidence that a bare forehead was inadmissible, for her fringe and veil reached her eyebrows. But the hemline was undecided, and skirts varied from near knee-high to ankle-length.

However, in the spring of 1924, Paris showed collections which no longer hesitated: skirts were short (they just reached the calf); waists no longer fluctuated, they were on the hips; bust and hips were obliterated. The *garçonne* was born in a beige jumper and pleated skirt which swished round her emancipated legs clad in flesh-coloured, instead of the customary black, stockings and, on her feet, strap shoes.

The collection which had the greatest success was that of 'Coco' Chanel who had been in business since before the war but now led the fashion world and offered a way of dressing which is not yet extinct. She specialized in the use of jersey which she had woven to her own designs and colours and used this hitherto humdrum fabric in a manner previously reserved for luxurious materials. Apart from the perfection of cut and finish, she added such fastidious details

Above: The couturier who more than any other was to change women's clothes from the shapeless to the chic was Gabrielle 'Coco' Chanel, whose collection in the spring of 1924 ushered in the 'garçonne'. She had started in business as a modiste in Deauville before the war and opened a couture house later, but did not achieve her great success until the early Twenties

LES PLUS JOLIES IDÉES DE LA MODE PARISIENNE SONT INTERPRÉTÉES DANS LES MODÈLES CRÉÉS PAR LE " BON MARCHÉ ".
AUSSI CES DERNIERS S'IMPOSERONT AU CHOIX DES ÉLÉGANTES, QUI EN PROMULGUERONT LE BON TON ET LE PRIX SANS RIVAL.
IMP. LAHURE

Mardi 7 Mars
et jours suivants
Au
Bon Marché
Maison A. Boucicaut

premières nouveautés
de la saison

as patterned silk linings with blouses to match, fine leather belts cut to slope downwards at the back, jewelled buttons, magnificent lapel-pins and carefully-chosen buttonholes.

The success of this new style was immediate and, as it was a genre eminently suited to the techniques of mass manufacture, it was soon copied extensively, and so fashion took a long step forward into a classless world. It also inaugurated an era when the ideal was to be an undeveloped adolescent, not a curvaceous woman.

At the Exposition Décoratif of 1925 some fabrics were shown which caused a furore. Sonia Delaunay, the Russian wife of the painter Robert Delaunay, was the first to bring together the tenets of the abstract painters, the possibilities of textile machinery and the demands of couture.

The small amount of fabric required for the skimpy fashions of the mid-Twenties necessarily threw great emphasis both on material and cut, for clothes were no longer laden with trimmings which obscured their outline and had to stand on their own merit. Rodier produced a novelty called *kasha,* a silk-soft woollen material woven from the fleece of a special

herd of sheep located on the Himalayas. Nearer home both Ducharne and Bianchini perfected methods of printing which made their flowered chiffons and crêpe de Chines a special delight. The latter were often used as linings to long 'clutch' coats which matched the dress beneath, and the accompanying hat, probably of Bangkok straw, was dyed to tone. Clothes were now composed to form an ensemble, not pieces bought separately. In winter, wrapover coats had upstanding fox collars to which, most unsuitably, orchids were frequently pinned. For evening wear the obligatory wrap or cape was of gleaming brocade or lamé.

The bateau neckline rivalled the low V, and scarves were wound round the neck with long ends hanging behind.

Though the silhouette was definitely slim, Lanvin continued to create her *robes de style* which never varied greatly from year to year but always managed to be in fashion; the main alternative, however, to the straight sheath with its fluttering panels was the clinging bias cut of which the chief exponent was Madeleine Vionnet. This great technician made exquisite dresses constructed of panels cut on the cross in which the original design was carried

Above: By 1925 skirts were slightly shorter, waists still ignored and bare bateau necklines preferred. Hats sat even lower on the head. More emphasis was placed on the cut and line of couture clothing, and less on the effect of sumptuous cloth or elaborate ornament

out with a great technical proficiency which frequently allowed the dress to fit with no fastenings.

The preferred colours were pale: beige for day with light brown as a runner-up and for evening almond green, soft blue or a misty rose. But white was top favourite.

Hair was parted on the side, cut into an 'Eton' crop and the enveloping cloche hat, inevitably of beige felt, entirely concealed the forehead. Among important accessories were pochettes dyed to match the ensemble, long strings of beads or pearls and dozens of 'slave' bracelets or narrow flexible diamond bracelets known as 'service stripes'.

The famous tennis champion, Suzanne Lenglen, always dressed by Patou, appeared on the courts in a sleeveless jumper, and so set another fashion in exposure. She retained the bandeau which hid her forehead, but her contemporaries soon followed the baring of their arms with the unveiling of their forehead, and the side parting with bare forehead became as ubiquitous as the bandeaux had been at the beginning of the decade. Pearl studs were the only earrings permitted. Danglers were 'out'.

Skirts were minimal; they began at the hip-line and only just covered the

Above left: In this drawing, the magazine La Vie Parisienne of 1926 caricatured a young girl whose skirts were so short that they revealed her rolled stockings. Corsets were no longer worn, her hair is shingled and a cigarette dangles from her mouth; the picture was not far from the truth in showing the high hemline of the period

Above: Van Dongen's portrait of Paulette Pax recorded the same type of figure in a rather more elegant manner

Left: A favourite accessory in the late Twenties was monkey fur, which trims this afternoon dress and jacket in lime-coloured panne velvet by Redfern. The skirt is cut with a bias front panel considerably longer than the sides and back. Redfern introduced the walking suit from his London salon to Paris; he was always noted for the detail of his tailoring

knees but in the evening the hem-line varied, and handkerchief-points, flared godets and fringes in uncertain lengths fluttered and swayed as the wearer walked or danced. The straight sheath bodices with no hint of bust or waist were often cut into a deep oval at the back. Over the shoulders printed shawls or triangles of lamé were thrown, sometimes composed of two or more colour sections, but the geometric designs of the mid-Twenties were beginning to be supplanted by flowered patterns.

Vionnet's bias-cut dominated the mode and dictated the construction of every garment in a woman's wardrobe from her satin, cut-on-the-cross chemise to her evening gowns composed of diagonal sections of chiffon or satin, often put together with hand faggot-stitching. Slender top-coats added upstanding collars and bands of fur round their hems in winter, and *grosgrain* was the newest material for the small close-fitting hats.

Another woman couturier, Louise-boulanger, one of the great artists of her time, was the most successful sponsor of a style which was as short-lived as was her House. This was the curious compromise on skirt length which in the

evening revealed the legs up to the knees in front but reached the ankles at the back and was a notable fashion of the late Twenties.

A fourth Englishman, after Charles Worth, Redfern and Creed, made a great name for himself in the competitive world of Paris couture and Edward Molyneux was now installed in the rue de la Paix. He excelled at creating apparently simple ensembles of pleated skirt, jumper, long coat and matching hat in such perfect proportions that his clothes became known as the best dress-investments to be found, for their classic qualities gave them a longer life than those of the more easily dated 'high fashion' models.

THE THIRTIES

A gradual increase in the femininity of clothes was noticeable at the beginning of the Thirties. The boyish girl tentatively exhibited a rounded bust, permitted a slight curve to be seen at her waist and allowed her hair to grow into a 'shingle'.

On this longer coiffure, which half hid the ears, tiny plate-shaped hats or small caps slid backwards and entirely revealed the forehead.

Skirts were lowered to mid-calf and tended to be longer at the back than in front. They showed godets or pleats let in below the knees instead of at hip-level, and were attached to bodices by slantwise or diagonal seams rather than at a definite waist line. Short boleros were added for day dresses, but, in the evening, gowns of trailing chiffon, velvet or satin had capes of the same material, often edged with fox. Draped décolletages added to the over-all effect of softness and fluidity, and small puffed sleeves contributed to a feminine silhouette which remained extremely slender, but with the torso moulded and exposed in diagonally-cut clinging materials. Colours were muted—pale aquamarine blues, *vieux rose* and parchment —but they were enlivened with matching or toning jackets of brocade.

Gloves were enormously important. Evening gowns usually had a special pair in matching or contrasting satin, while day outfits had striped or patterned fabric gloves with a hat or scarf to match.

Cotton entered the high-fashion world, largely sponsored by Chanel who came to London to stage a collection entirely made in British cottons, and débutantes went to balls in white

organdie, or to race meetings in white piqué instead of in silks and satins.

Pyjamas simultaneously appeared in three different spheres: as a 'nightijama' for sleeping in; as a glamorous alternative to a negligée or informal dinner-dress; and as a practical garment for beach-wear. The first two versions soon disappeared, but beach pyjamas became part of every woman's holiday equipment, made of shantung or heavy crêpe de Chine, with widely flared trousers and loose short coats, accompanied by large floppy-brimmed hats. An alternative was the sailor fashion, of navy-blue pants and blue and white striped tops stolen from the French *matelots* of Toulon.

The softly feminine fashions were soon rivalled by a masculine trend. Shoulders began to swell out until it seemed as if the leg-o'mutton sleeves of the Eighties might be revived, but this time the emphasis was rather on the width of the shoulders than on the rotundity of the sleeves.

Day-coats, suits and dresses were fitted with shoulder-pads which widened the top of the figure and minimized the size of the newly important small waist. Epaulettes appeared and were credited both to the Indo-Chinese temple

dancers who had enchanted everyone at the 1931 Exposition Coloniale in Paris, and to the dress uniform worn by the English Guards.

The most successful interpreter of this style was Elsa Schiaparelli, known as 'Scap', an Italian woman whose contribution to the couture of the Thirties was considerable. Her clothes were the antithesis of the soft, pretty style and her unquestionably chic models a godsend to plain women to whom fluttering chiffons in pale shades were unsuited. Her short, fitted jackets with their crisp shoulders in hyacinth or turquoise blue or pink tweed, teamed with dresses of brown or black wool became the high fashion of the moment.

Other unusual colour companions were russet-brown with pale green, and prune with a pinkish-magenta or aquamarine-blue. Fabric co-ordinations were equally novel.

Hats abandoned their brims and tiny berets were worn perched on one side of the head, weighed down with the same type of diamond clips which now replaced the extinct brooch, and which also clung precariously to the draped necklines of both day and evening dresses.

As the fashion for sun-bathing in-

creased, so did the importance of beach-wear, and the one-piece suit of dark wool and white towelling coat were superseded by fashions as diverse and as chic as any for more formal occasions. Beach wraps, floppy hats and duffle-bag shaped canvas hold-alls were all popular. Haute couture began to acknowledge the existence of casual clothes, with Schiaparelli in the lead, and her hand-knitted bathing suits caused a sensation when they were first seen at Antibes, then the smartest of the Riviera resorts.

Norman Hartnell designed a series of costumes for aboard ship and seaside wear, which included variations of the accepted grey flannel or navy pleated skirts, plus a lisle-thread jumper in navy, a basque beret, and a navy reefer with brass buttons. Chanel brought out her own version which was lined with scarlet silk, its cuffs turned back to show a flash of the bright lining, a steal from her friend Jean Cocteau who often wore such a jacket.

Trousers became acknowledged as the correct wear at all seaside resorts, but they were bell-bottomed and flap-fronted, not zipped.

In town the 'little black dress' was essential for afternoon wear, usually with some shirring at the bosom and

Above left: Tweed and woollen outfits in two colours designed by Schiaparelli and Marthe Regny

Above right: The padded shoulders which Schiaparelli used in order to minimize the waist and give an air of spurious masculinity to feminine styles are here added to a cape and a dress in which a multi-colour print is used to compose a geometrical pattern

always with large diamond clips clinging to the neckline. Small waists were emphasized by billowing sleeves and full accordion-pleated skirts, but such feminine detail continued to be counterbalanced by the military briskness of padded shoulders and epaulettes. A particularly androgynous fashion was one which allied a copy of a man's black evening coat, complete with white carnation and white silk scarf, to frilly chiffon dresses and tiny nonsense hats, flower trimmed and tilted over the forehead.

When the young Queen Elizabeth visited France in 1936, she wore an all-white wardrobe, because she was in mourning for George V, and all black had been thought unsuitable by her dressmaker, Norman Hartnell. She created a stir in her all-white toilettes of muslin, chiffon, satin and lace with white fox trimmings and white ermine wraps and a lace hat trimmed with white roses. An all-white craze in fashion became as ubiquitous as the all-white craze for decoration had been in the Twenties, and white satin evening gowns, cut on the cross and as slim and close-fitting as possible, though with flares at the hem for easy movement, were as much an evening uniform for women as black tails were for

men. Styles from Paris were adopted in London far more rapidly than in the previous decade and the hooded coats admired in the February Paris collections could be found the following autumn at Jaeger's.

One French fashion which did not cross the Channel was that of wearing a hat in the evening. In Paris tiny toques of tulle, flowers and feathers, sometimes tied on with a wisp of coloured veiling, were made to match evening gowns, but in London an Englishwoman so attired would be refused entry to a night club.

Most of these charming follies were accompanied by what became known as 'dinner-suits'. These consisted of long swirling gowns of lace or satin with short matching jackets with broad shoulders and neat flower- or jewel-trimmed lapels which were worn for cocktails, dinner and the theatre, and were among the most felicitous of the Thirties' fantasies, for they were both elegant and practical. Many of these suits were made of the shiny satin so typical of the decade, called *ciré* because its surface looked as if it had been waxed, and which was only seen in black.

Another Paris fashion which had no success in England was the short dinner

dress which was full-skirted, very décolleté and ballet-length—that is to just below the calf. This threw great emphasis on footwear, and Schiaparelli showed it with ribbon-tied tango shoes which drew further attention to the feet and ankles, but few women in Europe considered this hybrid adequate for dressing for the evening and ignored it. In America, where footwear was better designed and made, and where a more casual way of life was usual, it was welcomed as a good middle-of-the-road between day-clothes and full evening-dress.

In strong contrast to such sophisticated styles, Balenciaga, newly important in the world of couture and chiefly famous for sombre toilettes in black, proposed striped cotton dresses for summer evening wear: Brontë-ish gowns with bodices fastened demurely at the neck and full skirts in which the

bias-cut gave the fabric a new dimension.

This was an early indication of the fancy dress element which found its full flowering in the two seasons immediately before the outbreak of war. Every historical period and country in the world was ransacked by the couturiers for inspiration: they presented demure Jane Eyre dresses, glamorous Oriental houris, sophisticated black gowns, tulle crinolines recollecting the Empress Eugénie, Edwardian corseted figures, Empire highbreasted gowns, draperies very much like classical statues, the mid-calf ballet silhouette, and they even revived the bustle. There were loose-sleeved Mandarin jackets, high collared Russian coats, school-girl dresses in navy with white Buster Brown collars, and peasant dresses in gingham.

An attempt was made to bring back the corset, waists were reduced to a

Above: As for women, the expansion of sporting activity had a pronounced effect on men's clothing. New casual styles emerged: plus fours, windcheaters, open-necked shirts and pullovers were all in vogue

Above: Beach clothes became of great importance to fashion as the French Riviera summer resorts became more and more popular. The cover of Harper's Bazaar by Benigni for July 1930 shows a striking pyjama ensemble with a large hat to shield the shoulders

Top right: Stiebel, a new English fashion house, suggested a striped cotton shirt with a navy blue woollen skirt and jacket, and a dress and jacket in sky blue

Below right: By the middle of the Thirties dress had reached a lady-like extreme. Drooping skirts, drooping sleeves, flower-patterned silk, sideways tilted hats composed a figure totally contrary to the gay garçonne of the previous decade

Far right: Molyneux was the first to launch the fashion of contrasting colours for skirts and jackets or dresses and coats. These formed an ensemble but could be interchanged with other garments. Alix (centre) and Paquin (right) showed similar styles in 1938

Opposite page: To a printed silk gown with a black bolero, Schiaparelli in 1939 added a semi-medieval pointed headdress which covered the shoulders. Fancy dress was in the air and nostalgic glances looked back at the past as the future became more and more menacing. An alternative response to the current mood was surreal, like this fabric design for Schiaparelli by Salvador Dali, to simulate tears

minimum and tiny bodices, with no straps to uphold them, were stiffly boned. Not only did petticoats reappear with their starched embroidered frills showing beneath the skirt hem, but Vionnet permitted similarly trimmed pantalettes to be seen.

Shoulders were still emphasized, with padding for day-coats and jackets, puff sleeves for late-day and dinner dresses, and shoulder frills by night.

Hats were no more than doll size, perched over the eyes and feather-trimmed, or bonnets firmly fitting the head tied under the chin. Hair was worn long at the back and caught in fishnets of crocheted chenille such as Victorian ladies wore in the 1860s, or brushed up on top of the head with a curled fringe.

The trick of teaming light coloured jackets with dark pleated skirts was popular and for the first time manufacturers presented co-ordinated collections of bags, gloves and shoes.

A more varied, more picturesque and more extravagant fashion scene would be impossible to imagine and one more suited to a perpetual Mardi Gras rather than to everyday life, but the confusion of thought reflected only too truly the disorder of a world about to be plunged into the catastrophe of world war.

241

AUSTERITY AND THE NEW LOOK

The Forties and Fifties

Left: During the Phoney War, Molyneux showed in his spring collection of 1940 many outfits similar to this one. These showed slender skirts, loose three-quarter length coats of a contrasting colour or material with squared shoulders, topped with large, flat hats tilted to one side. Square handbags with handles were sensible accessories

The outbreak of war found women all over the civilized world with over-waved and over-curled hair on which shallow-crowned hats tilted sharply, with shoulders exaggeratedly square and skirts of medium length and of comfortable walking width.

A few of the younger and more dashing wore trousers in the country or at the seaside but never in town. House-pyjamas had not been a success and dinner gowns of supple crêpe were worn, most with puff sleeves and rows of shirring between the breasts, though some recalled the Gibson Girls of the Edwardian hey-day with a trim waist, emphasized bosom and leg-o'mutton sleeves. A popular newcomer was a 'top' of dark crêpe tied in front, with three-quarter-length sleeves, worn with a full skirt of a light-coloured print.

In France the situation was completely different and every effort was made both by the Government and the trade for couture to continue, since it was one of the country's most important industries and on it depended the huge silk mills in Lyons and the woollen mills in the north. The first wartime collections shown in January 1940 in Paris were attended by the more intrepid international journalists; active hostili-

ties had not yet commenced, but the tense atmosphere of the 'Phoney War' gave an artificial air to the whole proceedings. The models showed skirts which reached to just below the knees and, now that there were real uniforms in plenty, the jackets were less military in cut with softer outlines, no epaulettes and fewer buttons and braids. Pin-striped grey flannel was suggested for a spring which seemed uncertain to come, and jackets of stripes and checks were teamed with plain dresses or skirts. Molyneux came out with a new range of loose, casual coats of pillar-box red or yellow, swinging over printed dresses to match, while Schiaparelli tried in vain to introduce a sloping line but shoulders remained square.

After the German occupation fashion went berserk, and Paris produced vulgar, ill-proportioned clothes, with the object, it was later explained, of making the victors' wives look as ridiculous as possible. They certainly succeeded, and the huge ungainly hats allied to short skirts and ankle boots were supremely un-chic, but so completely were the two countries cut off from each other that none of this was known to the English public until the autumn of 1945.

Most men were in uniform of some

PEARLS .. LITTLE PRICE

"Utility" clothes, made under the Government controlled clothes order, are now finding their way into our big stores. The dresses, in fine woollens and soft spring colours, show how attractive they can be in variety of colour and design, and the suits and topcoats are remarkable for their excellent cut and tailoring.

● Left : From Peter Robinson, two smartly simple wool dresses in pastel shades. ● Above : From Derry & Toms, a topcoat in soft brown and cream tweed, with a rounded shoulder yoke.

PETER ROBINSON

DERRY & TOMS

JOHN BARKER

From John Barker ● Above : a pastel wool dress with rouleaux of its own material twisted on the bodice. ● And, right, a long-jacketed suit in nigger and off-white herringbone, and an all-purpose topcoat in off-white fleecy woollen.

JOHN BARKER

Right: This surrealistically posed ball gown from early 1940 shows Schiaparelli's sensitivity to drapery

Above: In 1940 when the Board of Trade decided to restrict the amount of clothing available they called in the help of the Incorporated Society of London Fashion Designers, composed of the leading English couture houses, and asked them to produce anonymous clothes which used the minimum of material. These 'Utility' clothes showed simple but acceptable variations on the theme of button-through dresses with revers or high necks, skirts flared for easy walking which reached just below the knees. Waists were belted and well-defined and dress-sleeves short to save material, with loose, easy sleeves for coats. Hats were unrationed, and were shallow-crowned with broad brims

Above right: In France the Chambre Syndicale de la Couture struggled to survive the years of German occupation. Those houses that elected to remain open and offer work to French people produced fashions which in retrospect reflected their hatred of the Germans: vulgar heavy dresses, with mannish squared shoulders, and unflattering high turbans

Right: In 1941, despite the real menace of war, a new, free woman emerged, seen here in a heavy tweed overcoat which is belted with large revers. This particular coat is longer than most worn at the time

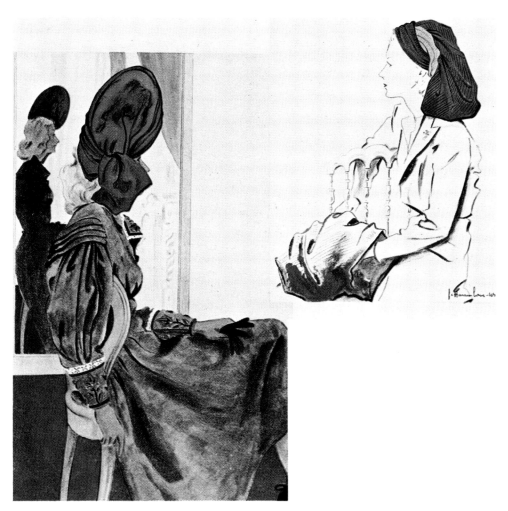

sort, for even civilians were Air Wardens or engaged in work which carried a distinguishing mark, but even this sameness did not prevent the arrival of a new fashion. General Montgomery's duffle coat, a loose knee-length garment of khaki wool fastened by wooden toggles, was adopted by both sexes and all ages and has continued to be worn ever since.

In England, in 1941, the Board of Trade brought out the regulations for 'Utility Clothes'—one of the best-kept secrets of the whole war. Every civilian was issued with twenty coupons bi-annually, and each garment was valued at a given number of coupons, one suit alone taking eighteen. Furthermore all manufacturers were forbidden to use more than a stated amount of material for any model, and no firm was permitted to create more than fifty styles during one calendar year.

In spite of such stringent regulations nothing short of a revolution took place because, for the first time in history, fashion (such as it was) derived from the proletariat, not from the privileged. Furthermore, a vast number of lower-class women who were drafted into the services experienced the discipline of good dressing and the feel of

what were comparatively good quality clothes.

To the typical wartime silhouette of shortish skirt and the long, square-shouldered jacket, the free English, now that their living standard was reduced to that of poor East European peasants, emulated them by tying handkerchiefs around their heads. Hats were unrationed, with large-brimmed, off-face models replacing the shallow-crowned, forward-tilting ones of the Thirties, but turbans and headscarves were the most usual headgear. Hair was shoulder-length, but often set in a roll at the nape with another across the forehead, with the head-scarf knotted on top of the head, a style which became associated with factory workers and cleaners in the following decade. Trousers were worn on the farm and in the factory, but they remained purely utilitarian garments and no attempt was made to glamorize them. Whenever coupons permitted, shoes were replaced by ankle-boots with clumsy soles and low heels.

At the end of the war Paris made an immense effort to revive its great fashion trade and to re-affirm its leadership. As is usual in France where the rapport between the arts and applied

arts has always been close, many of the best artists in Paris collaborated in creating a miniature *Théâtre de la Mode* which could show the current fashion. Each scene was exquisitely composed and the whole effect alluring, but the clothes themselves were not striking, and through the veneer of French taste and Parisian sophistication could be sensed the results of an oppressive occupation during which all sense of proportion had been lost.

It was not until nearly two years later that French taste rediscovered its equilibrium. It is rarely possible to give an exact date for any change of fashion, but Christian Dior's first collection was a real landmark. In 1947 this young man, before the war an art-dealer and after it a designer at Lucien Lelong's, was set up on his own by the great textile firm of Boussac, the success of whose business, like others of its kind, largely relied on France being recognized as the leader of fashion. Boussac was well known for his stable of racing-horses and for his luck on the turf, and in Dior he certainly picked a winner in the fashion stakes.

Dior presented a silhouette which became known as the 'New Look' though in fact it looked back to France's

golden age of elegance. This new ideal of feminine chic consisted of a tiny corseted waist, rounded bust and hips and skirts usually as low as twelve inches from the ground, though for country wear some rose to fifteen inches. Dior not only minimized the waist by means of clever cutting and by a mini-corset called a *guépière*, but padded out the front hip bones and set the sleeves into a rounded shoulder line, in total contrast to the masculine square-shouldered, man-tailored clothes of the end-of-the-war period. To these ultra-feminine costumes were added small flowered hats with veils, high-heeled shoes, coloured gloves to match a buttonhole or handkerchief, long slim umbrellas to tone with shoes and bag, and two or four strings of pearls.

Dinner gowns showed full ankle-length skirts of a different material to the bodice, and such contrasts as a lilac satin bodice buttoned up to the throat with a yellow plaid taffeta skirt were indicative of a return not only to elegance but to romanticism. This was particularly noticeable in ball-gowns which were as magnificent as any pre-war extravaganzas: immense white tulle crinolines covered with swirls of flimsy mousseline and draped overskirts, flat

On these pages: Toward the close of hostilities women were wearing short, full skirts, broad shoulders, ankle boots and high hats —the whole composing a vulgar and ill-proportioned figure. In the Théâtre de la Mode of 1945, so carefully prepared by the Chambre Syndicale de la Couture in Paris, the clothes displayed by the wire mannequins still showed some of these characteristics, but the man who was radically to change the silhouette was already one of Lucien Lelong's design team. Christian Dior (above) did not show his first collection until 1947 when his New Look showed lengthened skirts, with petticoats under them, a rounded shoulder line and a tiny waist. Some shoes had ankle straps, some had platform soles and some had both

CHRISTIAN DIOR

in front with the fullness at sides and back, which had tiny bodices that often dispensed with any shoulder coverage.

These lovely dresses were carried out in materials woven in mixtures of real and artificial fibres which had been developed during the War for want of anything better and had now reached a high pitch of perfection which made all concerned wonder if 'pure' silks would ever return to favour. Many of the characteristics of the new mode—the skirts held out by invisible means, the soft drapes which held their line without any visible support—owed their magical qualities to man-made fibres.

Previously an aura of non-U had clung to 'art silk' and 'rayon' and mixtures composed partly of synthetic and partly of 'real' yarn had been despised. In the Thirties Schiaparelli had experimented with several novelties, particularly with a crinkled silk, called 'Treebark', which in its weave presaged Crimplene, and in 1935 had made a 'glass' dress, complete with Cinderella slippers—prototypes of the cellophanes of today. At the same time Agnès brought out a variation of her famous turban made of this material, which demonstrated the full scope of her flair for sculpture. In 1947 Lurex, known in

America during the war where it was extensively used to enhance curtain materials and decorative furnishings, entered the fashion fabric world.

The international ready-to-wear trade took a stride forwards when in 1949 Christian Dior opened a wholesale house in New York which sold off-the-peg Dior models to stores throughout the continent. His narrow peg-top skirts with short, easy jackets, the waist emphasized by a cummerbund or belt, and his dresses with their built-in supports were eminently equipped with so-called 'hanger-appeal', that is, they looked as appetizing on hangers as they did on human beings.

America's own ready-to-wear was of a quality then unknown in Europe: Traina-Norell, Hattie Carnegie, Claire McCardle, Adrian and several other designers brought out clothes which illustrated the current fashion but also proclaimed the individuality of each designer. The Carnegie suit-look included neat jackets with slanted pockets on the hips worn over pleated skirts. Adrian was famous for his flower-printed, full-skirted evening gowns, and Traina-Norell for glamour wear, especially for his dinner-suits of black velvet with narrow slit skirts.

On these pages: The New Look was achieved by old methods. Dior revived the art of couture and used every known trick in the construction of his models. The most elaborate cutting kept its shape by the expert use of technical methods such as had not been seen for half a century. Every seam was reinforced by tapes, skirts held out by shaped linings, waists constricted by built-in belts or 'waspies', hips built out by padding, busts held in place both by cut and bones. No trick in the couturier's weaponry was omitted. Above all, the harmony between design and execution was achieved by the most recondite knowledge of what each material was capable of: these models would not have been possible without the assistance of such novel fabrics as feather-weight holland linings and the diaphanous but firm stiffened nylon

248

Slender dinner dress
with vast side panel;
from Dior

Straight skirt
but flying panels over;
from Dior

Among the most successful developments was that of the separate top and skirt, and innumerable variations were carried out with blouses of silk, muslin or shirred jersey teamed with full skirts of velvet or quilted silk.

For informal evening wear, the American short black dinner dress worn with pearls and coloured slippers, and little-girl day-dresses with white collars and white gloves became internationally adopted. Above all there was the mink stole, which was now not only coveted by all but acquired by many since methods of ranch breeding permitted the skins to become less exorbitant in price, and more varied in colour.

By 1951 fashion had settled down into two main day-time silhouettes, straight and slender for dresses and suits, wide and ample for coats. The waist, as tiny and as accentuated as possible, was outlined by a narrow belt, the rounded hips emphasized by basques and asymmetrical draperies, the shoulders soft, the sleeves short or three-quarter length. Skirts clinging to the hips reached exactly to the mid-calf, and below the knees often broke into flares. Collars were important—some were large and shoulder enveloping, some high-standing and chin hiding, while some were small and rolled and others were tied by a cravat.

Over slim suits and dresses were worn massive coats to whose bulk heavy materials contributed. The fullness was sometimes slit at the sides to give a cape effect and the sleeves were wide and mounted high on sloping shoulders. Broad fabric stoles were thrown over the suits and fur was everywhere, as an edging, as huge cuffs or collars, or as large pillow muffs—women were as well wrapped up in the winter of 1950 as they had been in 1910.

Dior presented a series of afternoon dresses which had an immense success. These showed wide-spreading, sun-ray pleated skirts in taffeta or shantung, with tight bodices fitted to a pinched-in belted waist and cleverly contrived necklines dipping to a V in front, pin-pointed by a large jewel. With these pretty dresses in caramel, beige and pink were worn broad-brimmed hats, long dark gloves and matching shoes.

Yet another instant fashion was the long-skirted cocktail-cum-dinner suit in black satin or velvet with white organza blouses. Rarely have women had more practical and becoming clothes.

In the evening, all was glamour. The theme of the tight sheath was developed into ankle-length skirts of faille (ribbed silk), taffeta and velvet which had one-sided folds or long draperies, or a sash tied at the back which formed a

Paris Sketch book

The most luxurious
evening coat in Paris:
grey satin with a
cloche hat.
Jacques Fath

Left: A white, flower-printed cotton dress in the summer of 1950 showed a short and wide skirt, puff sleeves and a deep, white-collared décolletage. The coquettish stance, the flower at the décolletage, the brimmed hat trimmed with a band of the same material as the dress and parasol to match, wrist-length gloves and stiletto-heeled court shoes were all typical of the short-lived lady-like style of the Fifties

Above: After a decade of difficulties in France and austerity in England, the Fifties saw an uninhibited return to luxury. No gown could be too picturesque, no combination of fabrics too rich, and the pictures above provide spectacular examples of this. Fath, always a lover of luxury, designed the voluminous dress on the left in filmy material and a jacket trimmed with collar and cuffs of fur

Above right: A beautifully extravagant evening gown, in a far more romantic mood than was usual with Schiaparelli, was made for the Duchess of Devonshire in a dreamy combination of pale pink silk overlaid with floating flower-appliquéd white organdie. It was among the models chosen by Cecil Beaton for his 'Dream of the Fifties' exhibition at London's Victoria and Albert Museum in 1971

train. Most waists were marked by a narrow belt buckled in front. Jacques Fath, a young couturier who had come to fame at the end of the war, liked pleated panels of patterned mousseline to spread out over a column of plain ottoman. The tiny, boned bodices, whose low décolletage descended to the waist at the back, were innocent of shoulder straps and accentuated the bust by asymmetrical folds or an envelope turn-over. Many were severely buttoned down at one side or at the back, and with them were worn long gloves always of a darker shade than the main fabric, and matching shoes.

The colours were exquisite: amethyst, maize, faded rose, turquoise, a bluish-violet and lemon yellow as favourites, with the combination of white and rose predominating.

Evening wraps were as luxurious as those of the long distant Edwardian era, long capes of rose-coloured satin were bordered with sable, voluminous coats of satin matched the slender dresses beneath and fox wraps covered the shoulders. Both patterned and striped materials were richly re-embroidered, and every single device was employed to make women look as luxurious and idle as possible at a time when they

were actually becoming more active in politics and business.

Most of the women who bought these beautiful clothes did not have jewellery of sufficient quantity or quality to match them and, since the gowns left the body above the bust entirely naked, and the hair revealed the ears, important parures were required. Dior came to the rescue with specially designed costume jewellery which was as splendid as anything made in the past with real gems.

In the mid-1950s, men's costume broke free from the restrictions surviving from war-time military dress. In England, the so-called Teddy Boys were noted for their slicked back, rather long hair, waisted coats and above all for their sharply pointed shoes whose winkle-picker toes recalled the excesses of their ancestors of the fifteenth century. Higher up the social scale men began to experiment with dinner jackets of coloured velvet, double breasted and fastened by brandenburgs, with matching satin collars. A few of the younger and more daring revived the frilled shirt of the Romantic period. White tie and tails were rarely seen and the dinner suit did duty for all but the most formal occasions.

Above: Men's clothes in the Fifties were as conservative as women's were elegant. Day suits with single-breasted jackets and double-breasted coats were worn with medium wide trousers creased down the front with no turn-ups. Neat collars and ties and plain shirts gave no hint of the revolution brewing in the male wardrobe

Right: Women wore extremely feminine dresses which combined great chic with comfort. Waists were no longer tightly pinched in, but the bosom was in evidence and a rounded, well-proportioned figure was required for simple, easy-to-wear styles executed in magnificent materials. Dresses and coats in the same satin or brocade were popular for evening-wear with mid-calf, rather than long, skirts for all except really formal occasions. Pearls and close-fitting hats added to an elegant but rather ageing ideal in fashion

Left: Balenciaga was a designer with a great influence on younger couturiers who passed through his salons. A master of sculptured shape and tailored detail, he produced grand, elegant but rather severe clothes

The lady-like figure of the mid-Fifties was rivalled by a very different type when the 'Sweater Girl' appeared. Lana Turner was the acknowledged star of this new fashion whose outward and all too-visible sign was a stiff-tipped brassière worn beneath a tight pullover. This vulgar style had one good result—more attention was paid to the design of knit-wear, which developed from a Cinderella into a high-fashion star.

Nowhere was this improvement more noticeable than in Italy, where chic and well-cut knitwear made an end to the dreary non-fashion garments hitherto regarded as proper to a sporting life, and Mirsa's neat models with dark Eton jackets and light slacks or pleated skirts entered every holiday wardrobe.

The Italian fashion market was centralized and publicized in Florence by Signor Giorgini, and the Italian government put at the disposal of the trade the Palazzo Pitti as a salon, the Palazzo Strozzi as an office, and the Boboli gardens as a scene for evening receptions. In these spectacular surroundings the collections of haute couture houses, such as Simonetta, Fabiani, Valentino of Rome, and Florence-born Emilio Pucci, were shown with the best

wholesale houses from Milan and Turin to large gatherings of buyers from all over the world.

The Italian influence invaded the shoe market of both sexes, and Englishmen went about wearing winkle-picker boots which in the length of their toes threatened to rival the ridiculous *poulaines* of the fifteenth century, and women added stiletto heels to their pointed shoes.

Spanish designers also attempted to enter the international fashion world and journalists and buyers of many countries went to Madrid to see the collections of Aissa (Balenciaga's Spanish branch), Rodriguez and Pertegaz, where the austere and magnificent evening

clothes were preceded by strictly tailored day clothes, uniformly black but never dull.

In Paris, Dior launched the A-line with belt-less, narrow-shouldered dresses widening gradually to the hem, worn under three-quarter length, tent-shaped coats whose collars slanted backwards from the neck. All skirts, whether for casual or formal wear, reached halfway down the calf, and the 'short' dinner dress tended to be even longer.

Cotton, now processed in a manner which made it almost uncrushable, became high fashion, and the cotton dresses designed by the firm of Horrocks' were worn not only by the

young and impecunious but also by the elegant Marina, Duchess of Kent. The most popular styles showed tight-fitting bodices and short sleeves cut in one, a trimly belted waist and full skirts set in gathers or deep pleats, held out by frilled petticoats. These were made of a new fabric, stiffened nylon, a prime example of a material permitting—or creating—a new style, for it allowed skirts almost as wide as crinolines to be as light as air and to keep their shape without any support. Furthermore these delightful garments were easily washed, and they dripped dry in a few hours. At first they were an accessory to couture gowns, but soon they were mass-produced and, by 1959, they were in every girl's wardrobe.

Cotton also entered the ballroom, and evening gowns with strapless bodices dipped to the waist at the back and were accompanied by matching stoles and long, very full skirts. Candy pink was the favourite colour, and, with these young-girl dresses, the classic fashion for a pony-tail coiffure was revived, sponsored by Brigitte Bardot.

The era of strict tailoring was over, suits were loose and easy with wide armholes, rounded shoulders, pouched backs and collars standing away from

Left: The illustration depicts a late 1950s evening ensemble of tight-fitting, ankle-length pants teamed with a slim-fitting matching top in a patterned, gold silk. It represents a move towards freedom and informality in style but suggests that entertaining at home or in public required 'dressing up'

Below: Synthetic fabrics, particularly the stretch type, were now becoming more and more popular. The model here wears black, stretch tights with a strap under the instep, ski-fashion

the neck filled in with soft, loosely knotted chiffon scarves. With these bloused jackets, often caught by a wide belt, were worn tight peg-top skirts. The whim for a centre seam either at the front or back of a skirt, previously considered a fashionable heresy, was characteristic of this epoch. Closely-fitting hats essayed brims deeper at the back than in front, but the summer mode preferred veiled flower toques worn straight on the head, and the winter brought fur hats similar to old-fashioned tea-cosies.

For dinner at home the craze for blouses teamed with thick mohair skirts was a godsend in a cruel winter. For more formal occasions pale-coloured lace or chiffon blouses were worn with long satin skirts. Further developments in synthetic fibres resulted in such materials as Acrilan, Banlon and Orlon which revolutionized sports and holiday clothes. Dresses of these materials were easily washed, did not require ironing and packed without creasing, and 'woollies', no longer of pure wool, and also washable, were lighter in colour and more fashion-conscious than ever before.

Stretch jersey was used by Helanca to make some of the first tights on the

Above: Schiaparelli used a new honey-comb piqué cotton for a 'casino dress' in 1952; the strapless top is typical of early 1950s evening wear

Above: Dior's line for 1958 showed a bloused top above a short, narrow skirt. It ignored the waist, dispensed with sleeves but laid the emphasis on a high turban and long gloves

Above: A sheath dress made in lamé by Carven (1959) showed a fitted princess line which displayed bust, waist and hips but allowed the skirt to flare out at the back

Right: A classic Chanel suit from the 1950s, lined in silk with matching fabric blouse, and accompanied by pretty fake jewellery which Chanel had popularised as early as the 1930s

market in a limited range of red, blue and green. These were often worn with a blouse of the same colour and a contrasting skirt, buttoned down the front.

Nylon stockings simulated nudity and dispensed with back seams and reinforced heels, and most summer shoes were open-heeled sling-backs, in different colours. Winter bootees favoured tiny turn-over fur cuffs, but black crocodile was a top favourite.

Both shoes and stockings were of particular importance since skirts rose to the knee. During the day they were usually slim, but in the evening there were a variety of shapes including the nonsensical puff-ball bloused over a tight hem which reached to just below the knee. Long sheath dresses of gleaming satin accompanied by short jackets of a different colour were correct for formal evenings, but velvet pants, very tight and barely reaching the ankles, were worn with satin blouses for informal dinners, with the short-skirted brocade dress the accepted half-way house for most occasions.

Waists were tightly belted at the normal line, but the décolletage was anything but normal, and wired brassières allowed it to be split to waist level in front. During the day wide necklines were softened by long strings of pearls, but in the evening elaborate necklaces of costume jewellery equalled nineteenth-century parures in their splendour.

England came to the fore once again in men's fashions which changed even more drastically than female fashions. The dull, grey city suit was hardly ever seen outside those precincts, and even there young men in light colours and fancy suitings and gay ties went bareheaded. The rest of the town, and indeed the whole country, paid more than lip service to the uniform of blue jeans which, in every shade of blue, embroidered with motifs and fantastically patched were teamed with shirts of many colours. Collars and ties were often replaced by polo-necked pullovers, worn both by day and night.

The frilled shirts so tentatively introduced a decade ago were common to all young dandies, and some were edged with lace and had frilled cuffs. The romantic coiffures of young Shelley and his contemporaries were seen at suburban parties as well as smart nightspots, and men's hair once again reached the shoulders, as it did just a century ago.

By 1962 most day skirts reached the mid-calf, with the slender line rivalled by pleats or a slight flare, but evening skirts continued to be ankle-length. Dior's long, slim satin skirts teamed with magnificently beaded tunics were every woman's ideal until he suggested the exotic alternative of silk culottes. Simonetta-Fabiani, recently established in Paris, also offered satin and brocade pants with lavishly trimmed matching jackets, and England experimented with novelty fabrics such as the ribbon woven tweeds of Bernat Klein and Ascher's mohairs.

KALEIDOSCOPE
The Sixties and Seventies

With the entry of Mary Quant and the opening of her 'Bazaar' in the King's Road in London, a new and unexpected chapter in fashion history began. By the early Sixties she had moved into premises in Knightsbridge, launched a wholesale range called the 'Ginger Group', made a tie-up in stores all across America, was exporting, largely to France, and had won *The Sunday Times* International and several other fashion awards. In 1966 she was given the OBE for her services to export, and, in 1974, the London Museum devoted an entire exhibition to her and her work.

In the early Sixties a myriad of boutiques was opened by enthusiastic young designers who made the sort of clothes they and their friends wanted, which turned out to be worn by both sexes. Many of these small shops failed, but some survived and made an important contribution to the London shopping scene, drastically changing both its methods of merchandising and its geographical boundaries. No longer was it necessary to go 'up West' to shop and, with the notable exception of Carnaby Street which evolved a style all its own, 'trendy gear' was more likely to be found in Chelsea, Kensington or Fulham than Mayfair. One of the most successful of

Far left: With the arrival of Mary Quant on the London fashion scene the last vestiges of English restraint vanished. The timid good taste which had dominated English fashion for more than two decades gave place to an uninhibited style suited to the new young, who had far larger pay packets and more freedom than their predecessors

Left: Together with social restrictions went those of race, so Mary Quant's satin shorts and shirt were worn by an African girl, while Cardin's favourite model in 1964 was a pretty Japanese. Here she wears a satin trouser suit over which is thrown a fur-edged cape

Left: When the mini-skirt appeared in 1965 it not unnaturally caused a sensation. Modesty was thrown to the winds, moralists thundered, textile manufacturers despaired and the aesthetes were appalled, for all too often legs so mercilessly revealed would have been better hidden. In spite of all said against it, however, the mini-skirt became current wear for several seasons. It brought an enormous boom to the underwear and stocking and tights manufacturers and generally laid great emphasis on a youthful, firm body

Mary Quant's rivals was Barbara Hulan-icki, who launched a boutique, Biba, famous for its distinctive black and purple interior. For a decade she traded on a fashion combination of romanticism and dark Hollywood: black satin, brown feathers, slippery Art Deco fabrics, and high-cut shoulder lines. After starting with a mail order business, she transformed a family grocer's shop in Church Street, Kensington, into an Aladdin's cave with myriads of lively clothes hanging from bentwood hatstands and velvet divans for the clients to lounge on.

From larger premises in Kensington High Street, Hulanicki eventually moved on to convert Derry and Toms – once a bastion of well-dressed elegance – into an Art Deco haven in which the freedom-loving young could buy or browse. This expansion was not at all successful, since most people browsed rather than bought, and the essence of Biba's appeal with its smallness and immediacy was lost. Hulanicki now works in Brazil, launching very expensive and extreme fashion on an international basis.

The Sixties also saw the rise of another English star, who has remained firmly in the ascendant ever since: Jean Muir, a London designer who began in ready-to-wear dresses but gradually moved into

Right: Among the most prominent names of the new London designers was that of Ossie Clark whose creations were worn by the young and chic. His pant suit for evening wear is composed of a plain satin jacket and trousers gaily patterned with an oriental design. Compare the practical styling and freedom of movement in this outfit with the trousers and cloak of a decade previously, shown on page 252

high quality design which is classic couture in price and quality. In 1969 she was invited by the French to show them her technique in handling jersey – the effect is somewhat reminiscent of Vionnet's work in the Thirties. Her trademark is as noticeable as Mme Grès: a loosely gathered and ruched range of feminine dresses, blouses or suits, manufactured predominantly in an extremely lightweight jersey, crêpe or silk, usually made in neutral tones or black.

However, in spite of a real flare of talent in London, the so-called Swinging Sixties did not seriously threaten the position of French designers as the arbiters of fashion for very long. For a while it had seemed that the ordinary mass of working- or middle-class girls on the London streets, wearing Quant or Biba minis, dictated fashion to everyone else in the industry, and eventually they devised new fashions for themselves with no reference to fashion authorities. They took to mini-skirts, clashing colour combinations, borrowed clothes from men (especially T-shirts and jeans) and broke down all classic fashion rules. Until the explosion of ready-to-wear activity in London, the Paris fashion houses had maintained a remote and formal control over the progress of

Left: During the late Sixties the Rolling Stones were among the most admired rock groups, and their tough, casual way of dressing was widely copied by the young. Tight trousers worn low on the hips, zip-fastened leather jackets and coloured shirts, shoulder-length straight, but determinedly untidy hair, formed the ideal figure for the male

Far left: The mid-Sixties saw a complete mixture of styles: young men began to wear fancy dress, living out their interests in American culture. Girls either wore baby-doll dresses, or emancipated minis, or one of a number of novelty outfits like the plasticized fabric raincoat and hood modelled by Twiggy, the British model who epitomized the androgynous female of the era

Below left: A further development of the fantasy dressing in the late Sixties was a unisex ethnic trend: men and women sported variations on Russian peasant clothing, as here, or Arab kaftans, Eastern kimonos, or Indian smocks and loose cotton trousers

fashion from the emergence of couturiers in the 1900s. Each decade had seen increasing authority, culminating with the imperial position of Dior, Balenciaga and Chanel. Suddenly all this had changed, and the couturiers began to realize that, for the first time perhaps in the entire history of fashion, new ideas or standards for men and women did not arise from the dictates of an élite, as in previous centuries, such as the court aristocracy. Now fashion was being invented by a newly affluent middle- and working-class, especially the very young element of society who were dedicated to the setting of a style, connected by sophisticated modes of communication in film, television and journalism, all over the western world. The phenomenon of the Sixties was principally that fashion was no longer a question of dictate, but of individual taste and invention – even though this came to be well marketed and exploited by clever young designers working in London.

Three young designers in Paris were among the first to respond to this wave of popular creativity and to channel it into the more accepted avenues of haute couture: Courrèges, Ungaro and Cardin.

Courrèges had begun his professional life as a cutter for Balenciaga (like the

Above: The late Sixties saw the emergence of several French designers who responded to the fashion revolution with energy and inventiveness. Courrèges designed the see-through mini-dress for a 1967 collection; he also experimented with shorts, trousers, and all-in-one suits, teaming them with thigh-length boots, as here, or short mid-shin boots for his dresses. His fancy for black model girls and immaculately tailored sporting clothes was caricatured accurately by a French cartoonist after his 1972 collection

great couturier he was a native of the Spanish-Basque area) and remained with him to learn his trade for ten years. This lent his clothes, however modern, a structured, sculpted look which he inherited along with Balenciaga's love of austere, rather statuesque outlines. He became independent in 1961, and significantly, he replaced himself at Balenciaga with Ungaro, his young protégé. The collections of greatest impact from Courrèges were shown in 1963 or 1964: he followed Mary Quant in grasping the new mood for a youthful iconoclastic style, and was the first couturier to raise hemlines to the rarefied heights of the mini, at mid-thigh. But his clothes remained essential couture, as opposed to ready-to-wear, in their quality of cut and cloth: fine quality gaberdine, light coloured plain wools matched with bold checks or contrasting stripes, particularly in white or beige. His basic shape was an 'A', bypassing the waist and ending with channel-seamed or bias-trimmed hem, supplemented by a lot of top-stitching, decorative double rows of buttons down suit fronts, and rather masculine mid-shin boots and mannish brimmed hats to match. The epitome of this particular look was shown in the spring collection of 1964.

Courrèges' other main offering to fashion in the mid-Sixties was his official recognition in couture circles of the trouser suit. For the first time, a matching jacket and trousers for women became acceptable formal wear for daytime professional life, more obviously for country or sporting occasions, and even more inventively for evening gala occasions. Courrèges became the socialites' couturier, and named among his clients the Begum Aga Khan, Princess Lee Radziwill, and the Duchess of Windsor. In the late Sixties and early Seventies, Courrèges continued with couture work, but he has not equalled the startling impact of his earlier collections. More significantly, his collections have been much copied by ready-to-wear manufacturers, and he has expanded his own boutique business internationally with great success. Jumpsuits, ribbed knitwear, men's sportswear, luggage, and other accessories have established the Courrèges name all over the world.

Ungaro, after serving his apprenticeship with Balenciaga for six years, joined Courrèges in 1964 for a year, after which he set up with a talented textile designer, Sonja Knapp. In 1965 he launched his own small first collection, inevitably bracketing himself with Courrèges as a

'Space Age' designer. The sharp-edged outlines of his neat dresses bore the inheritance of Balenciaga, but the stunning primary colours, pattern combinations and mannish cut indicated a new phase in modern fashion for women. Red on green, purple on yellow, spots on checks, stripes on flowers – all his hues, patterns and fabric mixtures passed into the ready-to-wear stock-in-trade for the following decade. The Sixties woman is symbolized by the model girls at Courrèges and Ungaro: the sophisticated 35-year-old of the Fifties with her thin crossed ankles and artificially high arched eyebrows, posing in her constricting straight skirt and stiletto heels was replaced by an outstandingly tall, bronzed athlete in jumpsuit and flat-heeled boots, or mini-skirt and tights with matching helmet. If the hair showed, it was a new version of the Twenties 'garçonne' look, created by London hairdresser Vidal Sassoon but soon copied by all women, pinheaded or moonfaced, throughout Europe and America.

Like Courrèges, Ungaro has also produced a successful range of ready-to-wear clothes, known as Parallèle, which by 1968 accounted for well over half of his turnover. The basic style of his ready-to-wear clothing is the same as his

Left: Glitter and fake, which had long been considered vulgar, made a spectacular return to popularity in the mid-Sixties. Without any intention of imitating expensive materials, synthetics shimmered and cheap shine became a virtue. Paco Rabanne in Paris made some of the prettiest outfits from them, like this gleaming mini from his autumn 1967 collection

couture look, but obviously the tailoring detail is reduced to cut down the cost, and the fabrics used are not so expensive or exclusive. The Parallèle range consists of extremely wearable, practical wool dresses and separates, light-coloured overcoats with small collars and often the neat double rows of buttons which are typical of the couturier's styling. Pastel coloured knits are teamed up with soft wool skirts or trousers (sometimes Bermuda shorts or divided skirts have been included) and there is also a full range of accessories. Sonja Knapp's fabric designs are used for the Parallèle range as well as for the more elaborate and expensive couture models. Her clear bright colours and bold geometrics are signatures of the Ungaro style.

The last and most important of the three Sixties couturiers is Pierre Cardin, who not only launched himself with futuristic clothes for both men and women, but diversified throughout the Seventies beyond pure fashion into hundreds of other projects, from furniture to hotels, to china and to glass. In pure fashion terms Cardin's contribution since the Sixties has been in his talent for combining couture skill with completely revolutionary clothing concepts. He uses architectural motifs and reduces gar-

ments to essential covers: tube dresses attached to breastplates or neck chokers in metal or leather; full flared coats springing from curved, stitched collars as wide as Elizabethan ruffs. In 1966 he launched in his couture range the first 'tubular moulded' knit dresses ever seen in Paris. Scallops, top stitching, appliquéd pockets in neat squared dresses are all marks of his style. As early as 1957 he moved into men's wear too, reflecting the new dandyism and adventurousness in male fashion, which had lain dormant for several decades, specifically in cut and colours. Cardin introduced the collarless jacket, tight-fitting double-breasted suits and a wide range of leather, ribbed-knit separates, zip-fronted track suits and other activity clothes. Not altogether successfully, he reintroduced tight-fitting stretch trousers with matching polo-necks and belted tabards for men.

Fashion for women in the mid-Sixties was very much a question of breaking rules. Successful designers in England and France reflected the youthful energy and gaiety to be seen in everyday clothing on the streets of London and Paris, or anywhere else in Europe. The most significant change was the dramatic rise in the hemline up to mid-thigh level.

Pierre Cardin (above) was the most successful and enduring of the Sixties French designers: this evening dress demonstrates his combination of classic couturier skill, simplicity of line and youthful taste for the unexpected

Left and below: Pierre Cardin's designs have always shown great variety, and an ability to see the modern woman's increased choices in life style and therefore clothing. He is equally successful in producing a gala evening dress, idiosyncratic day outfits, or characterful versions of classic clothes, like the overcoat shown below. This last model reveals his debt to Balenciaga, with whom he worked, in its generous cut and beautifully sculpted collar line

Skirts were of all shapes, culotte dresses (not a success) were no longer than Bermuda shorts and interest was focused on the legs. Teenagers' ankle-socks were taken up by big sister, who also borrowed her footballer brother's knee-high stockings. Legs began to appear in lacy stockings, at first obtainable only from speciality houses, but the amazed stocking manufacturers soon realized they had been offered the opportunity of a lifetime and began to create a wide variety of novelties – while the fabric manufacturers wondered how they could survive in a world where skirts were so short that they were almost at vanishing point.

Not only were stockings decorated with whorls, dots, flowers and trails of ivy, but the old-fashioned clock up the side reappeared and made plain flesh-coloured stockings appear as old-fashioned as black ones did in the Twenties. Even more novel were the stretch tights made necessary by the brevity of mini-skirts. When these had first appeared at the end of the Fifties, they made little impact outside active sportswear. Mary Quant in London and Valentino in Rome, among others, were quick to apply their talents to this new field. Though the modern leg-coverings could

not compare with the parti-coloured panache of Renaissance pages, which they resembled, they had one advantage denied their predecessors, and this was the invention of Lurex thread which enabled the modern girl to shimmer from ankle to thigh like a fairy prince.

Together with tights and conspicuous stockings came a radical change in shoes. Evening boots in silver or gold became popular, while others were of suede or doeskin, spur-chained, buckled or strapped, and some reached up to and over the knees, reminiscent of Edwardian pantomime boys. Plastic stocking-boots made their first appearance and Courrèges open-toed white boots were worn stoically by Parisians and Londoners alike all through a particularly cold and wet winter. A new substance, called Corfam, made a profound change in shoe fashions, for it not only kept out the wet but allowed the feet to breathe. Mary Quant was invited to style this novel material, with the result that the winter streets of the late Sixties were enlivened by hordes of gay red, green and yellow ankle boots.

The Sixties saw a drastic revision in underwear: slender pantees and minimal briefs replaced the pull-on girdle and the corselette; brassières were by-passed;

Above and above left: By the end of the decade, fashion photographers had arrived at a consciously playful rendering of the current mood. Shorts and kneesocks are accompanied by a provocative face and wild mane of hair, while the childlike frilled dress is worn by a girl with heavily stylized make-up, simulating an innocence which is no longer there. In the following decade, emancipation was to become more aggressive in tone

Above: The older-established Paris fashion houses responded more soberly to the new mood in women's dress. Dior produced this conventional response: grey flannel pants and double-breasted jacket. But there seemed little point in spending couture prices for a model that merely reflected ready-to-wear trends

and nightgowns were thrown away in favour of tiny sleep-suits.

Several young designers in the English wholesale market reflected the new tendency for unconventional clothes, chief among them Bill Gibb, Ossie Clark and Gina Fratini. The most original creator was probably Zandra Rhodes, who made up lovely fabrics, all designed and many painted by herself, into sensational dresses.

In 1967 'unisex' clothes, designed to be worn by both sexes, were to be found in all the collections, and by this date even the house of Dior carried trousers into evening wear by teaming them with

silk tunics in brilliant colours. Robin Hood leather jackets, Far West leather cowboy trousers and polo-necked pullovers were in feminine, as well as masculine, wardrobes.

An alternative to the unisex and mannish modes were flowing djellabas in gaudy stripes or heavily embroidered kaftans, forerunners of the free-for-all fancy dress epoch to which Gina Fratini added enchanting versions of Watteau dairy-maids in pretty cottons.

Modesty was a virtue no longer admired, and white satin hipster pants revealed the navel, but they were oddly teamed with a baby's bonnet and a full-

Left: Once again unisex — in the form of blue jeans — came to the rescue of a troubled fashion world, and the summer of 1969 saw the visitors to St Tropez and its environs — as well as to resorts all over the world — comfortably and well-dressed in jeans and bush shirts belted low on the hips

length lace coat. Perhaps the greatest iconoclast in Paris in the mid-Sixties to produce this state of chaos was Yves Saint Laurent, who had inherited the mantle at the house of Dior in 1958. He had been working as Dior's assistant for some time, and was already accepted as the great couturier's successor when Dior died in 1958. After military service, Yves Saint Laurent returned to revolutionize Dior in 1962. His most significant collection came in 1966 when he launched Pop Art on Paris. Black dresses with nude torsos printed dramatically down a length of plain sheath dress, see-through chiffons and other cartoon designs were the keynotes of this collection. Studded leather, copies of working-class street clothes, and the costumes of American pop culture idols took over in Yves Saint Laurent's salon. Slightly more marketable were the Mondrian-inspired geometric sheath dresses of 1965, which continued in vogue for some years. Like Cardin, Yves Saint Laurent soon followed into ready-to-wear with the launching in 1966 of the Rive Gauche chain of boutiques.

The general tendency throughout the Sixties was towards a more experimental, inventive, and youthful appearance. Clothes gained an ever more child-like

271

Above: 1969 was a year noted for its wild collections – Courrèges suggested the Egyptian look and produced strange figures such as the top one, which were partially covered in black sequin bands presumably thought to resemble mummy wrappings. He also gave one of the models a squared-off coiffure somewhat similar to those seen on the effigies of mummy coffin-lids

Right: No country was too far, no folk costume too fantastic for inclusion in the Paris scene of 1970. Féraud proposed an Indian mini-skirt of fringed and embroidered leather and added a warrior's head-band to an outfit that typifies the chaos and fancy of fashion at the end of the decade

look. Lanvin proposed capes similar to those worn by French schoolboys before the Second World War. These barely reached the knees, showed no skirt beneath but revealed a pair of legs clad in black stockings, with flat black shoes; with these was worn a beret, such as the boys also used to wear, perched on one side of the head.

In 1968 unisex fashions included feminine dandies wearing knickerbockers with coloured stockings and black shoes, or plaid trousers accompanied by matching jackets, contrasting waistcoats and fancy silk shirts. In the evening similar suits were proposed for both sexes, usually in velvet bound with braid and worn with wide Lavallière ties or white muslin and lace frilled shirts.

Several Paris houses essayed mid-length skirts both for coats and dresses. Saint Laurent's Hamlet-like ensemble of black tights allied to a black velvet jerkin and a floor-length maxi-coat presaged the ill-balanced costume of maxi-coat worn over mini-skirt which was prevalent if not fashionable during the winter of 1967. Dr Zhivago maxi-coats with high collars were seen accompanied by huge Cossack fur hats which ruined so many coiffures that wigs became an essential fashion item, not a luxury extra.

In summer the bare midriff was as much at home in the house as it had been for the last quarter of a century on the beach, but high fashion went one better and discarded the upper portion of the bikini. Cardin, among others, showed sarongs with only beads draping the torso, Ungaro offered some metal breast-plates, and to a simple transparent shift reminiscent of Queen Nefertiti's, Courrèges added only a few sequins.

Men's and women's clothes became increasingly similar, with blue jeans as the most popular common denominator. One young couple, after a conventional society wedding, discarded tulle and tails and left for their honeymoon as identical twins in pale blue hipster outfits, the hair of both heads similar in length and cut. Shops offered side by side the same styles so that He and She could do their shopping together. This new marketing style reflected the increasing freedom of women, enabling them to have careers and direct their own lives. On the whole, however, the unisex costumes tended to be conservative and those who set this fashion, Hardy Amies and Mr Fish in London, Bernard Lanvin and Ted Lapidus in Paris, were themselves crisply tailored – albeit colourfully – with collar and tie.

Three British designers emerged in the
Sixties, and have continued in prominence
through the following decade. Bill Gibb is
noted for his beautifully patterned knitwear
and combinations of leather or fur with
fabric (above). Zandra Rhodes (represented
by a Sixties design for Bianca Jagger, right)
is perhaps the most original and energetic of
the trio, slashing chiffons and frizzling silks
for a succession of outstanding evening
clothes; and Jean Muir produces endlessly
wearable but very modern outfits like these
three from a late Seventies collection (right).
Her use of soft jerseys and subdued glitter is
typical.

By 1970, peasant costumes were in most Paris collections. Féraud showed a dress of white wool printed in black and bright colours, full-sleeved and full-skirted, worn with short black suede boots. Cardin allied a floral printed skirt to a black leotard and high black boots. Ethnic fashions came from all countries. There were gaucho trousers tucked into knee-high boots, cheongsams from the Far East, sarongs from Malaysia and embroideries from Japan, and the display of national costume made the international journalists wonder if they had come to Paris, France, or had been set down in some more distant country.

In London the boutiques took full advantage of this individualistic and ethnic type of dress. Mongolian fur coats were to be seen everywhere in the King's Road, Chelsea or High Street, Kensington, flat Greek tapestry bags hung from shoulders and Laura Ashley's country girls in long printed cotton skirts with lace-trimmed bodices and puff sleeves became acceptable fashion at even the most formal of evening occasions. Status and luxury in clothing were no longer fashion requirements either for the established or the aspiring.

The general trend towards individuality and general commercialism con-

tinued throughout the 1970s. All the revolutionary elements of the 1960s continued to present themselves with greater confidence. It would not be at all surprising to attend a formal evening party and to find one woman wearing an original Fortuny, or a Poiret 1930s model dress, another in a jewelled Indian kaftan, and another in a denim or satin trouser suit. This variety in style was also seen in daytime wear for both sexes. The Seventies saw a sudden reversal in hemlines, with levels dropping to mid-calf. The aggressive emancipation of women seen in the Sixties has relaxed into a truly varied attitude to clothes. Denim jeans have remained popular for all occasions, and are permissible even in some offices. More men are able to wear casual sports-style jackets and slacks to work, instead of the regulation dark suit and tie. Perhaps less attractively, it is universally common for men to remain in informal clothing for evening wear while the women adopt their varied fantasies. The early Seventies saw great interest for both sexes in exotic floral prints for shirts and dresses, or rich coloured geometrics, as an off-shoot of the ethnic influences in clothing. The droopy skirts, boots and voluminous capes for women have gradually been left aside in

Right: In England Laura Ashley continued to produce simple cotton, peasant dresses which managed to be both old-world and absolutely new. Her contemporary versions of Kate Greenaway and Granny styles and her delightful flower prints, original and practical, were seized upon by the pretty, now impecunious young: in the Seventies money became gradually tighter

favour of a more tailored style, a 'layered' way of dressing which is practical and inexpensive. A typical mid-Seventies daytime outfit would be a shirt-style blouse, a cardigan with elbow length sleeves, or a bolero with matching skirt, possibly teamed with a co-ordinating knitted cardigan or blazer, and covered up with a loose-fitting wool coat or trench-style raincoat with wool lining. For casual wear, one of the most noticeable developments towards the end of the Seventies was a rapid expansion in athletic clothing, tracksuits and stretch fabric two-pieces, unisex outfits no longer confined to the running track or gymnasium. Teamed with diamanté jewellery and perilously high heels, they have passed for evening wear.

A significant Seventies trend was the increasing interest in lightweight clothing for both day and night. A beautifully simple wool or silk jersey two-piece from one of the better ready-to-wear manufacturers, such as Kenzo of Jap, Emmanuelle Khanh, Sonja Rykiel or Missoni, matches in quality or design and attractiveness the best of couture. (It is significant that Yves Saint Laurent has sensed the return to a simpler sophistication by producing some Hollywood collections, imitating the sharp-edged

elegance of Lauren Bacall and other stars in the Thirties and Forties.)

Italian designers, who participated less actively in the fashion upheaval of the 1960s, have gained authority over the past decade. The new centre for Italian fashion is not Rome but Milan, where over fifty new designers show in a massive exhibition building known as the Feria. A small initial group including Krizia, Missoni, Albini, and Cadette have since attracted a larger number of designers. They specialize in easy-to-wear separates using fine wools, jerseys and silks, none of the fabrics being at all bulky or substantial. The new essence of elegance is not to show status through the richness and thickness of the fabric worn, as in previous eras: this is obviously influenced by rising standards of living that bring warmer, more comfortable environments. The element of protection in modern clothing has been

reduced to a minimum for both the sexes. Men seldom wear the heavy Melton overcoats of the Fifties, and if women wear furs it is just as likely to be a trenchcoat lined in fur as a full-length mink. Scarcity of natural pelts is becoming an important factor in such choices, combined with modern attitudes about the preservation of wildlife, which makes the wearing of real, rare furs almost distasteful.

Two leading couturiers reflecting this trend are Mila Schon, recognized for her light unlined swirls of coats, remarkable for a suppleness of tailoring and an appearance of being without seams; and the knitwear of Missoni, where the combination of pattern and texture reaches new subtlety and beauty. Significantly, feather-weight knits have almost completely replaced double jerseys in the Seventies. In France the best exponent of the contemporary relaxed elegance is

Above and above left: Early Seventies softly casual styles, like the boy's patterned trousers, long hair, and the girl's floppy-brimmed hat, contrast sharply with popular fashion towards the end of the decade. Reflecting increasing social unrest, lack of money and unemployment, young people's clothing became aggressively ugly and anti-fashion, like these two Manchester 'punk-rockers'

Right: This end-of-the-Seventies suit by Krizia, the Italian ready-to-wear designer, shows the more widespread, general trend emerging from Italy: a combination of the classic and the revolutionary, with a return to couture standards of quality in fabric and finish

Far left: The wool ensemble from Missoni's autumn 1968 collection typifies the layered, comfortable style popularized by the Italians

Above: A similarly restrained and practical coat from another Italian designer, Versace

Left: A typical late Seventies ready-to-wear outfit by the British manufacturer, Cojana, demonstrating the trend towards practical, long-lasting clothes

Karl Lagerfeld, who sells his ready-to-wear clothing under the name of Chloe. He designs furs, knitwear, shoes and fabrics, besides his ranges of dresses, separates and coats.

These designers would claim that the issue of hemline or silhouette is now irrelevant. Sonja Rykiel once said, 'My fashion philosophy is really very classic. It's always the same sweater that I sell, the same shape but with different motifs . . . Fashion madness will force women to become more intellectual. I think it is impossible to tell women how to dress. The important thing is to offer slipovers, pullovers, dresses and let women do their own thing . . . we sell a lot of long dresses. If women feel like shortening them, that's no problem. It's the mood that counts.'

However, in the second half of the Seventies, two popular new styles moved away from this rule-less state. One is a tendency to break with the chaotic ethnic look of the Sixties. The extreme violence of the 'Punk Rock' look in England, with chain mail, leather jackets, safety pins pierced through ear lobes and nostrils, and violently coloured dyed hair, is giving way to a revival of the early 1960s 'Mod' look: neat cropped hair, immaculately groomed boys in tight-fitting suits, and girls in neat school blouses and slacks.

Left and above: Karl Lagerfeld, who designs under the name of Chloe, produced these styles in the late Seventies, showing the interest in soft fabrics, knitted textures and simple lines. The temporary experimenting with synthetics has gone

Left and above: The height of elegance in the late Seventies was not to look rich, but practical and economical. More designs by Karl Lagerfeld demonstrate a casual chic which became the present aim

Left: Three outfits by American designer Bill Blass illustrate the crisp, sporty elegance which is typically Transatlantic, and beginning to be emulated by women in Europe

Right: This evening gown by Yuki, one of Britain's most successful contemporary designers, is a reminder that for some women, mystery and allure are still essential aspects of their choice in dress

For the first time American designers and classic American taste may prove highly influential in Europe. The three main American designers in this area are Bill Blass, Halston and Oscar de la Renta, who produce neat elegant wool dresses, separates with small flower-sprigged blouses and heavily classical trench-style overcoats. More inventive and futuristic is the work of Bonnie Cashin, who designs principally with leather and knits, making enormous coats with capacious sleeveholes and rolled turtle-necks. She combines tweeds, knits and hides with an awareness of the return to modesty and natural-looking clothing — in keeping with a growing awareness of ecological balance and a need to conserve natural resources. The clean crispness of the American way of dressing may yet prove to be the most practical and feminine fashion for the Eighties.

The energetic growth and diversity of the fashion industry in the last twenty years is reflected in the growing internationalism of its products. Turning full circle, it is not surprising that Barbara Hulanicki of Biba should now find herself manufacturing high fashion in the Third World, with the centre of her empire in São Paulo, Brazil. As fashion journalist Serena Sinclair has pointed out, from Caracas through Europe to Tokyo, the status symbol has become the 'label' product. Luggage marked Vuittoni, blouses printed with YSL, Givenchy, Pucci or Hermes scarves, Cardin anything; the logo indicates a desire for an easily recognizable declaration of status and wealth. As the developed world moves into an era of modesty in its clothing styles, the rest of the world is anxious to acquire the symbols of material wealth, and the entire extravagant fashion cycle will assuredly begin once again.

Glossary

Abolla Short Roman military cloak, worn over one shoulder and fastened at the throat with a *fibula*, derived from the Greek, *Chlamys*.

Aglet, aiglet or **aiguillette** A metal tag attached to a ribbon used as a fastening device during the late Middle Ages and Tudor period, replaced during the mid-seventeenth century by buttons and hooks but still used today in some military and ceremonial costume.

Aigrette Term originally used to describe a plume of feathers worn in a woman's hair.

Alb Long white tunic of Roman origin, worn as a secular garment until the ninth century A.D., after which it was strictly liturgical.

Alençon lace An exceptionally fine hand-made French lace dating from the seventeenth century.

Amice A liturgical hood of white linen, worn by priests up to the thirteenth century.

Armseye Term used by dressmakers to describe the armhole where the sleeve is joined to the bodice of a garment.

Artois Eighteenth-century overcoat worn by both sexes and named after the Count of Artois, brother of Louis XVI. The coat was generally calf-length or longer and fitted with several overlapping capes.

Ascot A man's cravat with wide ends which became very fashionable in the mid-nineteenth century.

Astrakhan Tightly curled wool from the karakul lambs of Russia, widely used for collars and hats.

Bagnolette Short, hooded cape fashionable at the beginning of the eighteenth century.

Bag-wig Powdered wig with the ends tied into a black silk bag. Worn during the eighteenth century.

Balagnie cloak Cape with a deep collar which was fashionable in the seventeenth century. It fastened under the collar with a cord and could be worn draped either over one or both shoulders.

Baldric A wide sash of silk or leather worn diagonally across the chest and used to carry a sword, horn and other personal effects.

Basque A continuation of an upper garment a little below the waist forming a short skirt.

Bateau neck A straight, boat-shaped neckline running from shoulder to shoulder, usually the same depth front and back.

Birrus A thick hooded cloak similar to that worn by Roman citizens which was worn throughout the Middle Ages.

Blanchet A type of doublet of cotton, generally white, with sleeves and collar and sometimes fur-lined.

Bloomers Full trousers gathered in just above the ankles named after the American reformer, Mrs Amelia Jenks Bloomer, who first wore them in 1850.

Braccae Comprehensive term which described a piece of fabric wrapped round the hips and legs and worn by Asiatics, Barbarians and northern Europeans.

Braces Implements used to hold up trousers which were first used in the mid-eighteenth century, when shorter waistcoats covered less of the breeches. Originally they were simple cords, but, by 1840, elastic braces had been introduced.

Brandenburgs Ornamental fastenings on outer garments.

Bucksain Man's padded overcoat, popular in the mid-nineteenth century.

Buffonts A scarf of gauze used to cover the décolletage of women's gowns in the late eighteenth century.

Bum-roll or **roll farthingale** Padding, in the shape of a sausage, which was worn around the hips, and which served as a popular version of the farthingale.

Bustle Wire or whalebone cage worn by women after the decline of the crinoline to support the fullness of the dress at the back.

Camisole An underbodice or the fitted upper part of a petticoat.

Capa Wide, hooded cloak worn in Spain and France during the sixteenth and seventeenth centuries. The same word was also used to describe the evening cloaks in the Romantic period.

Caraco A gown fashionable in France during the late 1780s. It was very long-waisted and fitted with a peplum.

Cardigan Originally a short military jacket worn by the British Army during the Crimean war, named after Lord Cardigan.

Cardinal Woman's seventeenth-century shoulder cape with a hood.

Carrick A great coat fitted with one or more shoulder capes. It was originally a fashionable garment for gentlemen, but later it was worn only by coachmen.

Cassock A flared, knee-length coat with slit sleeves which was worn in the seventeenth century by soldiers and huntsmen. A longer version is worn by the clergy.

Challis A lightweight fabric originally made from a mixture of wool and silk but now made from fine wool, or wool mixed with rayon or cotton.

Chanmarre A full, early sixteenth-century coat. It was generally lined with fur and decorated with braid.

Chaperon A hood with shoulder cape, which was worn by men throughout the Middle Ages.

Chesterfield Named after Lord Chesterfield who sponsored it, an overcoat of the late nineteenth and early twentieth centuries, generally black with a velvet collar.

Chiton The basic linen garment in ancient Greece worn by both sexes.

Chitterlings Linen or lace frills worn on the front of men's shirts during the late eighteenth century and throughout the nineteenth.

Chlamys Short military cloak of ancient Greece. It was a simple rectangle of woollen material fastened with a fibula on the right shoulder, covering the left arm but leaving the right uncovered.

Codpiece A padded bag buckled to the front of a man's hose to conceal the opening.

Coif A simple white linen hood made to the shape of the head. It was sometimes worn alone but more often acted as an undergarment for a more elaborate headdress.

Cote-hardie A tunic worn by both men and women from the late twelfth century to the fourteenth.

Crinoline A petticoat stiffened with horse-hair which gave skirts a bell shape in the 1840s. By the 1850s, it had become a quilted cotton petticoat reinforced with whalebone. It was later replaced by a light metal cage.

Cucullus Name given by the Romans to the hood of working clothes.

Culottes Breeches worn by men in the late sixteenth and early seventeenth centuries. Since that time the word has generally been used to describe the divided skirt worn by women as casual dress.

Cyclas Tunic worn in ancient and medieval times.

Dagging Ornamental edging which originated in Germany and was popular from the fourteenth century to the seventeenth. The edge of the material was serrated, or cut, in a number of different patterns.

Dalmatic A long, wide robe with flaring sleeves, which originated in Dalmatia and was often made of white Dalmatian wool. It has been used for court ceremonies since Ancient Roman times and is still sometimes worn by Church dignitaries.

Djellaba A type of cloak, hooded and with long, wide sleeves, from North Africa and the Near East.

Faggotting An embroidery stitch, often

used in making a decorative join between two edges.

Farthingale A huge metal wheel worn round the hips over which the fabric of the skirt was stretched. The fashion started in Spain in the early sixteenth century, and from there it spread throughout Europe.

Fibula A safety pin, invented in prehistoric times and used to fasten clothes in almost all the ancient civilizations. They were often of gold and richly decorated.

Fichu A small lace scarf which was knotted round the neck with the points falling onto the chest, fashionable in the late eighteenth and early nineteenth centuries.

Fillet A head-band or any long strip of material suitable for binding.

Flammeum A saffron-coloured full-length wedding veil worn by Roman brides.

Flounce A strip of material, gathered and sewn on by its upper edge to a garment, usually to the skirt of a lady's dress.

Fontanges A hairstyle originating in about 1680 in which the hair was curled and worn at the top of the head, secured by a ribbon.

Frock-coat A knee-length overcoat, popular in Victorian England.

Frogs Decorative fastenings of long, braided loops and buttons.

Furbelow A term used to describe a decorative trimming, such as a flounce or frill.

Gabardine Originally a woollen cloak, the term now refers to a closely woven twill fabric.

Gaiters A covering for the ankle made from either leather or stout linen. They are generally buttoned down the side and were often fitted with a strap which passed under the sole of the shoe.

Garde-corps Full outer tunic introduced in the fourteenth century as a substitute for, or to be worn over, the surcote.

Gipon A very early form of quilted doublet, worn as an undergarment.

Godet, Gore or **Gusset** Any triangular piece of material inserted in a garment to give shape. In particular, *gusset* came to mean the triangular piece of elastic set into the side of boots in the nineteenth century.

Gonelle Long tunic worn by both sexes in the Dark Ages.

Guepière A type of corset which appeared in the 1940s.

Guimp Originally a simple piece of white linen worn on the head by women of the fourteenth and fifteenth centuries. In the nineteenth century, the word was revived and used to describe a short chemise which covered a deep décolletage.

Haïk An oblong piece of cloth, usually of hand-woven wool, which Arabs drape round the head and body, as an outer garment. The *Haïk Royal* is the name given by Egyptologists to the almost transparent, draped garments worn by royalty in ancient Egypt.

Haincelin A short houppelande, fashionable in France during the early fifteenth century.

Halter-neckline Fashionable neckline for ladies' evening dresses in the 1930s. It has a high panel at the front which is tied behind the neck, leaving the back and shoulders entirely uncovered.

Headrail Cotton or linen headdress worn by Anglo-Saxon women from the fifth to the eleventh century.

Himation Outer garment worn by both sexes in ancient Greece.

Hoop-petticoat English name for paniers of the eighteenth century.

Houppelande Long tunic worn by both sexes throughout the fifteenth century. It was a very long voluminous gown with enormous sleeves and a high belted waist. It was generally made from a richly embroidered fabric lined with fur.

Kaftan A long full coat or gown worn by both sexes in oriental countries which came into fashion in the West during the 1960s.

Kaunakès A long-haired fur pelt, or a garment made from such a pelt, worn by the Sumerians in the third millenium B.C. Later the term was used to describe a tufted fabric made from wool which was very similar in appearance to animal fur.

Kerchief A cloth used as a headcovering.

Kirtle A woman's chemise or petticoat worn from the fourteenth century to the seventeenth. It was one of several terms used to describe this garment.

Lacerna Long, flowing cloak with fitted hood, originally from Gaul, but later adopted by the Romans for protection against the cold. It was full enough to be worn over the toga.

La Modiste A piece of lace which was used to conceal the deep décolletage of women's eighteenth-century gowns.

Leg-o'mutton sleeves Sleeves fashionable for women's gowns during the 1830s and, again, at the end of the nineteenth century. They were fitted from wrist to elbow, but from elbow to shoulder they ballooned out and were pleated into the armseye.

Liripipe A long strip of material, originally used in the thirteenth and fourteenth centuries to decorate chaperon hoods. At

one stage they were so long that they hung to the wearer's feet and there was a fashion for wrapping them round the neck and throwing the loose end over the shoulder.

Macaroni A derogatory term to describe the young dandies of the 1760s who were extremely fussy about their appearance and were considered effeminate by their contemporaries.

Macramé A knotted lace originally made in Arabia but later made in Italy. It is used in the manufacture of scarves and shawls.

Manta Most commonly used to describe the Spanish shawl of the poncho type, a simple rectangle of cloth with a hole cut in the middle through which the head was placed. The remainder of the fabric was then allowed to fall freely round the wearer's shoulders.

Mantilla A shawl worn to this day by Spanish women. It is generally worn so as to cover the head, shoulders and part of the face.

Mantle First used during the fifteenth century, this describes any form of sleeveless cloak.

Mathilde A broad strip of embroidery which was used to decorate the front of dresses at the beginning of the nineteenth century. It was named after the supposed maker of the Bayeux tapestry, Queen Matilda, whose handiwork was put on public display in 1804.

Mob cap Linen night-cap worn by ladies in the eighteenth century. In the second half of the eighteenth century the garment was worn under large hats.

Muff A cylinder of padded fur carried to keep the hands warm. They originated in France in the early seventeenth century.

Neckstock A form of cravat worn in the late eighteenth and early nineteenth centuries.

Norfolk jacket An essentially English belted jacket of the late nineteenth century, pleated at the front and back and generally made from tweed. It is still worn now with knickerbockers for sport and for travelling in the country.

Opera cloak A knee-length cloak worn from about 1850, generally of velvet with a large standing collar which was tied with tasselled cords.

Opera hat A collapsible hat invented in 1823 which could be snapped open or shut by means of internal springs. It is also known as a gibus hat.

Orby An American single-breasted cutaway

frock-coat which became fashionable at the beginning of the twentieth century.

Oxford Bags Englishmen's trousers of the 1920s with enormous flared bottoms, often up to 24 inches wide.

Oxford gillie Man's late nineteenth-century sports-shoe which laced at the instep, with the laces fastened round the ankles.

Paenula A Roman outergarment made in heavy wool or leather for wear in bad weather. It was formed like a poncho and could be worn with or without a hood.

Pagne-skirt A loin-cloth or short petticoat.

Pagoda sleeves The term was first used to describe the sleeves of men's coats during the 1730s which had a deep cuff almost reaching the elbow, becoming narrower as opposed to flaring out. The term was revived during the nineteenth century when women of the second Empire had similar sleeves on their gowns.

Paison Greek word for the trousers worn by the Persians.

Palatine At first, this was a small fur stole inspired by the Palatinate Princess, Charlotte Elizabeth of Bavaria, in the late seventeenth century. It later referred to a deep collar of lawn or lace.

Palisade or **commode** A wire frame covered with silk used in the Fontanges headdress.

Palla Latin word for Greek peplos.

Pallium The Greek outergarment, equivalent to the Roman toga.

Paniers Reed or whalebone cages which were worn at the hips by women at the beginning of the eighteenth century. At their most exaggerated they filled the skirt out to a circumference of more than eight feet.

Pantalettes Little girls' pantaloons which were worn in the mid-nineteenth century and fell below the skirt hem.

Passement The name given to all forms of lace in the sixteenth and seventeenth centuries. Later the word changed to *passementerie* and described all kinds of woven ornamentation.

Pattens Wooden platform soles designed to keep shoes clear of the dirt in the streets.

Peascod-bellied doublet Padded doublets of the late sixteenth century which gave an exaggerated, pointed pot-belly to the wearer.

Pelerine Woman's cloak of the nineteenth century made from silk, velvet or fur. It was usually short, covering the shoulders.

Pelicon Fur-lined tunic worn in the thirteenth, fourteenth and fifteenth centuries between the chemise and the cote.

Pelisse A term which has been used to describe several different fashions. It most commonly refers to a long cloak, usually fur-lined and padded, which was worn by both sexes in the Middle Ages (often called a *pelisson*). This fashion was revived by ladies of the Romantic era, who wore fur-lined, fur-trimmed coats for evening outings. By the end of the nineteenth century it was men who were wearing the pelisse, again as a heavy fur coat for evening wear. In the mid-eighteenth century the term was used to describe ladies' ankle-length cloaks of silk or velvet either with slits for the arms or sleeves. A century later it described thick outdoor coats worn by children.

Peplos Outer garment worn by the women of Ancient Greece. It was a large rectangle of material fastened on both shoulders with fibulae.

Peplum The Roman version of the Greek word *peplos* was *peplum*. The word came to mean a short over-skirt or flounce attached to the waist-line of a dress, blouse or jacket.

Petticoat breeches Loose flowing breeches, fashionable in the mid-seventeenth century.

Phrygian bonnet A primitive cap with chin strap of felt or leather, which was worn by the Ancient Greeks. In Roman times, a freed slave was presented with such a cap and the Phrygian bonnet came to be a symbol of liberty. It was later adopted by the French Revolutionaries.

Pileus Felt cap worn by men in Rome.

Plus-fours Very baggy breeches which originated in Britain in the 1920s, so called because they reached four inches below the knee where they were fastened in the same way as knickerbockers.

Points Metal-tipped laces which were used to fasten sleeves into the armseye and doublets to breeches.

Polonaise A late eighteenth century gown with a boned bodice fastened at the neckline and cut away at the waist to show a waistcoat.

Pompadour Hairstyle in which the hair is brushed off the forehead into a high roll at the top of the head.

Postillion A gathered basque attached to the bottom of the bodice during the late nineteenth century.

Poufs Padded cushions worn under hooped skirts or under the voluminous hair-styles of the late eighteenth century. The term was also sometimes used to refer to the coiffures themselves.

Pourpoint An alternative name for a doublet.

Princess dress Dress popular in the last third of the nineteenth century. The skirt and bodice were cut in one piece and the fullness was at the back.

Raglan sleeve A method of sewing in the sleeve devised by Lord Raglan during the Crimean War. The seam runs from underarm to neck without any other shoulder seam, which allowed greater mobility. The word *Raglan* alone is used to describe a man's overcoat fitted with sleeves of this type.

Redingote A man's double-breasted top-coat worn in France during the eighteenth century. It had a large collar, revers, and sometimes a short shoulder cape. It was adopted by women towards the end of the century.

Reefer A thigh-length top-coat particularly favoured by seamen.

Reticule Small handbags, used during the Directoire period in France.

Robe Anglaise A child's dress of the late nineteenth century; also the plain white muslin dress which became fashionable in Paris in Marie-Antoinette's day.

Ruche A frill of fluted or crimped lace or gauze, used as a trimming, particularly around the neck. Ruching at the neck developed into the ruff in the late sixteenth century.

Ruff A starched collar of lawn or cambric which encircled the neck, worn during the late sixteenth century and early seventeenth.

Ruffle A strip of fabric pleated to a straight edge as a frill.

Sack-coat Any short loose masculine coat.

Sagum A rectangle of cloth originally worn by the ancient Celts. It was draped round the left shoulder, fastened at the right, and, at night, it doubled as a blanket.

Sailor suit Child's outfit worn from the mid-nineteenth century to the beginning of the second World War. It was inspired by the uniform of the French and English navies.

Schenti The loincloth worn in Ancient Egypt.

Siren-suit A one-piece overall worn during the second World War in England. It was so called because it could be put on with the minimum delay when the air-raid sirens sounded.

Slashing The Renaissance fashion for making slits in an outer garment, through which were revealed areas of contrasting colour of the fabric of the under-garment.

Slicker A waterproof overcoat made either from oilskin or a rubberized material.

Snood A form of coarse hair net worn from

the thirteenth century onwards to keep women's hair in place. During the fifteenth and sixteenth centuries snoods became more elaborate and they were frequently decorated with pearls and precious stones.

Soccus A wide cloak, fastened at the shoulder, generally worn by royalty in the Middle Ages on ceremonial occasions.

Sottana A woman's tunic worn in the twelfth and thirteenth centuries in Italy. It was often of striped material and worn as an undergown by adults or as an upper gown by young girls.

Spat A short gaiter, covering the upper part of the foot and the ankle, which fastened under the shoe. Spats were widely worn in both America and Britain during the late nineteenth and early twentieth centuries. They were generally made from linen and decorated with buttons down the side.

Spencer A very short-waisted jacket originally worn by women in the 1790s over their Empire dresses. Later, a similar style was adopted by some regiments of the army as a mess jacket.

Stola Long, lightweight robe worn by Roman women, belted—often in two places—and fitted with short sleeves.

Stomacher A decorative V-shaped panel attached to the front of a woman's bodice during the sixteenth, seventeenth and eighteenth centuries.

Strophium A band of linen used to support the breasts of women in ancient Rome.

Subucula An additional under-tunic of wool, worn by the Romans under their tunic proper, for protection against the cold.

Succinta A belt worn in ancient Rome. It was generally worn at the waist and was used to tuck up excess material while walking.

Surcote Term used throughout the Middle Ages to describe the top tunic worn by either sex.

Swag Hanging folds of material used to decorate women's gowns towards the end of the eighteenth century.

Tab A small flap sewn into a garment either for a practical or decorative purpose.

Tabard A military or ceremonial tunic top worn from the thirteenth century to the sixteenth. It was a simple garment, similar to a dalmatic, put on over the head and open at the sides.

Tablion An oblong embroidered panel which decorated Byzantine mantles. The panel, worked in metallic and coloured threads, usually portrayed the emperor.

Tails English slang for a man's formal evening dress. It comprises a black serge swallow-tail coat with silk lapels, and black serge trousers which are decorated with braid down the side seam.

Tassel A bunch or thick fringe of threads or small cords tied at the top to make them hang in an ornamental pendant.

Tatting A narrow strip of lace, normally used for edging, which is made by knotting each loop of thread using a small shuttle.

Tent Term used to describe an inverted V silhouette, pioneered by the great Spanish designer, Balenciaga, in 1951.

Tholia High, pointed hat with a brim worn by the women of ancient Greece.

Tippet A long, thin streamer of material, used to decorate medieval costume, and which is usually attached to the sleeve.

Toga The most important outer-garment for Roman citizens and an indication of their status. The toga changed in both size and in the manner of folding through the centuries, but it was basically a single piece of white woollen material draped elaborately round the body. Different coloured stripes decorated the toga to denote some particular government office or position of respect.

Toggle A simple fastening method with buttons constructed from a wooden peg, held in place with a piece of cord and pushed through a loop for fastening.

Toque Term used today to describe a woman's small, close-fitting hat, usually without a brim.

Torque A ring-like neck or wrist ornament of Celtic origin, usually of twisted gold wire or hollow gold tubing with decorative ends.

Tricorne A hat with the brim turned up on three sides.

Trotteur French term for woman's early twentieth-century costume, comprising a tailored suit and sturdy shoes, suitable for outdoor wear.

Trunk-hose Name for the garment which extended from the waist to the knee in the Middle Ages, before the word 'breeches' was adopted.

Tunic à la Mameluck A woman's tunic fashionable in France in 1801. It was short with sleeves, and was named after Napoleon's campaign in Egypt.

Ulster A loose-fitting, calf-length man's overcoat, usually double-breasted with a full or half-belt. It was originally made and worn in Northern Ireland, but, during the early twentieth century, it was widely fashionable in America.

Vair One of the most valuable furs of the Middle Ages, probably the squirrel.

Venetians Balloon-shaped breeches of the late sixteenth and early seventeenth centuries.

Verdingale An alternative name for the farthingale.

Visagière The open part of a hood which surrounds the face.

Visite A large buttoned shawl with two front slits, fashionable in the late nineteenth century as a form of cloak.

Vitta A headband worn by Roman women which not only held their hair in place but also denoted their status as free-born citizens.

Volant (1) French word for a flounce or ruffle. (2) A light jerkin worn in the second half of the eighteenth century. It was sleeveless, open at the front and fastened with a single button at the neck.

Watteau gown One of several early eighteenth-century styles named after the French painter, Jean-Antoine Watteau. This was the principal form of ladies' gown of the period; it was a loose sack-dress worn over a tight bodice with a very full underskirt.

Wimple A simple piece of linen worn by women in early medieval times. It was worn in a number of ways, but it generally covered the head, neck and sides of the face.

Costume Collections

A selection of costume collections around the world

Australia
National Gallery of Victoria,
180 St Kilda Road, MELBOURNE, Victoria

Austria
Kunsthistorisches Museum,
VIENNA 1, Burgring 5

Belgium
Musées Royaux d'Art et Histoire,
10 Parc du Cinquantenaire, BRUSSELS

Canada
Glenbow-Alberta Institute,
902 11th Avenue South West, CALGARY 3

Royal Ontario Museum,
100 Queen's Park, TORONTO 5

Denmark
De Danske Kongers Kronologiske,
Samling Paa Rosenborg, COPENHAGEN

France
Musée du Costume de la Ville de Paris,
11 avenue du President Wilson, PARIS 16e
(This museum, which is attached to the
Musée Carnavalet, houses a collection of
costumes dating from 1725.)

Musée des Arts Décoratifs,
Palais du Pavillon Louvre, de Marsan,
107 rue de Rivoli, PARIS 1er

Musée de Bretagne, 20 quai Emile Zola,
RENNES, Ille-et-Vilaine
(Nineteenth-century costume collection)

Federal Republic of Germany
Historisches Museum,
Untermainkai 14, FRANKFURT

Museum für Hamburgische Geschichte,
Holstenwall 24, HAMBURG

Bayerisches Nationalmuseum,
Prinzregentenstr 3, MUNICH 22

Italy
Museo Stibbert,
via di Montughi 7, 50139 FLORENCE

Museo Correr, Piazza San Marco,
Procuratie Nuove, VENICE

Raccolta Delle Stampe,
Achille Bertarelli, Castello Sforzesco, MILAN

Museo Diocesano d'Arte Sacra,
Palazzo Vescovile, VOLTERRA

The Netherlands
Rijksmuseum,
Stadhouderskade 42, AMSTERDAM

Norway
Kunstindustrimuseet i Oslo,
St Olavsgate 1, OSLO

Portugal
Museu de Arte Popular,
Praça do Imprevio Betern, LISBON

Spain
Museo del Pueblo Español,
Plaza de la Marina Española, MADRID

Sweden
Kungl. Livrustkammaren,
115 21 STOCKHOLM

Nordiska Museet,
S-115 21 STOCKHOLM, Djurgårdsvägen 14/18

Switzerland
Industrie – und Gewerbe museum,
Vadianstr 2, ST GALLEN

Bernisches Historisches Museum,
Helvetiaplatz 5, BERNE

United Kingdom
The Museum of Costume, The Assembly
Rooms, Alfred Street, BATH BA1 2QH

City Museum and Art Gallery,
Congreve Street, BIRMINGHAM B3 3DH

Bolling Hall Museum, Brompton Avenue,
BRADFORD, Yorkshire BD4 7LP

Snowshill Manor, Snowshill,
BROADWAY, Worcestershire WR12 7JU

The Red House Museum and Art Gallery,
Quay Road, CHRISTCHURCH,
Hants BH23 1 BU

Carnegie Dunfermline Trust,
Abbey Park House, Abbey Park Place,
DUNFERMLINE, Fife KY12 7PB

Churchill Gardens Museum,
Venn's Lane, HEREFORD HR1 1DE

Hereford City Library and Museum,
Broad Street, HEREFORD HR4 9AN

Ipswich Museum and Art Galleries,
High Street, IPSWICH, Suffolk IP1 3QH

Worcestershire County Museum,
Hartlebury Castle, Hartlebury,
KIDDERMINSTER, Worcestershire DY11 7XX

Wygston's House (Costume Museum),
25 St Nicolas Circle, LEICESTER LE1 5LD

Bethnal Green Museum (branch of
Victoria and Albert Museum),
Cambridge Heath Road, LONDON E2 9PA

British Museum (Department of Prints
and Drawings),
Great Russell Street, LONDON WC1B 3DG

Horniman Museum and Library,
100 London Road, Forest Hill,
LONDON SE23 3PQ

The London Museum, Kensington Palace,
LONDON W8 4PX

Victoria and Albert Museum,
Exhibition Road, LONDON SW7 2RL

The Gallery of English Costume,
Platt Hall, Wilmslow Road, Rusholme,
MANCHESTER M14 5LL

The Symington Museum of Period Corsetry,
R. & W. H. Symington & Co. Ltd.,
Church Square, MARKET HARBOROUGH,
Leicestershire LE16 7NB

Central Museum and Art Gallery,
Guildhall Road, NORTHAMPTON NN1 1DP

City of Nottingham Museum and
Art Gallery,
The Castle, Castle Place,
NOTTINGHAM NG1 6EL

Museum and Art Galleries, High Street,
PAISLEY, Renfrewshire PA1 2BB

Castle Howard Museum, YORK YO6 7DA

USA
Boston Museum of Fine Arts,
BOSTON, Massachusetts 02115

Brooklyn Museum,
188 Eastern Parkway, Brooklyn,
NEW YORK 11238

Cincinnati Art Museum,
Eden Park, CINCINNATI, Ohio 45202

The Metropolitan Museum of Art,
Fifth Avenue and 82nd Street,
NEW YORK 10028

The Traphagen School of Fashion,
257 Park Avenue South, NEW YORK 10010

Philadelphia Museum of Art—Fashion
Wing.
Benjamin Franklin Parkway at 26th Street,
PHILADELPHIA 2, Pa 19101

Costume and Textile Study Collection,
University of Washington,
School of Home Economics,
SEATTLE, Washington 98105

Bibliography

The Age of Worth, Couturier to the Empress Eugénie by E. Saunders (Longman Group Ltd., London, 1954)

Ages of Elegance: five thousand years of fashion and frivolity by G. D'Assailly (Macdonald & Co., London, 1968)

The Changing Face of Beauty by Madge Garland (Weidenfeld & Nicolson Ltd., London, 1957)

The Changing Form of Fashion by Madge Garland (J. M. Dent & Sons Ltd., London, 1970; Praeger Publishers, New York, 1971)

A Concise History of Costume by James Laver (Thames & Hudson International Ltd., London, 1969; Harry N. Abrams Inc., New York, 1969)

Costume by P. Cunnington (A. & C. Black Ltd., London, 1966; Dufour Editions Inc., Chester Springs, Pennsylvania, 1970)

Costume by James Laver (Cassell & Co. Ltd., London, 1963)

Costume: an Illustrated Survey from Ancient Times to the Twentieth Century by Margot Lister (Barrie & Jenkins Ltd., London, 1968; Plays, Inc. Publishers, Boston, 1968)

Costume in Antiquity by James Laver (Thames & Hudson Ltd., London, 1964)

Costume in Detail, 1730–1930 by Nancy Bradfield (George G. Harrap & Co. Ltd., London, 1968; Plays, Inc. Publishers, Boston, 1968)

Dandies by James Laver (Weidenfeld & Nicolson Ltd., London, 1968)

Dress Art and Society 1560–1970 by Geoffrey Squire (Studio Vista Ltd., London, 1974)

Dress: how and why fashions in men's and women's clothes have changed during the past 200 years by James Laver (John Murray (Publishers) Ltd., London, 1950)

English Costume from the Second Century B.C. to 1972 by Doreen Yarwood (B. T. Batsford Ltd., London, 1972; Dufour Editions Inc., Chester Springs, Pennsylvania, 1953)

The Evolution of Fashion: Pattern and Cut from 1066 to 1930 by Margot Hamilton Hill and Peter A. Bucknell (B. T. Batsford Ltd., London, 1967; Van Nostrand Reinhold Co., New York, 1968)

Fashion by Madge Garland (Penguin Books Ltd., Harmondsworth, Middlesex, 1962)

Fashion: an anthology by Cecil Beaton by Madeleine Ginsburg (HMSO, London, 1971)

Fashion: From Ancient Egypt to the present day by Mila Contini (The Odyssey Press, New York, 1965)

Fashion through Fashion Plates 1770–1970 by Doris Langley Moore (Ward Lock Ltd., London, 1971)

The Fashionable Lady in the Nineteenth Century by Charles Harvard Gibbs-Smith (HMSO, London, 1960; Pendragon House Inc., Palo Alto, California)

Handbook of English Costume in the Sixteenth Century by C. Willett and Phillis Cunnington (Faber & Faber Ltd., London, 1970; Plays, Inc. Publishers, Boston, 1970)

Handbook of English Costume in the Seventeenth Century by C. Willet and Phillis Cunnington (Faber & Faber Ltd., London, 1973; Plays, Inc. Publishers, Boston, 1973)

Handbook of English Costume in the Eighteenth Century by C. Willett and Phillis Cunnington (Faber & Faber Ltd., London, 1972; Plays, Inc. Publishers, Boston, 1972)

Handbook of English Costume in the Nineteenth Century by C. Willett and Phillis Cunnington (Faber & Faber Ltd., London, 1970; Plays, Inc. Publishers, Boston, 1970)

Handbook of English Costume in the Twentieth Century 1900–1950 by Alan Mansfield and Phillis Cunnington (Faber & Faber Ltd., London, 1973; Plays, Inc. Publishers, Boston, 1970)

A History of Costume in the West by François Boucher (Thames & Hudson International Ltd., London, 1966)

A History of English Costume by Iris Brooke (Eyre Methuen Ltd., London, 1972; Theatre Arts Books, New York, 1973)

A History of the Umbrella by T. S. Crawford (David & Charles (Holdings), Newton Abbot, Devon, 1970; Taplinger Publishing Co. Inc., New York, 1970)

History of World Costume by Carolyn Bradley (Peter Owen Ltd., London, 1970)

Kings of Fashion by A. Latour (Weidenfeld & Nicolson Ltd., London, 1958)

The Mode in Costume by R. Turner Wilcox (Charles Scribner's Sons, New York, 1969)

Paris Fashion: The Great Designers and their Creations edited by Ruth Lynam (Michael Joseph Ltd., London, 1972)

Patterns of Fashion: I—Englishwomen's dresses and their construction c1660–1860;

II—Englishwomen's dresses and their construction c1860–1940 by Janet Arnold (Macmillan Publishers, Ltd., London, 1972)

The Pictorial Encyclopaedia of Fashion by Ludmilla Kybalová, Olga Herbenová, and Milena Lammarová. Translated by Claudia Rosaix (Hamlyn Publishing Group Ltd., Feltham, Middlesex, 1968)

Quant by Quant by Mary Quant (Cassell & Company Ltd., London, 1966)

Royal Courts of Fashion by Norman Hartnell (Cassell & Company Ltd., London, 1971; International Publications Service, New York, 1971)

Style in Costume by James Laver (Oxford University Press, London, 1949)

Taste and Fashion by James Laver (George G. Harrap & Co. Ltd., London, 1945)

A Technical History of Costume Volume I: Ancient Egyptian, Mesopotamian and Persian Costume by Mary G. Houston (A. & C. Black Ltd., London, 1964; Barnes & Noble, Inc., Scranton, Pennsylvania, 1954)

A Technical History of Costume Volume II: Ancient Greek, Roman and Byzantine Costume by Mary G. Houston (A. & C. Black Ltd., London, 1931; Barnes & Noble, Inc., Scranton, Pennsylvania, 1965)

A Technical History of Costume Volume III: Medieval Costume in England and France by Mary G. Houston (A. & C. Black Ltd., London, 1939; Barnes & Noble Inc., Scranton, Pennsylvania, 1965)

Theory of the Leisure Class: an economic study in the evolution of institutions by Thorstein Veblen (George Allen & Unwin Ltd., London, 1971; H. M. Gousha, San José, California, 1973)

Tudor and Jacobean Portraits (Volume I text, Volume II plates) by Roy Strong (National Portrait Gallery) (HMSO, London, 1969; Pendragon House Inc., Palo Alto, California, 1969)

The World in Vogue by B. Holme, K. Tweed, J. Davies & A. Liberman (Martin Secker & Warburg Ltd., London, 1963)

Victoria and Albert Museum *Costume Illustration: The Nineteenth Century* with an introduction by James Laver (Ministry of Education, London, 1947)

Victoria and Albert Museum *Costume Illustration: The Seventeenth and Eighteenth Centuries* with an introduction by James Laver (HMSO, London 1951)

Index

Page numbers in italics refer to illustrations

Acknowledgments

The following abbreviations have been used: A Above; B Below; L Left; R Right; M Middle; and combinations of these, e.g. AR Above right, BL Below left

We are grateful to the following for permission to reproduce illustrations: frontispiece Mme Poiret—G. Lepape, Coll. Mme Poiret, Paris/Scala; 7 Vatican Library/IGDA; 8A *The Painter and his Family*—C. de Vos, Brussels Museum; 8B Henry II of Lorraine—F. Elle, Rheims Museum; 9 *Mlle Rivière*—J. Ingres, Louvre, Paris/Scala; 10 *The Balcony*—E. Manet, Jeu de Paume, Paris/IGDA; 11 *Dreams*—V. Corcos, Museum of Modern Art, Rome/Scala; 12 Sumerian mosaic, Snark International; 14A Limestone plaque of Ur-Nansche of Lagash, Louvre, Paris/IGDA; 14B Sculpture of Ebih-il, Louvre, Paris/IGDA; 15 Mosaic from Royal Standard of Ur, Michael Holford; 16 Diorite statue of Gudea, Louvre, Paris/IGDA; 18 Babylonian boundary stone, Michael Holford; 19 4th century BC frieze from Susa, Louvre, Paris/IGDA; 20 Sassanian silver dish, Ronald Sheridan; 21 Egyptian wall painting, from *The Book of the Dead*, Scala; 22L Wooden figure of La Dame Tui, Louvre, Paris/IGDA; 22R Painting from a Noble's Tomb at Thebes, Su Gooders; 23A Wall painting from tomb of Mebamun, Thebes, Michael Holford; 23B Panel from throne of Tutankhamun, Roger Wood; 24 Painted relief of Seti I, Louvre, Paris/IGDA; 25L Statue of Rameses II, Scala; 25R Figure from 11th dynasty, wood and plaster, Roger Wood; 26 Polychrome terracotta figure of snake goddess, Scala; 27 Late-Minoan fresco from Palace at Knossos, William MacQuitty; 28 Late-Minoan sarcophagus painting from Hagia Triada, Mella; 29A Mycenean warriors and helmets, National Museum, Athens/IGDA; 29B Fresco from Royal Palace, Knossos, C.M. Dixon; 30 National Museum, Naples/IGDA; 32 Dish showing Doric costume, Elettra Cliche; 33 SEF; 34 Hellenistic sculpture of Persephone, Michael Holford; 35A Detail of geometric pot from Acropolis, C.M. Dixon; 35B Statue from Acropolis, 6th century BC, C.M. Dixon; 36 The Girl from Verona, Michael Holford; 37 Two figures from Triclinium Tomb, Tarquinia, C. Bevilacqua/IGDA; 38AL Musician from Tomb of the Leopards, Tarquinia, C. Bevilacqua/IGDA; 38AR Dancer from Tomb of the Leopards, Tarquinia, C. Bevilacqua/IGDA; 39 Painting in House of Mysteries, Pompeii, 50BC, IGDA; 40L Roman statue, Alinari; 40R Roman statue, Alinari; 41 Wall painting of the marriage of the Aldobrandi, Imperial period, Scala; 43A Roman mosaic, National Museum, Naples/IGDA; 43B Statue of Dogmatius, Scala; 44 Mosaic of Salome from St Mark's, Venice, Scala; 46 Mosaic in Church of Sant' Apollinare Nuovo, Ravenna,

Elenco Fotocolors; 47 Byzantine mosaic at Ravenna, IGDA; 48 Mosaic from Church of San Vitale, Ravenna, IGDA; 49 6th century book of Genesis, National Library, Vienna; 50AL 9th century relief, C.M. Dixon; 50AR 9th century relief, C.M. Dixon; 50B 6th century bronze plate, Björnhofda, Sweden, National Museum, Stockholm; 51 Gold statuette from Le Mans, France, courtesy of the Dumbarton Oaks Collection, Washington D.C.; 52 9th century Apocalypse, Bibliothèque Municipale, Valenciennes; 53 Mid-12th century illustration from St Albans, Bodleian Library filmstrips; 55 Bronze statuette of Charlemagne, Louvre, Paris/Giraudon; 56 Miniature showing Otto III, Staatsbibliothek, Munich/Elenco Fotocolors; 57 Tapestry in Baldishol Church, Norway, Kustindustrimuseet, Oslo/C.M. Dixon; 58 Bayeux Tapestry, Michael Holford; 60 By courtesy of the Syndics of Cambridge Univ. Lib.; 61A & B Illustrations from Encyclopedia by Rabanus Maurus, Scala; 62A Statues from Chartres Cathedral, C.M. Dixon; 62B Manuscript from Museum of Catalan Art, Barcelona, Museum of Art, Barcelona/IGDA; 64A Manuscript from Stuttgart, Wurttembergische Landesbibliothek, Stuttgart; 64B Scala; 65L Portrayal of Brother William, by courtesy of the Board of the British Library; 65R Illustration from Matthew Paris, Bodleian Library filmstrips; 66 Scala; 67 Statues from Chartres Cathedral, C.M. Dixon; 68 13th century manuscript. M.636,ff.17, Pierpont Morgan Library, New York; 70 Scala; 71L By courtesy of the Board of the British Library; 71R By courtesy of the Board of the British Library; 72 Illustration from Alfonso's Book of Chess, Biblioteca Real de San Lorenzo de El Escorial; 73 M.635,ff.18, Pierpont Morgan Library; 75 *Fountain of Youth*—Jaquerio, La Manta, Turin, Scala; 76 Fresco in Assisi—street musicians, Scala; 78A Scene of feasting, Bibliothèque Nationale, Paris, 78B Luttrell Psalter, 14th century, by courtesy of the Board of the British Library; 79 Scala; 80A Fresco in Spanish Chapel in Florence, 1365, Scala; 80B Scene from Luttrell Psalter, by courtesy of the Board of the British Library; 81A National Gallery of Art, Washington/Snark; 81B By courtesy of the Board of the British Library; 82–3 Scene from Spanish Chapel, Florence, Scala; 84 Bibliothèque Nationale, Paris; 85A *Guidoriccio da Fogliana*—Simone Martini, Elenco Fotocolors; 85B Giraudon; 86 Drawings of courtly dress—Pisanello, Musée Condé, Chantilly/Giraudon; 88A Scala; 88B Musée de Versailles, Cliché Musées Nationaux; 89 By courtesy of the Board of the British Library; 90L Scala; 90R From *Les Très Riches Heures du Duc de Berry*, Giraudon; 91 *Arnolfini and his Wife*—Jan van Eyck, National Gallery, London; 92L Michael Holford; 92–3 Bibliothèque Royale, Brussels; 93AR C.M. Dixon; 93B From *Les Très Riches Heures du Duc de Berry*, Musée Condé, Chantilly/Snark

International; 94 *Henry VIII*—Hans Holbein, The Walker Art Gallery, Liverpool; 96–7 *The Marriage of Ottavio Farnese to Margherita of Austria*—Taddeo Zuccari, Caprarola, Viterbo, Villa Farnese, Scala; 98L & R *The Duke of Saxony and his Wife*—Lucas Cranach, Staatliche Kunstsammlungen, Dresden-Gemaldegalerie Alte Meister; 100 Detail from *La Messa de Bolsena*—Raphael, Vatican Museum/IGDA; 101 Biblioteca Querini, Stampalia, Scala; 102 *Sir Philip Sidney*—anon., National Portrait Gallery, London; 104 *The Ambassadors*—Hans Holbein, National Gallery, London; 105 *The Money Lenders*—M. van Reymerswael, Alte Pinakothek, Munich/IGDA; 106–7 *Tapestry made for Catharine de Medicis*, Scala; 108L *Anne of Cleves*—Hans Holbein, Louvre, Paris; 108C & R Mary Evans Picture Library; 109 *Two Courtesans*—Carpaccio, Correr Museum, Venice/Scala; 110L *Portrait of Philip II of Spain*, Michael Holford; 110R *Sir Henry Unton*—anon., National Portrait Gallery, London; 111 *Conrad Rehlinger*—B. Strigels, Alte Pinakothek, Munich/Scala; 113 *Robert Dudley, Earl of Leicester*—anon., National Portrait Gallery, London; 114L *Portrait of a Young Man*—Hilliard, Victoria and Albert Museum/Snark International; 114R Philip II of Spain, Prado, Madrid/MAS; 115L *Alexander Farnese*—A. Sanchez-Coello, National Gallery of Ireland; 115R *The Tailor* (detail)—G. Moroni, National Gallery, London; 116 *Sir Walter Raleigh and His Son*—anon., National Portrait Gallery, London; 117 Michael Holford; 118–19 *Lord Cobham and Family*—H. Eworth, by courtesy of Marquis of Bath/R.B. Fleming; 120 *Sir John Hawkins*—H. Custodis, Plymouth Corporation/Tom Mollard; 121 *Armada Portrait of Elizabeth I*—M. Gheeraedts, Woburn Abbey Coll., by courtesy of His Grace the Duke of Bedford; 123 *The Ditchley Portrait of Elizabeth I*—M. Gheeraedts, National Portrait Gallery, London; 124 *Rubens and His Wife*—P. Rubens, Alte Pinakothek, Munich/IGDA; 126 *The Merry Company*—F. Hals, Metropolitan Museum of Art, New York; 127 *Henry Rich, First Earl of Holland*—D. Mytens, National Portrait Gallery, London; 128 *Dirk Jacobs and his Family*—D. Santvoort, Mauritshuis, The Hague; 129 *Charles I*—A. van Dyck, Louvre, Paris; 130 *William II of Orange and His Wife Mary Stuart*—G. van Honthorst, Collection Haags, Gemeentemuseum, The Hague; 131 *Princess Mathilda Sybil*—anon., the Royal Collection, Copenhagen/Snark International; 132 *Portrait of the Artist's Wife and Son*—J. Tradescant, The Ashmolean Museum, Oxford; 133 *The Visit*—G. ter Borch, National Gallery of Art, Washington D.C.; 134A *Samuel Pepys*—J. Hayls, National Portrait Gallery, London; 134B *Anne Corten*—S. Mesdach, Rijkmuseum, Amsterdam; 135 *Margaret Bromsen*—M. Hiert, St Anne Museum, Lubecq/Snark International; 136 Snark International; 137

C.M. Dixon; 138 *Tric-Trac Players*—attributed to M. le Nain, Louvre, Paris; 139 *Game of Skittles*—P. de Hooch, Cincinnati Art Museum, Gift of Mary Hanna; 140 *Man in Black*—G. ter Borch, National Gallery, London; 141L *Dancing Partner*—G. ter Borch, Polesden Lacey, Surrey/R.B. Fleming; 141R *Charlotte Landgrave de Hesse*—Robert Bonnart, Victoria and Albert Museum, London; 142 *Mlle de Lavallière and Her Children*—Mignard, Château de Versailles, CFL-Giraudon; 143 *James Francis Edward Stuart and His Sister*—N. Larqillière, National Portrait Gallery, London; 144 *La Barre and the Musicians*—Tournières, National Gallery, London; 147 *Sir John Stanley*—G. Romney, Louvre, Paris; 148 L & R Su Gooders; 149 *Marie Theresa of Savoy*—Dagoty, Versailles Museum; 150 *Declaration of Love*—J. Detroy, Staatliche Schlossen und Garten, Berlin; 151 *Mr and Mrs Andrews*—T. Gainsborough, National Gallery, London; 152 *La Comtesse de Rumain and Her Daughters*—Carmontelle, Musée Condé, Chantilly/Giraudon; 153 *The Graham Children*—W. Hogarth, Tate Gallery/R.B. Fleming; 154 *John Peyto, 14th Baron Willoughby da Broke and His Wife Louise*, by courtesy of the Mountbatten Collection/R.B. Fleming; 155L *October*—R. Digton, Victoria and Albert Museum, London; 155R *Mme Mole Raymond*—V. Lebrun, Louvre, Paris/Giraudon; 156 *The Morning Walk*—T. Gainsborough, National Gallery, London; 157 Su Gooders; 158 *Nelly O'Brien*—Sir J. Reynolds, reproduced by permission of the Trustees of the Wallace Collection, London/Freeman; 159 *La Belle Strasbourgeoise*—N. Larqillière, Musée des Beaux Arts, Strasbourg/Giraudon; 160 *The Actor Chénard as a Sansculotte*—L. Boilly, Musée Carnavalet, Paris/Snark International; 162–3 *Family Portrait*—F. Sablet, Musée Cantonal des Beaux-Arts; 164 *The Point of Convention*—L. Boilly, Louvre/F. Arborio Mella; 165 *Napoleon Bonaparte at the Malmaison*—F. Gérard, Château Rueil Maison/Giraudon; 166L & R Musée Carnavalet Paris/Bulloz; 167 Bulloz; 168 *Walk on the Italian Boulevard*—anon., Musée Carnavalet, Paris/Bulloz; 169 *Mme Recamier*—J. David, Louvre/Mercurio; 170 *Marie-Louise and the 'King of Rome'*—F. Gérard, Versailles/Bulloz; 171A Plate from *Gallery of Fashion*—Niklaus Wilhelm von Heideloff, Victoria & Albert Museum, London; 171B Su Gooders; 173 *Marie-Julie Queen of Spain*—Lefèvre/Bulloz; 174 Su Gooders; 176 Guildhall, London/Su Gooders; 177 Hulton Picture Library; 178 Mary Evans Picture Library; 179 Hulton Picture Library; 181 Mary Evans Picture Library; 182 Hulton Picture Library; 183 Mary Evans Picture Library; 184 The Mansell Collection, London; 185L Hulton Picture Library; 185R Hulton Picture Library; 186 Mary Evans Picture Library; 187 *The Duchess of Aumale*—Winterhalter, Château de Versailles/CFL-Giraudon; 188 Mary Evans Picture Library; 189 Hulton Picture Library; 190 The Mansell Collection; 192–3 *Derby Day*—W.P. Frith, Tate Gallery/Cooper-Bridgeman Library; 194 Editions Robert Laffont; 195 *Empress Eugénie and Ladies*—Winterhalter, Musée de Compagne, Paris/Snark International; 196 Hulton Picture Library; 197 Hulton Picture Library; 198A Mansell Collection; 198B Mary Evans Picture Library; 199 Hulton Picture Library; 200A Mary Evans Picture Library; 200B Mary Evans Picture Library; 201 *A Summer Day in Hyde Park*—J. Ritchie, London Museum/R.B. Fleming; 202–3 *Omnibus Life in London*—W. Egley, Tate Gallery, London; 204 Hulton Picture Library; 205 *Women in the Garden*—C. Monet, Jeu de Paume, Paris; 206 *Lady with a Glove*—A. Carolus-Duran, Louvre, Paris/Lauros-Giraudon; 208AL Mary Evans Picture Library; 208AR *Woman in Blue*—J.B. Corot, CFL-Giraudon/Louvre, Paris; 208B Mary Evans Picture Library; 209L Mary Evans Picture Library; 209R Mansell Collection; 210 *La Grande Jatte*—G. Seurat, Chicago Art Gallery/Cooper-Bridgeman Library; 211 *Les Parapluies*—A. Renoir, National Gallery, London; 212A R.B. Fleming; 212B Mansell Collection; 213A Mansell Collection; 213BL Mander and Mitchenson Theatre Collection; 213BR *Robert de Montesquieu*—G. Boldini, Nat. Mus. of Modern Art, Paris/Giraudon; 214A *Festivities aboard Ship*—J. Tissot, Tate Gallery/CFL-Giraudon; 214B Mansell Collection; 215 Mary Evans Picture Library; 215BL Mary Evans Picture Library; 215BR Editions Robert Laffont; 216 Mansell Collection; 217A William Gordon Davis; 217B Mander and Mitchenson Theatre Collection; 218–19 *Cinq Heures chez Paquin*—N. Gervex, House of Worth/Cooper-Bridgeman Library; 220A Mary Evans Picture Library; 220BL Julian Robinson Collection/A.C. Cooper; 220BR Julian Robinson Collection/A.C. Cooper; 221 *Girl with Parasol in Cornfield*—C. Monet, Louvre, Paris/Ziolo; 222AL Barnaby's Picture Library; 222AR Popperfoto; 223AL *L'Eau Mysterieuse*—E. Bieler, Ziolo; 223AR Julian Robinson Collection/A.C. Cooper; 223B Mander and Mitchenson Theatre Collection; 224 Mary Evans Picture Library; 225AL *Bank Holiday 1912*—W. Strang, Tate Gallery/John Webb; 225AR *Corporation Street, Birmingham*—E. Southall, published by permission of Birmingham Museum and Art Gallery; 225BL & R Mary Evans Picture Library; 226AL Mary Evans Picture Library; 226AR Mary Evans Picture Library; 226B Mary Evans Picture Library; 227 *Bank Holiday, Hampstead Heath*—P. May, Mansell Collection; 228AL & R Mary Evans Picture Library; 228BL & M Mary Evans Picture Library; 228BR Mary Evans Picture Library; 229 Mansell Collection; 230 Popperfoto; 231 Julian Robinson Collection/A.C. Cooper; 232 Julian Robinson Collection/A.C. Cooper; 233L Hulton Picture Library; 233R Popperfoto; 234 Editions Robert Laffont; 235AL Harper's Bazaar, London/Geremy Butler; 235AR *Paulette Pax*—van Dongen, Ziolo; 235B Harper's Bazaar/Geremy Butler; 236AL Julian Robinson Collection/A.C. Cooper; 236AR Harper's Bazaar, London/Geremy Butler; 237AL Julian Robinson Collection/A.C. Cooper; 237AR Harper's Bazaar, London/Geremy Butler; 238L Harper's Bazaar, London/Geremy Butler; 238R Julian Robinson Collection/A.C. Cooper; 239 Bobby Locke in 1939, Hulton Picture Library; 240AL Harper's Bazaar/Geremy Butler; 240AR Harper's Bazaar/Geremy Butler; 240BL Julian Robinson/A.C. Cooper; 240BR Harper's Bazaar/Geremy Butler; 240L Cecil Beaton. By courtesy of Southeby's Belgravia; 241R Harper's Bazaar/Geremy Butler; 242 L'Officiel, Paris; 244A Harper's Bazaar/Geremy Butler; 244B Harper's Bazaar/Geremy Butler; 245A L'Officiel, Paries; 245B Harper's Bazaar/Geremy Butler; 246L Julian Robinson Collection/A.C. Cooper; 246R L'Officiel, Paris; 247L Camera Press/Karsh of Ottawa; 247R Camera Press; 248L Harper's Bazaar, London; 248B Album du Figaro; 249L Harper's Bazaar/Geremy Butler; 249R Harper's Bazaar/Geremy Butler; 250 Camera Press; 251L Harper's Bazaar/Geremy Butler; 251R Camera Press; 252 Richard Dormier; 253AL & R Camera Press; 253B L'Officiel, Paris, 254 Kobal Collection; 255A Michel Molinare; 255B Camera Press; 256L Richard Dormer; 256M Camera Press; 256R Camera Press; 257 Richard Dormer; 258 Sunday Times; 259 Sunday Times; 260 Sunday Times; 261 Sunday Times; 262 Richard Dormer; 263A Camera Press; 263B Michel Molinare; 264L Sunday Times; 264M Sunday Times; 264R Editions Robert Laffont; 265 Camera Press; 266 Jeanloup Sieff, Vogue, Condé Nast Publications; 267L Richard Dormer; 267R Pierre Cardin; 268AL Pierre Cardin; 268AR Pierre Cardin; 268BL Pierre Cardin; 269BR Pierre Cardin; 269L Sunday Times; 269R Michel Molinare; 270–75L Sunday Times; 275R Yves Saint Laurent; 276L Bill Gibb; 276R Sunday Times; 277L, AR & BR Niall McInerney/Jean Muir; 278 Sunday Times; 279 Sunday Times; 280L Camera Press; 280R Syndication International; 281 Harvey Nichols, London; 282 Krizia; 283L Harvey Nichols, London; 283R Harvey Nichols, London; 284L Chloe, Paris; 284R Chloe, Paris; 285L Chloe, Paris; 285R Chloe, Paris; 286L Michel Arnaud; 286AR Michel Arnaud; 286BR Michel Arnaud; 287 Richard Dormer